Growing Wings on the Way

SYSTEMS THINKING FOR MESSY SITUATIONS

ROSALIND ARMSON

Published by:
Triarchy Press
Station Offices
Axminster
Devon. EX13 5PF
United Kingdom

+44 (0)1297 631456
info@triarchypress.com
www.triarchypress.com

A catalogue record for this book is available from the British Library.

Cover design and image by Heather Fallows -
www.whitespacegallery.org.uk

Typeset in Palatino Linotype, Arial and Bookman Old Style

ISBN: 978-1-908009-36-4

Contents

Acknowledgements

A hundred times every day I remind myself that my inner and outer life are based on the labors of other men, living and dead, and that I must exert myself in order to give in the same measure as I have received and am still receiving.

Albert Einstein

In writing this book, I find myself indebted to very many people. First, to my friends and colleagues, past and present, in the Open University Systems Group, I offer my heartfelt thanks. They have supported me in learning and developing my skills in systems thinking and in learning how to teach the skills to others. They have, over many years, provided a community of conversation that has been critical and supportive. In particular, I treasure the care, stimulation and challenge I have received from John Hamwee and Ray Ison. Truly,

If I have seen further it is only by standing on the shoulders of giants.

Sir Isaac Newton in a letter to Robert Hooke, 1676

I also acknowledge the important contribution of workshop participants and Open University students who, over the years, have participated energetically in summer schools and workshops. They have given me generous stimulus and feedback. Above all, together with consultancy clients, they have shown me that systems thinking is not only fun but almost magical in its ability to reveal opportunities in intractable situations.

This book would not have happened without Maria Smith who helped me recognise that writing it was the most important thing for me to do at this point in my life.

Writing a book can be a lonely business at times so I have greatly appreciated conversations with Ray Ison, Sue Holwell and Martin Reynolds. All, in their different ways and at different times, helped when I got stuck, gloomy or both. Ray helped me address the conundrums of writing from a particular epistemological position. Martin gently showed me the limits of what I could do and Sue challenged me to 'say what I mean and mean what I say'. I also acknowledge the importance of Peter Checkland's Soft Systems Methodology (SSM). SSM is a great gift to the world at large and a constant reference point for me.

Many people have participated in the book-writing process. Roger Packham, Tony Netherclift, Jitse van Ameijde and Matthew Fairtlough gave thoughtful and affirming feedback on the book proposal. Tony Netherclift has been ruthless in pursuing deficiencies in grammar and style. Patrik Germann, Sue Holwell, Nick Pandya and Karen Shipp gave critical feedback that enabled me to find my voice in the early chapters. Patrik Germann, Sue Holwell, Ray Ison, Steve Johnston and Glyn Martin read the whole draft to a tight deadline and gave affirming but challenging critical feedback. Patrik Germann helped me track down quotations.

I have drawn on a wide range of resources in preparing this book. In particular, I would like to thank my sister for permission to use our shared story from an uncomfortable time in our lives.

> *Children of the same family, the same blood, with the same first associations and habits, have some means of enjoyment in their power, which no subsequent connections can supply.*
> Jane Austen in *Mansfield Park*, 1814

Jitse van Ameijde, Dana Cordell and Paul Carr gave permission to use their rich pictures. Jitse van Ameijde also initiated me into the mysteries of Adobe Illustrator. Francis Meynell let me use my photograph of him. Windrush Willow provided the lobster-pot photograph. Michael Leunig, whose drawings I have enjoyed for several years, gave permission to use his two drawings.

I am immensely grateful to my editor at Triarchy Press, Andrew Carey. I enjoyed every moment of our work together, pressured though it was. He was ruthless but gracious in pursuit of a well-put-together book.

I made life difficult for the other clever people at Triarchy with my many diagrams, generated with a non-standard font in diverse formats. They sorted them all out in next to no time. It was important to me to get the diagrams right, so I am thrilled they were able to find solutions that met the need. Thank you everybody.

I also acknowledge the Open University for allowing me a study-leave year during which to write the book.

Most of all, my beloved Tony Netherclift who, as well as providing critical support, put up with my self-absorbed lifestyle for eighteen months. I owe him more than I can say.

Rosalind Armson
April 2011

Introduction

Life is not a problem to be solved, but a mystery to be lived.
Thomas Merton[1] (1915 – 1968)

I was at my wits' end. My elderly mother was becoming ever frailer. I drove three hours there and three hours back twice a week to support her but it was not enough. Her friends and neighbours were becoming ever more reluctant to meet her growing needs and Mum was unwilling to face up to the situation. Every possible course of action seemed to entail some insuperable obstacle.

This book is about what to do when you don't know what to do.

Some problems demand urgent attention but offer no starting point. Even the most competent people, the best-run organisations and the happiest families run into issues that need attention. The worst of these turn out to be much larger than anticipated, to have one problem leading to another, to be immensely uncertain (although everyone has a different opinion) and to have no obvious outcome. Even worse, when someone does tackle them, it either makes no difference or makes things worse.

Problems like these are genuinely different, I believe, from the kinds of problems we learn to solve at school – the ones with right answers, the ones where we know what the problem is and where we simply need to work through them to discover the solution. Problems like the one I had with my Mum are different and need a different approach. They are messy situations. No prescriptions or recipes can tell you what to do in a messy situation because each messy situation is unique.

So this is not a 'how to' book. It does not offer solutions. It does not even tell you what to do. It offers ways of *finding out* what to do.

The ways of finding out that it proposes all come under the heading of 'systems thinking'. Whether you are new to the term or an old-hand, this book is an invitation to develop and extend your own unique thinking skills to become more adept at dealing with complex, uncertain and interconnected issues through the ideas and insights of systems thinking.

Thinking is a very personal business so, while I know what works for me, systems thinking will only work for you if you make it your own. Because thinking is so individual, I have imagined this book as a conversation between you, the reader, and me, the writer. We cannot literally share each other's experience but observations that make sense of my experience may make sense to you in terms of your own experience of complex and perplexing issues. My image of how this book works leads to another feature that makes this book somewhat different. I use first person language, talking about my experience and how I make sense of it and how systems thinking has helped me manage complex situations. This is not because I think my experience is particularly special but because I want to avoid any sense that some ways of thinking are 'right' and others 'wrong'. There is no right way to manage messy situations and no right way to think systemically. My only claim in this respect is that I, and many other people, have found systems-thinking insights to be *useful and effective*. So, my first invitation to you, the reader, is to use this book to find your own way to be a systems thinker.

> *The teacher, if indeed wise, does not bid you to enter the house of their wisdom, but leads you to the threshold of your own mind.*
>
> Kahlil Gibran[2] (1883 – 1931)

You and me with our mirrors

I imagine the book you are reading as a shared space where you and I stand, reflecting in our mirrors on our own experience. I tell you about my experience of dealing with messy situations using systems-thinking ideas, insights, tools and techniques. You make sense of what I say in terms of your own experience.

There are many diagrams in this book: diagramming is a useful systems-thinking skill. All the diagrams were originally hand drawn and, had my handwriting been clear enough, I would have preferred to present them just as I drew them. In the interests of clarity, I have settled for a 'handwriting font' because I intend handwriting to convey 'this is the way I see it' rather than 'this is the way it is'.

There are plenty of books about systems thinking. They describe what it is, why it is important and what it has achieved. What seems to be missing are the skills to do it – and that is why I wrote this book. My second invitation, should you choose to accept it[3], is to go beyond *learning about* systems thinking and instead *learn to think systemically*.

Like swimming, systems thinking is a skill. As such, theory can only convey a context for the skill, not the skill itself. Eventually, you have to get into the water. You also have to risk not being very good at it at first. Learning systems thinking is a bit like 'jumping off cliffs and developing our wings on the way down'[4]. My next invitation, therefore, is to develop your skills with a messy situation of your own.

> *I hear and I forget. I see and I remember. I do and I understand.*
> Confucius (551 B.C.E – 479 B.C.E)

From Confucius to clinical training for doctors, experiential learning[5] has been the preferred way of learning new skills. If you would like to take up the challenge of experiential learning, look out for an issue that you have been avoiding. A suitable issue may be quite hard to spot because humans tend to ignore situations they cannot deal with, hoping they will go away – even though experience shows they often do not go away, usually get worse and always drain enthusiasm and energy.

A suitable messy situation to work with will have some or all of the following characteristics:

- you have been putting it off because you do not know where to start
- there have been arguments about what the problem is
- there have been arguments about what should be done
- you do not know important information about the situation and you don't know how, or what, to find out
- the problem seems too big even to think about
- the problem seems too complex to think about

- you have tried to deal with it but the problem reappeared later, or got worse

- you would like to be able to do something about it.

Whatever your chosen mess, I suggest you look for one in which you have some influence or ability to improve the situation. Almost certainly, the ideas and thinking described in this book will open new avenues for managing the situation. Most people who engage with these ideas find the problem becomes much less problematic.

Systems thinking is about more than *management*. Systems thinking is about *managing* – something everyone does. Systems thinking is applicable all the way from personal and family issues to international strategy. It can certainly be a useful skill for managers; but anyone who manages anything – most of us – is likely to find it useful in contexts that range across work, leisure, politics, family, campaigning, environmental and community action. I have used a family example to explain some of the ideas in the book, hoping that most readers will be able to relate to it. In other cases, I have drawn on stories from my consultancy work. All of these stories are 'real' although I have disguised details for confidentiality reasons.

My Open University colleagues and I have been teaching the ideas in this book for 30 years. More than 10,000 Open University students and others have tried and tested them, both as theoretical constructs and as practical ways of thinking about complex problems and situations. More recently, I directed an Open University project in which university staff engaged with systems thinking in order to improve the university's ability to deal with the complex and changing challenges of the higher-education environment. This proved to be an exciting time as together we refined ideas that made a difference to busy managers, team leaders and executives. The project engaged colleagues and others in working with the issues raised in a rapidly changing and often difficult higher-education environment, usually in workshops. These workshops were designed to support people in learning to use systems thinking experientially by engaging directly with their issues. Many of the ideas in the book, and my approach to them, were developed in these and other workshops.

In consultancy work, the person bringing the problem will always know more about the complexities of their issue than I do. My role is always that of problem helper and skills developer. I bring no direct experience of the client's situation but systems thinking gives me skills for finding out so that, together, we can find our way to an improved situation. This book is intended to do the same job, developing your skills for finding ways to work through messy situations.

In consulting, I often start out feeling overwhelmed by clients' messy situations. I wonder if I have anything at all to offer as I discover the enormity of the challenges they face. However, having trust in the tools and ideas and applying them conscientiously always delivers positive results. I continue to be amazed by this and I have learned that feeling overwhelmed is a normal response to a messy situation. It need not frighten me off. It has also been my experience that clients always realise important benefits from systems thinking. Our combined expertise often helps us identify straightforward routes to significant improvement. My experience is far from unique. Using systems thinking, many organisations (business, governmental, public sector, health-care and not-for-profit) have improved their performance, overcome crises, restructured and seized new opportunities when they seemed completely stuck.

Systems thinking is especially suitable for complex and ambiguous problems that defy definition: where any definition of the problem somehow seems to miss the point or changes the problem, so that it is no longer the problem I experience. I often think of such problems as log jams. In the late nineteenth and early twentieth century, the lumberjacks of the Pacific Northwest felled trees and floated them down the rivers to the sawmill on the high water from melting mountain snow. From time to time, the logs would stick and cause log jams. Some log jams became famous, involving thousands of logs and flooding many square kilometres[6]. The photograph shows one such log jam.

A 1907 log jam on the Coquille River at Prosper, Oregon (from a contemporary postcard). The river was prone to log jams because incoming tides had the effect of 'blocking' the river at the estuary where the mill was located. This small log jam was 210 metres long and contained over 5,000 logs.

Dealing with intractable situations is rather like my mental picture of the log drivers as they jump from log to log across the jam, freeing it up to get both lumber and river moving again. A skilled driver, I imagine, can spot which log to move and how to move it: freeing surrounding logs and creating movement. Skilfully moving a small number of logs, perhaps rocking them rather than removing them, would be enough to get the water flowing: dislodging neighbouring logs and breaking up the jam until eventually the flowing water once again carried the logs downstream. Systems thinking allows me to spot the 'logs' that, if moved, will improve the situation. I don't have to solve every bit of the puzzle created by the messy situation. I just have to set it on a path to continuing improvement.

How to use this book

Above all else, I intend this book to be useful. I have described the tools, techniques and ideas that clients and workshop participants have found most useful in working with their own messy, ambiguous, sensitive and puzzling issues. This book provides resources so that you can *learn to be* a systems thinker. If you want to learn to think systemically, *use* the ideas.

> *I am always doing what I cannot do yet, in order to learn how to do it.*
>
> Vincent van Gogh (1853 – 1890)

Most of the chapters can be read independently so this is not a book you need to read straight through. If the ideas in any particular chapter seem useful, try them. If not, then try something from another chapter. Not every idea works every time and most people prefer some ideas and use others less often. The book does have a structure, however, intended to help you find an effective route to dealing with your messy situations and thorny problems.

- Part 1 is about engaging with the situation you want to address. It describes the big ideas of systems thinking and how to use them. In particular, Chapter 1 looks at why some problems defy our best attempts to solve them. Whatever route you take through the book, Chapter 1 is a good place to start.

- Part 2 is about understanding any particular issue. It describes tools and techniques that help make sense of complex situations.

- Part 3 is about exploring purposeful action, being sure about what you can do to improve the situation, why, and how it will work and fit into the context. Clarifying these issues eliminates ambiguity and misunderstandings for you and others.

- Part 4 is about acting to improve the situation in ways that simultaneously improve your understanding of the situation and your appreciation of further options for more improvements. Part 4 also introduces a model for ongoing inquiry.

In a difficult and complicated situation, it is tempting to jump to the tools and techniques set out in the later parts of the book. This may not be a good idea, for reasons explained in Chapter 1. Instead, I suggest taking a chapter from each of Parts 1, 2, and 3 if you are in a hurry. If you have a little more time and the inclination, I suggest reading Part 1, selecting one or more chapters from Part 2 and then reading the first chapter of Part 3. You can then come back to Part 4 to think about the context of your actions.

> *That is what learning is. You suddenly understand something you've understood all your life, but in a new way.*
>
> Doris Lessing[7] (b. 1919)

Finally, there are further resources, links and systems-thinking tools and techniques online at:

www.triarchypress.com/GrowingWings

Notes, resources and explorations for the Introduction

1   *Thomas Merton*

Thomas Merton, an American Trappist monk, became one of the foremost writers on spirituality of the twentieth century. His work transcended his Catholic background to include spiritual insights from the East. He was passionately committed to radicalism, social justice, civil rights and pacifism. His writings, including his poetry, inspired a whole generation to explore spirituality and its meaning for social action. His knowledgeable engagement with Buddhism and Sufism, and his own deep commitment to his monastic calling, make his writings a source of wisdom and delight.

2   *Kahlil Gibran*

Kahlil Gibran's poetry, it is claimed, outsells all but Shakespeare and Lao-Tzu. Born in the Ottoman province of Mount Lebanon, Kahlil Gibran wrote his famous prose poem *The Prophet* in English after he emigrated to the United States. *The Prophet* has never been out of print since its publication in 1923 and was a great favourite of the 1960s' counter-culture. This quotation comes from the section on *Teaching*.

Gibran, Kahlil. (2011). *The Prophet*. Portsmouth, NH: William Heinemann.

3   *Invitations*

Mission Impossible's catchphrase captures something essential about my experience of teaching systems thinking. By *inviting* you to develop some systems-thinking skills, I also offer you an opportunity to reject the invitation. While I believe the world might be a saner place if there were more systems thinkers around, I do not believe anyone should engage with it because they think they ought to. One's own thinking skills are deeply personal and an intimate part of one's self. It would be presumptuous to suggest you should think differently. On the other hand, most people who engage with systems thinking find it immensely useful and some become enthusiasts. The invitation to engage with this book is a warm one but not, I hope, a pressing one.

4   *Developing our wings on the way down*

This quotation comes from Kurt Vonnegut's 1997 novel *Timequake* in which 2001 is folded back to 1991 and everyone has to re-live their bad choices.

Vonnegut, K. (1997). *Timequake* (1st ed.). New York: G P Putnam's Sons.

5   *Experiential learning*

Experiential learning is 'learning from your own experience' in a context that matters to you.

6   *Shifting log jams*

Metaphors are only ever a partial fit to the realities they describe but I was somewhat disappointed to discover my imagined notion of log-jam clearance is only partially true. In really big jams they used dynamite. I am somewhat reassured by a still later discovery that the frayed ends of dynamited logs destroyed the value of the timber and risked still worse jams. Using an ill-judged 'solution' to a problem may simply make it worse.

7 *Doris Lessing*

The quote comes from *The Golden Notebook* (1982), Lessing's exploration of some twentieth century themes. It concerns the heroine's attempts to make sense of her experience of central Africa, of communism, of the novel she is writing and of her dreams, emotions and memories. She explores each of these themes in a differently coloured notebook, using the golden notebook to synthesise and make sense of the different strands of her life.

I recommend the use of a notebook, journal or diary as a resource for making sense of messy situations and of systems thinking itself.

Lessing, D. (2007). *The Golden Notebook* (reissue edn.). New York: Harper Perennial.

Part 1: Engaging with messy situations

Part 1 explores complex, intractable and interconnected messy problems – the ones that seem to defy resolution. It proposes engaging purposefully with such problems by including the problem solver and the problem context in the process of dealing with the problem itself.

The structure of Part 1

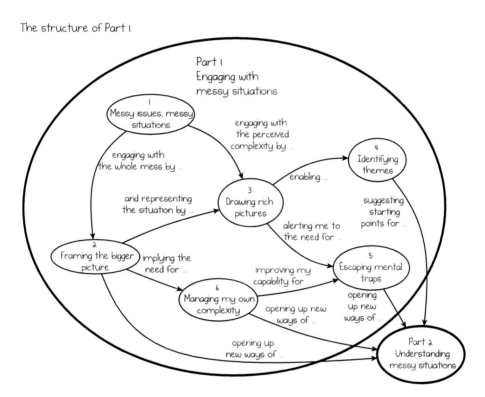

The starting point for Part 1 is the idea of messes: apparently intractable problems that seem to affect everything around them. Chapter 1 provides the foundation for the book and the problems it addresses. Chapters 2 and 3 present ideas for engaging with the problem and its context. Chapter 4 suggests starting points for other tools and techniques in the book. Chapters 5 and 6 bring you – the problem solver – and your thinking, into the picture by reviewing how your thinking can enable, or disable, improving the situation. Part 2 provides techniques for understanding the situation.

Messy issues, messy situations

It's not the tragedies that kill us, it's the messes.

Dorothy Parker[1] (1893 – 1967)

In many books, Chapter 1 begins with a story. This chapter follows the pattern but here it will be *your* story. In my workshops, the first activity creates an important 'Aha! moment.' I invite you to take a few moments to tell yourself the stories that begin this chapter.

- First, think of your plans for this evening or the weekend. I imagine you have some task or issue you intend to sort out. It may take an hour or more but dealing with it will improve your life in some small way. Just identify one of these issues.

- Next, take yourself back to the trickiest, most puzzling and most troubling issue you ever had to address. It may even be a current issue. What is going on? Who is involved? Why is it an issue? What approaches have you tried? What was the outcome?

- Finally – and this is where, if you can resist the temptation to read on, you will set yourself up for this book's adventures – identify the key differences between the 'deal-with-it-this-evening' issue and the tricky-and-troubling issue. It might help to make some notes.

I asked you to do the exercise because it builds on your own experience. Experiential learning – learning from experience – is a powerful launch pad for learning new skills for dealing with tricky-and-troubling problems. You already know almost everything in this chapter but may not have thought about it before. What follows will help you to think about the implications for dealing with problems.

Workshop participants quickly spot differences between their deal-with-it-this-evening issues and their tricky-and-troubling issues. It enables them to recognise that while some problems are soluble with a bit of effort, others defy our best efforts. Together we have worked out some of the characteristic differences. The tricky-and-troubling issues, which I call *messes*:

- are bigger

- are more worrying

- are more puzzling

- go on longer

- take more time

- draw in more people

- create more conflict

- are emotionally charged

- have more things to think about.

The routine deal-with-it-this-evening issues are simpler and smaller. I call them *difficulties*. It may take longer than one evening to deal with difficulties but, for the purposes of the exercise, I want to be sure you recognise the difference between a difficulty and a mess.

DIFFICULTIES AND MESSES; TAME PROBLEMS AND WICKED PROBLEMS

The differences between these two types of issues began to emerge in the planning context of the 1970s. Russell Ackoff[2], the American management scientist and systems thinker, named them *difficulties* and *messes*. At the same time, Horst Rittel and Melvin Webber noticed a similar distinction, which they labelled *tame problems* and *wicked problems*. Rittel, Webber and Ackoff were all responding to the same observation – the inadequacy of most problem-solving approaches when dealing with messes. In this book, I use the more general terminology of *difficulties* and *messes*, building on the ideas and insights of Ackoff, Rittel, Webber and the many clients and workshop participants with whom I have explored the ideas.

Almost all the well-known strategies for understanding, managing and dealing with issues, only work for difficulties. *They do not work well for dealing with messes*. Either they do not work at all or they make things worse. Most problem-solving strategies are designed for difficulties. Many of these start with 'defining the problem' – stating the problem in a way that makes it soluble. But the problem with messes is that they defy definition. This is the Aha! moment[3] many people experience when they understand that messes and difficulties are different. It explains why their best efforts sometimes have very little result.

This book is about dealing with messes. Dealing with messes is harder than dealing with difficulties so it is tempting to ignore them. People often persevere with the strategies designed for difficulties, even when they fail or make things worse. Strategies for dealing with difficulties are often simple to understand in the abstract or through examples but *experience* is the best way to learn strategies for dealing with messes. This may explain why strategies for dealing with messes are less well known.

In this chapter, I reflect on my experience of difficulties and messes – and the experience of people I have worked with – and I invite you to look at your experience through the mirror of 'difficulties and messes' (see the figure in the *Introduction*) as I reflect on my own experience of messes. Your experience will be different from mine but, by drawing on your experience, I hope you will develop a richer understanding than if I were just to present lots of theory.

I asked you to think of your own two stories because your stories will enable you to make sense of what follows. Most people *experience* rather than *know about* the differences between difficulties and messes, so it makes more sense to explore the differences by drawing on your experience. You will then *recognise* some of the differences rather than just reading about them. If I had offered an example of a mess, you might have been tempted to treat it as a difficulty and so miss the point. It is harder to dismiss your own experience of messes as puzzling, worrying and frustrating.

TWO SORTS OF ISSUES

Humans are problem-solving animals and, while we do not always welcome problems, dealing with problems is what we do. When we do not have a problem set by our outside world, we set about improving the routine stuff. Human problems range from minor irritations to near or actual catastrophes, from private to global, from hitches to persistent and intractable tangles. They are the very stuff of human experience.

Difficulties are routine. They may be a bit tricky but we know where we are going, what the main steps are, and the order in which to do things. We can even anticipate where obstacles may arise and take steps to deal with them. We can make a reasonable estimate of how long it will take. For example, I recently bought a car. I knew what sort of car I wanted and I knew what my budget was. I knew it might take a few days but if I tackled it carefully, I could find some suitable cars and choose between them. There were several stages but it was a difficulty not a mess. I wanted a car with good fuel economy and a reputation for reliability but I am not an expert on cars or on what I should look for. I would spend a few evenings working out what the issues were, refining my ideas about what I wanted and researching the market. I would then spend a few evenings looking at cars on sale locally and getting likely candidates checked by an independent expert. I guessed it would take about a week but I allowed two weeks for unplanned hitches. When I thought I had found the one I wanted, I discovered that the dealership I was going to buy from had been caught making fraudulent claims about their cars. Back tracking and deciding on a different car added an extra stage but did not change the essence of the task of deciding on a new car.

Difficulties involve fewer people than messes, reducing the need to negotiate. In a difficulty, I can confidently predict the consequences of my own, and others', actions because the component tasks form a simple sequence. Deciding on and then buying a car benefited from a few moments of mental rehearsal but, despite some irritations, it was not something that worried me. Although I had predicted some potential pitfalls (I would need to make sure my friendly expert would be available when I needed him), I had correctly foreseen that they would be easy to deal with.

Messes are nothing like this. They are bigger, worse, more worrying and more serious than difficulties. In a mess, everything seems interconnected and offers no clear starting point. Everything seems to depend on everything else and getting it wrong may precipitate serious consequences. This makes messes worrying. Messes often involve more people, each with their own idea of what the issue really is. Negotiating any plan of action is tricky when it is unclear who is affected and how. Messes take a long time to resolve, if they get resolved at all. They tend to haunt affected people over months – or even years. They cover a larger area and touch on a wider range of concerns. They can feel overwhelming with many more things to think about than a difficulty.

For most people, however, scale on its own does not capture the most troubling features of messes. *Uncertainty* is part of the essential nature of a mess. It starts with the mess itself – it is unclear what the problem is. It is also unclear what a solution would look like or how it might be found. In a mess, it does not seem to make sense to talk about a 'solution' because parts of the mess seem immutably problematic. People argue about the nature of the problem and its possible solutions. They may even deny that a problem exists. Messes cannot be pinned down like difficulties and I cannot specify a solution. In a difficulty, I know *what* to do even if *how* to do it is a little less clear. In a mess, I may have no idea where to start or what to do. Learning my way through is the only way to make progress without making it worse. Quick fixes will not work because the problem and the priorities are unclear. Instead, I try to look for *improvements* rather than solutions: a solution for one person may make things worse for others. It is not just that people will disagree or have different agendas in mind, but 'solving' one part of the mess may significantly reduce the options available for solving other parts of the mess. An improvement, in this context, should at least make things no more difficult for anyone. Aiming for improvement rather than solution allows me continuously to re-evaluate the mess as it evolves alongside my growing understanding. In a mess, improvement is not a second-best alternative to a solution. Single solutions simply do not exist for a complex of interconnected problems – unless one chooses to treat the mess as if it were a difficulty and risk the consequences. Improvement is a positive way of managing the situation and, as systems thinkers often discover, improvement can often lift one onto a spiral of continuous and sustainable improvement that everyone involved recognises.

Improvement seems to have three elements in the context of a messy situation.

All those involved are able to recognise that the situation has improved. There may be no unity about what has improved but everyone will assent to the claim that things have improved, even if only some experience local improvement. A client once captured this effect by saying, 'I'm glad it's improved for them and it's certainly no worse for me'.

Improvement generates learning about the mess, its internal interconnections and its relationship to its context. This allows greater confidence in further actions for improvements.

New opportunities for improvement appear. As a messy situation improves, it also changes, partly because the context evolves and changes and partly because an improved situation is not the same as the original situation. And partly, too, because I and other people in the situation change, and our relationship to the mess changes[4].

A mess offers no clear starting point, no clear priorities and no clear end-point. Large parts of it lie outside my control. A mess calls into question my assumptions, my goals and perhaps even my values. It can be hard to imagine a desirable outcome. When all the options seem blocked, any favourable outcome seems far-fetched, impossible or simply unimaginable.

I do not know enough about a mess. But how can I find out if I do not know what I need to find out? There may be serious, but unknown consequences if I get it wrong. How can I avoid them or know what they might be? With a difficulty, I have enough knowledge and understanding to tackle it or, if not, then it is clear what I need to find out. This is not the case for messes. Former US Secretary of State for Defense, Donald Rumsfeld, famously drew attention to different forms of ignorance:

> *[...] as we know, there are known knowns; there are things we know we know. We also know there are known unknowns; that is to say we know there are some things we do not know. But there are also unknown unknowns – the ones we don't know we don't know.*
>
> Donald Rumsfeld, 12th February, 2002

Although widely ridiculed at the time, Rumsfeld was making an important point and would probably have benefited from a diagram like Figure 1.1 to make his point more clearly.

Over the course of questioning, he identified what the Department of Defense knew about Iraq:

that it had invaded Kuwait

threatened and harmed the Shi'a in the south

attacked the Kurds in the north

claimed its neighbours' regimes were illegitimate.

These were known knowns. But at the time, despite inspections, there was no evidence Iraq had weapons of mass destruction (WMDs). WMDs were known unknowns: the Department of Defense knew it did not know whether Iraq had WMDs[5]. The upper quadrants of Figure 1.1 represent these two forms of knowing. Messes contain unknown unknowns – the worrying bits that catch you out – in the bottom-left quadrant. The outcome of a mess is less certain than the outcome of a difficulty.

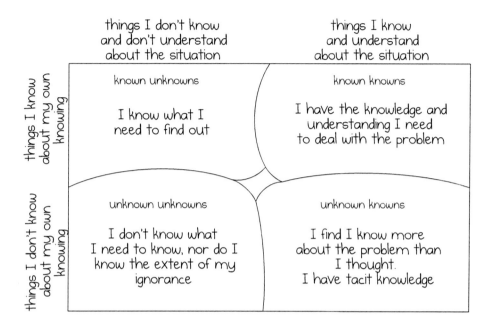

Figure 1.1 *In a difficulty, I may already know what I need to know about the problem (top-right quadrant) or I may know what I need to find out (top-left quadrant). In the terms used by Donald Rumsfeld, these are known knowns and known unknowns. In messes, I do not know yet about elements that I will need to know about. These elements may surprise me. Messes require awareness that the bottom-left quadrant of unknown unknowns exists and contains elements of the mess that I have yet to discover. In the bottom-right quadrant, I delightedly discover that I know more than I realised: elements of the problem that I believed were messy but prove to be just difficult rather than messy. The wavy lines between the quadrants in this diagram indicate softness of the boundaries. Areas of guessing lie along the boundaries between the quadrants.*

Scale and uncertainty may be hard to separate. For example, the larger number of people involved in a mess may itself contribute to the uncertainty as goals and priorities are contested and negotiated. Scale and uncertainty contribute to each other.

Evolution and change, in the issue and its context, are much less likely in a difficulty. Evolution – change through time – makes the idea of a 'solution' for a mess more problematic. Over the longer timescale of a mess, things happen and circumstances change in unforeseen ways. A solution devised and painstakingly constructed at one point in time may no longer fit the mess by the time it is ready. The nature of the mess will have changed (Figure 1.2). The future trajectory of a mess is fraught with uncertainty because it extends into the future, and the future becomes less and less predictable.

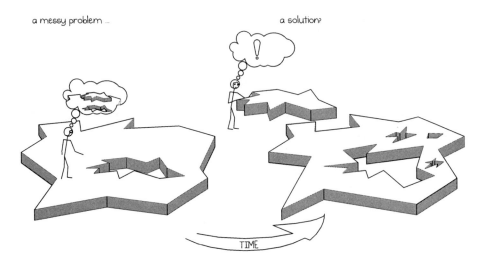

Figure 1.2 *In the time it takes to devise and implement a solution, messes change and evolve. The problem solver imagines a solution to a messy problem (on the left). Returning with the solution (on the right), the problem solver finds the problem has changed shape and fragmented. The solution no longer fits.*

Because solutions are unlikely to work once-and-forever, I can instead look for sustainable improvements. Sustainable improvements create opportunities for further improvements and opportunities for learning more about the mess. Managing a mess involves *learning* my way through, changing my approach as I understand more about the mess. Systems-thinking approaches do not tell me what to do. They enable me to *work out* what to do.

I can disentangle a difficulty from the broader context. But a mess is fuzzy. Its implications seem to entangle everything around it, drawing the context into the mess. It is hard to say who, or what, is part of the issue; and who or what is separate.

As well as being entangled with its context, a mess is itself a tangle of interacting concerns or issues. The Haiti earthquake in 2010 illustrates this interconnectedness.

As the international community sought to bring aid in the immediate aftermath of the earthquake, it began to seem as if every problem needed all the other problems solved first. The lack of heavy-lifting plant made digging people out of the ruins and clearing the roads difficult. The deep-water port was unable to operate, delaying the landing of vital supplies and equipment, including heavy-lifting gear. Port-au-Prince became dangerous without sanitation and the removal of the thousands of dead. Extracting the dead and still-buried survivors from the ruins was dangerous without equipment and clear roads. A lack of equipment to dig mass graves complicated safe burial. With 90 per cent of buildings devastated or unsafe, the population was close to despair. Lack of water and medical care for traumatised survivors, many of them badly injured, triggered localised looting. The earthquake wrecked Government buildings although, even with a functioning civil society, it would be hard to manage such a situation. Solving each problem depended on solving several other problems first. What should be tackled first? Getting the roads clear would have made it easier to get heavy-lifting gear in but clearing the roads was impossible because heavy-lifting gear was either on ships that could not land it at the harbour, or was blocked by destroyed roads and collapsed buildings. Repairing the port would have made it possible to land essential equipment, the huge tonnages of food and water needed, and medical supplies. But the port could not be made usable because of the lack of heavy-lifting gear. Even clearing using manual labour was impossible. Port-au-Prince was dangerous because of looting, unburied bodies and lack of sanitation and food supplies. Every avenue to recovery was blocked because solving each problem depended on solving other problems first. Cholera added to the complexity of the situation.

A difficulty is uncontroversial. Everyone agrees what should be done and can converge quite quickly on how it might be done. A mess involves more people, with their conflicting values and interests, and it can seem as though there are as many interpretations of 'the problem' as there are people involved. Emotions can run high where values are at stake and this adds to the ambiguities of a mess. Ethical issues acquire added importance. At what point do you stop looking for buried earthquake survivors? After medical advice says no-one will survive? When only one or two are found each day? When the needs of survivors becomes pressing? In the aftermath of the Haiti earthquake, there was a clear ethical imperative to support survivors with food, water and medical aid but even repairing infrastructure presents ethical issues. Should temporary sanitation be provided quickly or should it wait until some of the rubble is cleared and reconstruction of the sanitation system can begin? Providing for immediate needs in emergency-aid situations always risks undermining recipients' long-term recovery.

A DIFFICULTY OR A MESS?

Figure 1.3 summarises what I and workshop participants have learnt together about how we experience difficulties and messes. It clusters the differences into five groups: scale, certainty, stability, clarity and boundedness. You may want to compare these features with your own experience, either of a mess you are currently facing or the tricky-and-troubling issue you identified earlier.

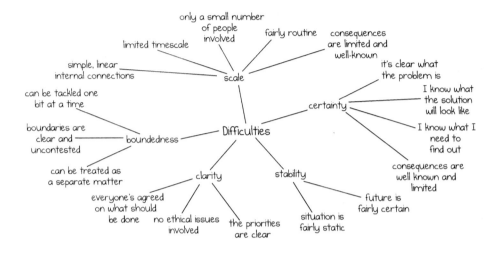

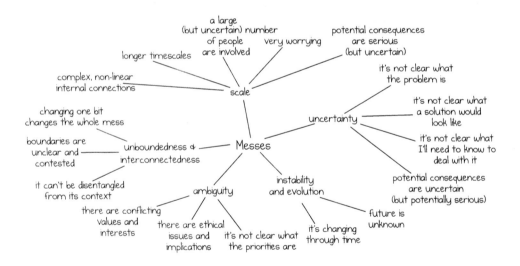

Figure 1.3 *Spray diagrams of the characteristics of difficulties and messes. Messes are bigger, more complex, more uncertain, more ambiguous, more unstable and less bounded than difficulties. They need a different approach.*

Difficulties and messes lie at the two ends of a spectrum. Some issues show only some of the characteristics of messes or the messy bits may not be serious.

Some appear as difficulties with a few messy features and some as messes with some easier-to-deal-with parts. So how do I know if any particular problem is a difficulty or a mess?

In some ways, this perfectly reasonable question is unhelpful. It implies that studying the issue will enable me to decide. Let me ask another question first. Does the distinction between a difficulty and a mess arise from some external reality or does it come from the way I perceive the problem? The first possibility seems awkward. Do problems exist before someone notices? They seem to exist as threats (the earthquake that is about to happen, the virus that will undermine my health, the faulty valve that will lead to a major pollution incident) but not as problems-to-be-solved. So it seems rash to suggest that difficulties or messes are independent of the person who perceives them. So is it simply a matter of my perception? The observation that one person's mess might be another person's difficulty seems to lend weight to this view. It seems perfectly reasonable to say that if I perceive a mess, then it is a mess. The converse, if I perceive a difficulty, then it is a difficulty, seems less plausible, however. If it is just a matter of perception, then this argument implies that finding out a bit more about a mess will turn it into a difficulty. Neither independent existence nor perception seems to provide a satisfactory basis for deciding whether an issue is a difficulty or a mess.

Counselling

The resolution lies, I think, in the *experience* of working with real problem situations. It is as if 'being a difficulty', or 'being a mess' comes from the *interaction* between me and the problematic situation and not from the problem on its own nor simply from my perception of it. When I fail to resolve something I had perceived as a difficulty, or observe my solution re-creating the problem in a different form, I become aware of the messiness I am dealing with. This implies that my inability to separate it from its surroundings or my experience of scale, uncertainty and ambiguity makes the issue messy. The distinction between a difficulty and a mess lies in *my experience* of trying to deal with an issue.

If my experience of an issue determines whether it is a difficulty or a mess, then I have choice about how I want to continue my engagement with it. I can choose to ignore the messiness by, for example, ignoring its context, ignoring other viewpoints, breaking the problem into smaller parts, deciding on a 'core problem' and ignoring other parts of the issue. In fact, I can choose to continue treating the problem as a difficulty.

But, if I choose to treat messes as if they were difficulties, I may find:

> *There is always an easy solution to every human problem – neat,*
> *plausible and wrong.*
>
> H. L. Mencken (American newspaperman, 1880 – 1956)
> in the essay *The Divine Afflatus*, originally published in 1917

Treating messes as if they were difficulties triggers consequences that arise from the characteristics of messes. In fact, it involves solving an *idealised problem* rather than the *problem as experienced*. It is a decision to solve a problem we would *like* to have rather than the one we *actually* have. Moreover, a solution reached this way may be difficult to implement or not have the desired effect. More often, the problem moves somewhere else, to another time or to another group or individual. It may re-appear later in another (possibly worse) form[6].

A seaside town in the South of England provides an example of displacing a problem to another group of people. Many of its holiday guest houses were no longer up to the standard visitors expected and the owners could not raise the capital needed for improvements. Government funding was available for towns that provided rehabilitation centres for drugs offenders so the town council encouraged the purchase of guest houses for conversion. There was a national demand for rehabilitation centres from courts, which saw rehabilitation as an effective alternative to prison. Property developers were keen to acquire properties and let them to the contractors providing rehabilitation services. It looked like a solution to several problems: the courts' problem, the council's problem and the property owners' problem. For property developers and contractors, it was a revenue opportunity. The centres acquired contracts to treat specified numbers of drug addicts for rehabilitation.

Things did not go as expected. Drug rehabilitation programmes have huge failure rates, especially when ordered by courts. The drug users lack self-motivation and their 'sentence' lasts for a prescribed time, often without consideration of their progress. In this case, once their rehabilitation period ended, un-rehabilitated drug users, having no homes or support networks elsewhere, moved into low-cost accommodation in the town. This depressed property values and created no-go neighbourhoods. Local demand for heroin, cocaine and other substances increased, attracting dealers to the town and increasing the crime rate as addicts sought money to support their habit. Parks became no-go areas for children and dogs because of discarded needles. Life became difficult for local residents. Demands on local social services rocketed. The town acquired a 'dangerous' reputation and families no longer came to enjoy the town and its beach.

The solution had passed problems onto residents and visitors. The situation had become even messier than before[7]. Messes, when treated as if they were difficulties, invariably produce unintended and unwanted consequences.

All of this suggests that messes need a different approach – one that respects their complexities, uncertainties and interconnectedness. But first, we have to recognise that we are dealing with a mess.

SPOTTING A MESS

Education accustoms us to problems that have solutions. Indeed, at school we often only encounter the sorts of problems that have solutions at the back of the book. We enjoy the tick that tells us we have the right answer. We are equipped to deal with difficulties and few people are educated to deal adequately with messes. Our instinctive preference is not to notice messes. Even if we do, we may have few skills for dealing with messes. Ignoring them becomes an attractive, or perhaps inevitable, strategy.

The good news is that systems thinking offers a wide range of ideas, tools and techniques to deal with messes. Systems thinking has been around for a long time and provides thinking tools for complex situations. It offers an alternative to treating every problem as if it were a difficulty.

If you do not have the right tools, a mess is simply a source of anxiety that you cannot address. Indeed, psychological health depends to some extent on ignoring things we cannot deal with. We deny that there is a problem but that does not make it go away.

A mess is more intimidating than a difficulty. In behavioural-psychology terms, discovering something unpleasant, like messiness I cannot deal with, is likely to discourage future exploration. Immediate rewards or punishments are more effective in establishing future behaviour. It takes patience and skill to deal with a mess so the avoidance strategy embeds itself firmly. Deciding to tackle a mess may involve unlearning the preference for ignoring it.

Humans are typically insensitive to information they do not expect. We use 'static filtering' to avoid noticing the unexpected. We like to believe that we, other people, and the world we live in, are mostly rational and orderly. Evidence to the contrary, such as symptoms of a mess, is not only unwelcome but genuinely difficult to perceive. This is picked up nicely by the idea of 'Sunnydale Syndrome', a fictional idea that has passed into wider use. Sunnydale Syndrome is derived from *Buffy the Vampire Slayer*. (Buffy tells an unsuspecting Sunnydale resident about the ubiquity of vampires in the town[8]. He responds, 'This explains a lot.') Similarly, in *Life, the Universe and*

Everything[9] the intergalactic travellers hide their spaceship at Lord's Cricket Ground – during a test match – under the cover of an 'SEP field'. In the story, an SEP (Somebody Else's Problem) field is cheap form of invisibility field because, although people may notice the spaceship, everyone will assume it is 'somebody else's problem' and ignore it. On TV, *Dr Who* and *Torchwood* use similar devices called 'perception filters' generated by 'chameleon circuits'. In fact, the idea appears so often in science fiction that sci-fi fans call it the 'weirdness censor'. Weirdness censors get round some of the plotting difficulties of fantasy fiction but also resonate with everyday experience. This resonance explains why terms like Sunnydale Syndrome and SEP fields have passed into usage beyond their fictional origins. SEP fields occur in real life with surprising frequency, disguising messes of all kinds, especially in organisations[10].

Other strategies are observable in everyday life. 'Ignoring it and hoping it will go away' is a strategy related to both the SEP field and the lack of adequate tools. When hints emerge into consciousness that there may be a mess, we often choose, without further investigation, to ignore it and to hope it goes away. A slightly more conscious version is 'hope for the best' optimism based on little evidence. *OR BLAME SOMEBODY*

Donald Schön[11] likened organisational messes to a swampy landscape where paths detour around the swampy bits. Gradually, intersecting paths, each taking extensive detours, wind their convoluted routes across the landscape, slowing progress from A to B. Vegetation grows up around the paths, obscuring the view of the swamp. Opening alternative routes by draining the swamp is no longer imaginable. This metaphor translates into taboos, work-arounds, traditions, inefficiencies and eventual paralysis. The organisation chooses, usually unconsciously, to find ways around its messes. Messes become 'the elephant in the room' – an immense obstacle that no-one acknowledges.

It takes courage to spot a mess and then take responsibility for addressing it. Recognising one's own strategies for avoiding messes is the first step. My own, and many other people's, strategy is *procrastination*. If I notice myself procrastinating, it is often symptomatic of a mess I do not want to acknowledge. Recognising a mess can be an invigorating awakening.

GOOD NEWS OR BAD NEWS?

Is it not dispiriting to work with messes – with problems that are much bigger, much less soluble than 'ordinary' problems?

I am often asked this and my answer is 'no'. It is certainly not as dispiriting as trying to get solutions meant for difficulties to 'stick' in messy situations. Moreover, many people report a huge sense of relief when they realise how different difficulties and messes are. It is neither incompetence nor stupidity that dooms their dealings with messes to frustration. Once I recognise a mess, then I can anticipate the excitement of making major improvements in the situation.

Lila was a senior manager in a large organisation. She had recently taken responsibility for the organisational-change and development team. Lila decided to learn systems thinking, hoping it would help her manage the complexity of her new role, about which she had some anxiety. She had a significant Aha! moment when she understood the difference between difficulties and messes. The situation in her department – with its identity confusion and its conflicting roles – she could now see was 'a real mess'. It was a 'huge relief', Lila said. Her approach and expectations about her role changed. Her anxiety about her role dissipated. She did not have to struggle for the *right* answers. Instead, she could embark on a programme of continuous organisational improvement. Lila later said that her life would have been much easier had she understood the distinction years earlier.

This book is about systems-thinking tools for dealing with messes. The next chapter describes how messes can be approached in ways that attend to their complexities.

Notes, resources and explorations for Chapter 1

1   *Dorothy Parker*

I make no apology for using quotes from Dorothy Parker. I love her acerbic wit. You can find some of her one-liners on the web (search for "Dorothy Parker" and "quotes"). For more of her witty and acid writing see:

Parker, D. (2004). *The Portable Dorothy Parker*. (Revised edition). London: Longman.

The quotation at the front of this chapter predates Ackoff's distinction between a difficulty and a mess but it seems apposite. It comes from an interview with *Paris Review,* Summer 1956.

2   *Russell Ackoff*

Russell Ackoff was born in 1919 in Philadelphia, PA. He introduced systems ideas to management. He became a gifted educator and management theorist, firmly committed to enabling people to find their own solutions to messy problems. A gifted speaker and a lively and readable writer, he was committed to the idea of 'fun'. He wrote an engaging summary of his experiences to mark his 80th birthday and, more recently, a book of *Management f-Laws*. He died in 2009. His final book has an introduction by John Pourdehnad and a forward by Charles Handy.

Ackoff, R. L. (1974). *Redesigning the Future*. New York: Wiley.

Ackoff, R. L. (1999). On Passing Through 80. *Systemic Practice and Action Research* 12:425-430.

Ackoff, R. L., Addison, H. J. and Bibb, S. (2006). *Management f-Laws: How Organizations Really Work*. Axminster: Triarchy Press.

Ackoff, R. (2010). *Differences That Make a Difference: An Annotated Glossary of Distinctions Important in Management*. Axminster: Triarchy Press.

3   *Aha! moments*

I am not particularly fond of this neologism but it captures the essence of the moment one 'gets it'. Aha! moments happen a lot with systems thinking.

4   *New opportunities for improvement*

The changes in Northern Ireland since the 1998 Good Friday Agreement illustrate this continuous process of improvement very well. As the cease-fire held, people's confidence grew, the economy gradually improved as violence subsided and inward investment began to create new jobs and opportunities. As the improvements went on, defecting from the negotiations became too costly so that, even when major political challenges emerged, no-one could afford to withdraw from the on-going talks. Almost no party got what they wanted but everyone got an improvement on the 1998 situation, as well as further opportunities for negotiating their way towards still greater improvement. Although it is still hard for participants in the talks to admit it, they have changed themselves. They are better able to work with people whose views, culture and aspirations are very different from their own and the language of warfare and entrenched conflict has given way, on a day-to-day basis, to the language of 'getting things done' and 'making it work'.

5 *Knowing about my knowing*

Donald Rumsfeld was not the first to distinguish between known and unknown Knowns and Unknowns but he certainly made it well known. He also noted, in the same briefing, that absence of evidence (of WMDs) was not the same as evidence of absence. This became the rationale for invading Iraq a year later. War is often seen as a difficulty but always turns into a mess.

Nasir al-Din al-Tusi , the 13th century Persian astronomer, mathematician, biologist and philosopher, captured Rumsfeld's point with much greater eloquence in a verse that begins, 'Anyone who knows…'.

Axworthy, M. (2008). *Iran: Empire of the Mind*. London: Penguin Books.

Nassim Nicholas Taleb's excellent book *The Black Swan* has some of the best discussions about knowing and not knowing:

Taleb, N. N. (2007). *The Black Swan: The Impact of the Highly Improbable*. London: Allen Lane.

6 *Moving the problem on*

For some problem solvers, moving the problem on is not problematic. They can by-pass tricky issues and 'spin' their way out of it.

7 *Drug addiction*

Governments and judicial systems would love to have a simple solution to the problem of drug addiction, ideally in the form of a simple cure. Alas, whether from the point of view of the judicial system, social services, welfare programmes, society or the drug-dependent individuals, addiction to illegal substances is messy. It typically involves not only physical dependency but the collapse of supportive families, networks, stable home-life and employment and their replacement by a loose community of similarly addicted people on the edge of criminality. Treating physical dependency as if it were 'the problem', even if it succeeds in breaking the addiction, leaves the person still homeless, unemployed, unsupported and without friends other than drug users. Without huge personal resources of determination, self-belief and energy – most of which addiction destroys – the temptation to seek solace in substance abuse with other addicts is overwhelming. Few societies are willing to take on such a mess, despite the encroachment of the mess into communities, the cost of the associated criminality, health-care costs and the cost of destroyed lives.

8 *TV programmes*

In *Dr Who*, the world's longest running science-fiction programme, the Doctor travels through time and space in the TARDIS. The TARDIS takes the form of a British police box. (Before two-way radio and mobile phones, police boxes were miniature police stations from which the public could phone the police. They were common all over the UK until the mid 1970s.) The TARDIS's chameleon circuit had enabled it to blend into its surroundings until it broke, leaving the

TARDIS as a police-box. Curiously, in more recent series, the TARDIS can still avoid attention, despite the anachronistic police-box form.

Torchwood is a spin-off series from *Dr Who*. The Torchwood Institute's mission, 'separate from the government, outside the police, and beyond the United Nations', is to deal with extraterrestrials. Its Cardiff city-centre entrance, next to a fountain, is disguised by a perception filter that allows the Torchwood team to appear and disappear without the public noticing. *Dr Who* and *Torchwood* are produced by the BBC.

Buffy the Vampire Slayer (Mutant Enemy Productions) ran for six years from 1997 and is set in Sunnydale, California. Its High School is located above Hellmouth, a portal between 'our' world and the world of demons, vampires and other nightmarish creatures. Despite many clues indicating the presence of vampires, most Sunnydale residents do not notice anything odd about their town.

9   *Douglas Adams*

Life, the Universe and Everything is the third part of the 'five-part trilogy': *The Hitchhiker's Guide to the Galaxy*. Its author, Douglas Adams (1952-2001), was fascinated by the implications of the complexity sciences. Numerous references to systems effects appear in his books.

Adams, D. (1982). *Life, the Universe and Everything*. London: Pan Macmillan.

10   *Ignoring the evidence*

SEP fields, Sunnydale Syndrome and other weirdness censors are discussed (in more traditional psychology language) by Stuart Sutherland.

Sutherland, S. (2007). *Irrationality*. London: Pinter & Martin.

I come across Sunnydale Syndrome as a consultant in organisations but it usually takes a while before I recognise it. It is almost as if I have Sunnydale Syndrome about Sunnydale Syndrome. It is a term used informally in jurisprudence and in psychology discussions, where it is commonly observed that defendants have justified their actions (or inactions) to themselves by denying they had any power to act in any other way.

11   *Donald Schön on swamps*

Donald Schön was a founding spirit in *reflective learning* – the way professionals learn by reflecting on their experience. He had a lifelong interest in how societies, organisations and individuals absorb new technologies and how they adapt or fail as a result of their competences for learning and change. He was interested in how metaphors influence or inhibit learning. The swamp metaphor for messy situations arises in:

Schön, D. A. (1983). *The Reflective Practitioner: how professionals think in action*. San Francisco: Basic Books.

Schön, D. A. (1987). *Educating the Reflective Practitioner: Toward a New Design for Teaching and Learning.* , San Francisco: Jossey-Bass.

CHAPTER 2

Framing the bigger picture

If there is any one secret of success, it lies in the ability to get the other person's point of view and see things from that person's angle as well as from your own.

Henry Ford (1863 – 1947), car manufacturer

We know far less about the external world than we think – perhaps even less than St Paul imagined in his first letter to the Corinthians (between 54 and 57 C.E.) when he wrote, 'For now we see through a glass, darkly'. The findings of cognitive psychology and neurobiology and reflection on human ability to deal with messy situations, all confirm that what we can know about messy situations will be, at best, partial and provisional. Our brains, our histories, our interests and our senses all conspire to trap us within ourselves with only the narrowest slivers of light reaching us within the dark cave they create for us[1]. Successful mess-management requires us to face this alarming but fundamental idea and minimise the limitations it imposes.

This chapter explores the limitations of human perception and how to transcend them by accessing a wider view – a bigger picture – using *holistic thinking* and *multiple perspectives.*

HOLISTIC THINKING

Holistic thinking attends to 'wholes' and the relationship between a whole entity and its context. Whether the entity is an organisation, a project, an artefact, a person, an idea or a concept, holistic thinking attends to the entity in its context and in relationship with other entities. For example, a teacher seeking to understand a child in his care may choose to look at the child's relationship with her peers, her family and himself. He is responding to the underlying idea that he can only fully understand the child *in relationship to her environment.*

In this section, I use photographic metaphors to explore holistic thinking.

Focus and framing

Holistic thinking stands in contrast to reductionist thinking, the habitual approach to finding out and understanding in Europe and North America. Reductionist thinking seeks understanding by looking at the internal structures, reducing the entity to its component parts. By understanding the component parts, I come to understand the whole. Reductionist thinking has been immensely successful as a way of understanding the world and has developed into a powerful tool for science. It looks at finer and finer details to understand how something works, or how it might work better. For example, the great successes of medicine have come from understanding the detailed workings of human cells, the mechanisms that control them, how these go wrong and how to put them right. The great discoveries of science mean we tend to value explanations in terms of the details rather than the broader picture. So might it be, as Stafford Beer[2] has suggested, that it is reductionist thinking that has got the world into the mess it is in?

The staggering insights of science have earned reductionist thinking a privileged place in Western thinking and education. Education encourages students to 'break the problem down into its component parts' and to understand underlying structure as an 'ideal model' stripped of irrelevant details. All this has contributed to a relative neglect of the knowledge, understandings and insights gained by looking at a wider view rather than a detailed view and by looking at the whole rather than the parts. So, is reductionist thinking the best way of thinking about and understanding the world? Holistic thinking looks at the broader picture with less detail in order to understand the whole. A reductionist approach to improving the performance of a football team would look at the individual skills of individual players and seek to improve them. An holistic approach would look at the performance of the whole team, the circumstances under which it performed well and the circumstances under which it performed badly, and would make adjustments at the level of the whole team.

Holistic thinking is neither better, nor truer, than reductionist thinking, and reductionist thinking is neither better nor truer than holistic thinking. Holistic thinking and reductionist thinking reveal different features as complementary ways of looking at the world. Exclusive use of either approach can lead to impoverished understanding. Messes do not have clear internal boundaries. Indeed, I usually experience them as 'everything connects to everything else'. This means that improving one part of the mess risks making things worse in other parts. In a messy situation, people who only see part of the mess will often try fixing 'their' bit of the mess and create unintended consequences for other people. Having an holistic view enables me to discover improvements that do not have negative impacts in other parts of the mess.

Systems thinkers consciously move through different levels, deliberately seeking wholes at different levels. Systems thinking looks at the individual team members, the team as a whole and at the context and circumstances in which they train and play. It looks at how the relationships *between* players create the performance of the whole team. It moves consciously between the bigger picture and the more detailed picture, distinguishing wholes at each level. It encounters each player, his skills, his fitness and his individual muscles as it moves towards a more detailed view and, in the opposite direction, the relationships between players, their movements relative to each other on the field, their ability to make use of each other's talents and the whole team's performance. At each level, each of these is a whole. If I am interested in the star-shaped something in Figure 2.1 (b), then in reductionist-thinking mode, I will take an interest in the elliptical elements that seem to be a major part of it (a). I could then focus still more closely on the zigzag sub-components to find out more about them. This is the direction Western science has taken, with enormous success, but to the exclusion, until recently, of any other approach. In holistic-thinking mode, I take an interest in the star-shaped entity's neighbours, in its relationship with them and in the Chinese-cloud-shaped entity they are part of (c). Thus systems thinking calls on both reductionist and holistic ways of looking at the situation, and the parts, wholes and contexts that emerge at each level.

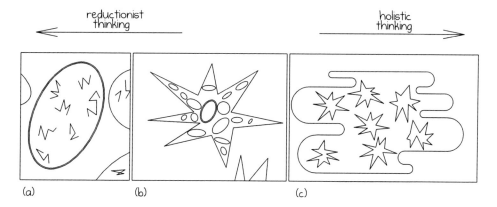

Figure 2.1 By changing focus, different entities come into view. In reductionist-thinking mode, I zoom in on the star-shaped element (b) and find it has elliptical components (a) with zigzag sub-components. In holistic-thinking mode, I zoom out to observe context (c). In systems thinking, I move freely between these views.

Figure 2.2 offers a specific example for exploring reductionist and holistic understandings. It is a greyscale version of the original print. The fiery glow at the top of the funnel, the soldiers' cap bands, the screaming mouth of the drowning soldier at the centre front and the seal at the bottom left are the only spots of red to alleviate the wintry palette of greys, pale blues and browns. A train of at least four carriages, drawn by a steam engine, is falling through the ice into the water below. A plume of hazy white steam rises from beneath the water in the centre panel, contrasting with the rhythmic swirls of black and grey smoke from the funnel. Soldiers fall and leap from the train into the water. The artist conveys horror by using strong diagonals for the engine, the carriages, the ice and fences, contrasting them with the orderly horizontals of the following train. All this is a way of describing the picture as we see it.

Figure 2.2 Kokunimasa (Ryua), Japanese, active 1894–1905: **An Enemy Troop Train Falling through the Ice of Lake Baikal** *- from: Telegraphed Reports of the Russo-Japanese War, March 1904. The inscription in the top-left says the steam locomotive and all its carriages sank, dozens of officers and soldiers died, and Russian transport capacity was greatly damaged.*

Color woodcut triptych. 36 x 72.5 cm (image)
The Fine Arts Museums of San Francisco, Achenbach Foundation for Graphic Arts,
1963.30.5655

Looking at this picture in even more detail – the reductionist approach – reveals more about Utagawa Kokunimasa's skill. The lines vary in thickness much like brushstrokes. The water is rendered as gentle wavelets in the centre but explosively where the carriages hit the water. The ink lines of the smoke are almost calligraphic but Kokunimasa describes the steam using only colour shading. Small details add to the sense of panic: soldiers' fingers are splayed; they crowd the windows with their bearded faces. The rough-hewn logs function as sleepers for the temporary ice railway. What is happening on the footplate between the engineer and the smartly-dressed man? Who is he, and what is a civilian doing on a military transport? Further back in the train, a soldier attempts to rouse his sleeping companion, another climbs over his comrade and an officer steadies himself against the window frame as he leans out to see what is going on. Looking closely brings all these (and many more) details into sharp focus.

An holistic approach alerts us to the context. A picture like this exists in a number of contexts. It exists in our own context. It is a picture, in a book you are reading. Our twenty-first century context may include our memory of previous encounters with Japanese prints and their conventions. It may also evoke contemporary Japanese graphic art such as manga comic-book images. The contemporary viewer may also think in terms of the picture's collectability and monetary value as an art object. The picture also has an historical context. Placed somewhere between ephemera and fine-art objects, prints were acquired by the Japanese viewer as cheap and easy-to-buy images of events and places. In this context, the print is an image of the Russo-Japanese War. Before the widespread use of photo-journalism, such prints brought images to the public from the frontline. It was an image for study and discussion. The Russo-Japanese War (February 1904 to September 1905) – a war about railways – is yet another context in which the picture can be considered. Japan had undergone a period of rapid technological development while Russia struggled against its own vast size and inefficient administration. There is no evidence that there ever was a disaster such as Utagawa Kokunimasa depicted[3] but it was incompetence like this, and defeat in the East, that led to the 1905 revolution in Russia. The engine depicted has been identified as one from the Railway Museum in Tokyo, a 30 year-old import from Britain that was significantly out of date in rapidly-changing, technologically-advanced Japan. Perhaps Kokunimasa was using it to show Russia's backwardness and its disaster-prone transport system. A piece of war-time propaganda? Holistic thinking often yields surprises. It reveals unexpected connections with unexpected other entities.

Both reductionist thinking and holistic thinking can follow different paths. For example, reductionist exploration of a Japanese print may identify details of technique or ink chemistry, or follow stories and questions prompted by the content. An holistic approach reveals multiple contexts such as the historical context; the viewers, contemporary and contemporaneous; and the purposes attributed by the artist.

Returning to the photographic metaphor of framing and focus, I notice I do not need to be constrained by the 'frame' implied by name or boundary; the edge of the picture in the example above. I can instead zoom in and out to focus on detail or to show the context; including perhaps observers, viewers and others in relation to the object of my interest.

If you have a mess of your own in mind, I suggest you pause to ask yourself the following questions:

- Labelling your mess as 'The Mess' and thinking of it as a whole, what other wholes are present in the context of The Mess but not as part of it? (Hint: your list may include other projects and activities going on around the mess; other things that you or others need to attend to; ethical frameworks you espouse; resources such as money, time, energy, enthusiasm and political considerations.)

- What are the relationships between these things and The Mess?

- What is the relationship between you and The Mess?

- What essential problems become invisible if you break the problem down into components?

There are no right or wrong answers to these questions: it is your experience of the mess that counts. I am simply inviting you to look at the mess holistically (as a whole) and to look at some of the interactions between the mess and other features of its context. Being aware of the context is important in managing messes because mess boundaries are unclear. This means I need to address the *context* of the mess as well as the mess itself. In this book, I write as often about the *messy situation* as about the mess.

Lighting

The second part of my photographic metaphor concerns the lighting that reveals, conceals or highlights visual features. I want to consider two aspects of this metaphor: the effect of illuminating everything in only one colour and the effect of 'high contrast' lighting.

Seeing everything in terms of one particular value, performance indicator, interpretation or theory is equivalent to illuminating everything in, say, red light, or blue light. Some things stand out and other things recede or become almost invisible. Over-emphasising one value, interpretation or theory is another form of reductionism.

'The economy, stupid', James Carville's famous slogan for Bill Clinton's 1992 presidential campaign, was often taken to mean that the economy was the only important issue[4]. The economy is an important issue for any government but, while a healthy economy is important, voters see the economy as enabling or disabling other aspirations like improving education, healthcare, welfare provision or crime. An attitude that 'it's all about the economy' is reductionist and obscures or distorts other important issues. In managing messes, I treat any attempt (whether mine or someone else's) to define 'the core issue', 'the real problem' or 'the essential challenge' as provisional. This contrasts with many problem-solving approaches that start with a problem-definition stage. Identifying 'the problem' highlights one version of the problem, pushing other versions into the background. Defining the problem also specifies *and limits* possible outcomes. It obscures other, potentially better, solutions and improving actions by directing attention to a single solution. For example, defining the problem as 'how to get addicts off illegal drugs' suggests treating individual addicts for their addiction and obscures other possible improvements such as managing and preventing addiction, de-coupling addiction from criminality, and social-inclusion strategies.

Considering your own mess, ask yourself:

- Have I limited my thinking by identifying a 'core issue' or 'the real problem'?

- What other possibilities might there be, if I let go of this idea?

The history of ideas since the Enlightenment[5] has seen many 'big ideas' based on single interpretations come and sometimes go. For example, some of Freud's followers have adopted stances in which *all* psychological disorders arise from psychosexual development in childhood. Freud's own views were less reductionist but he never lost his conviction that the sexual urge was the root of all neuroses. Ultimately, this conviction limited his view and his exploration of some of his own best insights[6]. In a similar way, Marxism shrank from Marx's own broad view of the origins of capitalism and the resulting exploitation of the working class. Marxists of various persuasions saw economics, politics, history and indeed almost every field of human activity in terms of class warfare, dialectical materialism or some other single element of Marx's often elegant analyses. It will take some time, I suspect, before history rescues Marx and his ideas from the influence of Marxist reductionism.

Further questions arise here concerning your own thinking about a mess that you are dealing with.

- Are you using one 'big idea' to understand the mess? Such a big idea may come from your own education, from habit or from the organisation you are part of.

- Are there other ideas that may be relevant? They may be 'big ideas' but small ideas are helpful too. The point is not to hold onto one single idea but to have several ways of interpreting what is happening. Even having no idea at all is better than one single idea.

Reductionist thinking extends beyond big intellectual ideas. For many years, clinicians and surgeons saw saving life as their primary task. Now that technology can keep hearts beating and blood flowing almost indefinitely, this simple idea has created circumstances where preserving life seems pointless on its own. While legislative frameworks and codes of practice take some time to catch up, most medical practitioners now recognise that quality of life is an important consideration and that simple clinical guidelines have to yield to more complex decisions – including ethical concerns that may be the practitioners' alone. The reductionist idea of the primacy of preserving life cannot match the complexities exposed by life-preserving technologies.

Performance targets, often set for public-sector services as a proxy for market disciplines, are dramatically reductionist. There are numerous stories to be told. A typical example concerns the UK National Health Service. In the 1990s, taxpayers, politicians and patients were all concerned by the long delay between doctors' referrals and patients seeing a specialist. The NHS was set targets for the maximum waiting time. Sanctions were applied where hospitals failed to meet the new targets. The effect was to decrease the waiting time but patients often experienced unsatisfactory outcomes. Often the consultant sent patients to another consultant with another waiting list and hospital culture began to feel as if 'seeing the patient', however cursorily, was the only criterion for success. Meeting the government-set target competed with caring for patients. The intention had been to improve patient care but, by reducing the complex phenomenon of 'good patient care' to a single target, patients experienced a reduction in the quality of their care.

Profit is often seen as the single and perhaps only organisational value of importance. Stafford Beer told a story of Selfridges[7], the up-market London department store. Seeking to drive up profits in the late 1950s, they commissioned a study to see which part of their retail floors generated the most profit per square foot. To everyone's surprise, the ladies' room, with its coin-in-the-slot cubicles, came out top by quite a margin, implying that Selfridge's prestigious store should greatly extend its ladies' loos. Fortunately Selfridges had the wit to realise their reductionist approach was too simplistic.

With your own mess in mind, ask:

- How do I measure success? Do I have one value in mind or am I able to run several values in parallel? It is not that a single value is 'wrong' but it can be unhelpful in the midst of a mess.

Reductionist thinking can also become limiting when it becomes dualistic. Dualism is a big subject and I am using the term *dualistic thinking* to mean the habit of mind in which things, ideas, theories, concepts, people, etc. are seen as *either* one thing *or* another. It is a kind of 'high-contrast lighting' which shows things only in black or white. Dualism often involves right-or-wrong or true-or-false and often appears in subtle forms. A senior executive once said to me, describing a particularly messy situation, 'the Marketing people all think the product is the problem but really it's about their failure to reach the customers'. He was making a statement that different interpretations of the problem were right (his) or wrong (Marketing's). In some contexts, deciding between different interpretations of an event or phenomenon may be important. When I am dealing with a mess, however, dualistic thinking can be a severe limitation. Holistic thinking takes a 'both-and' approach, treating different interpretations of the problem simply as observations: 'Marketing thinks the product is the problem. The senior executive thinks it is about not reaching the customers'. In a messy situation, it is simply more helpful to suspend judgement and accept that there are a number of interpretations. I do not have to decide between interpretations. It is also likely that each interpretation will add something unique to my understanding of the messy situation.

In the context of your mess, ask yourself:

- Am I discarding important data in order to maintain one single version of the mess?

- What alternative interpretations are available to me?

Holistic thinking and managing messes

Extending the photographic metaphor a little further, in the next section I will think about perspective and the photographer's viewpoint. A skilled photographer can create different interpretations of a scene using lighting, focus and filters to highlight different aspects. Focus, as we have seen, can direct viewers' attention to details, to an object or to surroundings. Similarly, lighting an object in different ways and with different colours will highlight and bring particular qualities to viewers' attention. Different coloured filters will highlight otherwise almost-invisible features. For example, some surface features on Mars, Jupiter or Saturn are almost invisible, even with large telescopes.

Inserting a coloured filter into the telescope's eyepiece reveals astonishing and previously unnoticed details. Holistic thinking is the equivalent of taking all these photographic ideas and experimenting with different ways of seeing the messy situation.

 As you engage with a messy situation, it is helpful:

- to move between detailed views and broader views

- to resist the temptation, at least initially, to break the problem down

- to access the wider picture by asking questions about the context (different perceptions of the context will add to your understanding of the situation)

- to be prepared for surprises, especially as you engage with the bigger picture that includes the context

- to notice reductionist thinking in the form of valuing things in terms of a single value. Supplement this with holistic thinking that looks for features that get excluded

- to notice less obvious forms of reductionist thinking and supplement either-or, right-wrong and true-false thinking with both-and thinking that suspends judgement.

In the next section, I want to explore the idea of multiple interpretations and multiple views and include them in the frame of the bigger picture.

PERSPECTIVES

In this section, I will look at the metaphorical photographer's viewpoint. The image the photographer creates is not separate from the photographer's position when the photo is taken. It is always a 'view from somewhere'. It is a unique position; it may reveal things that can only be seen from that viewpoint. But it is also limited. Some things cannot be seen from that viewpoint. They are too far away or are hidden behind other things. As I encounter a messy situation I wish to improve, I am in a similar situation. My mental image of the mess, and ultimately my understanding of it, is always 'a view from here', behind my eyes, using my mind, my previous understandings, my preferences and my expertise (and lack of it). In systems-thinking terms, perspective is more than a simple viewpoint. A perspective also includes the way someone categorises, codifies and makes sense of their experience. Understanding how my perspective enables me to understand and how it limits my understanding alerts me to features of the mess that lurk invisibly, obscured by the more obvious features. Until Luna 3 orbited the moon in 1957, no human had any idea what the far side of the moon looked like. 41 per cent of the moon's surface is simply not viewable from Earth. It turned out that it has almost no *maria* – the dark patches seen on the earth side – and is heavily cratered. How could this be? Observations from these first photographs, confirmed by Apollo 8's astronauts – the first humans to see the far side of the moon – opened a new chapter of ideas on how the earth and moon formed[8].

My habitual ways of seeing the world also filter my 'view-from-here'. Just as news editors select stories they think will interest TV viewers, I have filters that decide, before I even notice, whether something is relevant or not. I then fail to notice some features of the mess. The problem arises because my brain decides what is relevant based on experience. I may fail to notice things that were irrelevant in the past but might be relevant now. My history of making sense of the world enhances my ability to make sense of experiences similar to those encountered before but limits my ability to deal openly with new experiences – or even to experience them at all.

Perhaps even more startling is the limited bandwidth of my senses. Emerging evidence shows that humans perceive the world in ways that reflect their own needs and interests. As I walk around my neighbourhood, I encounter an overwhelming amount of data. My senses receive 400 thousand million bits of data every second. My brain only deals with 2,000 bits per second so I only notice a very small fraction – a half a millionth of one percent – of what I see, hear and smell. More extraordinary still is the observation that the 100 bits per second that trigger my visual perception are not enough to form any image of what is going on around me. My brain fills in the deficiency[9]. My expectations and previous experience create my sense of the outside world. It is hard to defend any claim to an objective view under such isolating circumstances. As St Paul observed, we see through a glass darkly.

My perspective is unique. No-one has access to the view-from-here that I have. But my perspective is also limited. Humans place huge trust in their senses. We tend to treat what we see, hear and understand through our senses as being 'the way the world is'. But it is, at best, only partial and provisional. I only ever see the world through my own eyes and my eyes are always in some physical location. I do not have a view that is 'outside it all'. So accessing other perspectives begins with the wisdom of acknowledging that I do not see everything, know everything or understand everything. Everything I know about a messy situation is known *relative to me*. Unless I recognise that my own viewpoint is partial, I risk trapping myself – with my own unchallenged assumptions – so I cannot change my understanding of the mess I am trying to deal with. (There is more about mental traps in Chapter 5.) Once I recognise that my view is partial and limited, I can also recognise that my understanding of the mess is always provisional – it is open to development and change as I seek to learn more. I am impelled to adopt an attitude of openness, provisionality and learning if I am to enrich my perception and understanding of the world.

The uniqueness and limitations of my perceptions come into sharp focus when I face a messy situation. My perspective means that what I 'see' when I look at a messy situation is at least as much to do with me as it is to do with the mess itself[10]. I bring to the mess my previous experiences, my understandings, my expertise (such as it is) and my commitment to improving it. All these are unique to me. But there are features of the mess that I cannot, do not and will not see. None of us can escape from the limitations of our own perspective. I cannot escape from the filtering effects of my senses and perceptions. There is no objective 'me' that can be separated from my previous history and my habitual ways of understanding what I see.

There are three ways I can attain a more complete view of the messy situation:

- by exploring the limitations of my own perspective

- by extending my own perspective

- by accessing other partial views to supplement my own.

Exploring the limitations of my own perspective

How do I learn to see a mess differently? The chapters that follow describe some of the many ways. Some will be familiar already. Describing the mess to a friend who is prepared to listen can be helpful. Sorting it out enough to describe it can reveal new ways of thinking about it. 'Sleeping on it' can be helpful, especially if anxiety has become part of your response. Anxiety can become a mental trap that keeps one going round in circles. Sleep (and dreams, perhaps) can break the fretful cycle. Physical activity, a movie or a good meal may also work.

Another way of attaining a new perspective is to use 'what if?' thinking. Ask yourself the following questions about your messy situation. (If you are reading this book with a specific mess in mind, I suggest taking brief notes about your answers and any insights that occur.)

- Thinking about your needs and aspirations, what do you most need from this situation?

- Imagine you are assured of getting what you need. What new possibilities and opportunities become apparent?

- What would be the least favourable outcome from your point of view?

- Imagine that this least favourable outcome were certain. What new possibilities and opportunities become apparent?

- What features of the situation constrain you from doing what you would like, or need, to do?

- Imagine that each constraint no longer exists. What new possibilities and opportunities become apparent?

This exercise can yield unexpected but powerful results. Margrit, a woman in her late fifties had reached the top of her profession and had an international reputation for managing the legal technicalities for large one-off events. She had previously set up the legal framework that enabled the host city to purchase land for, and then build, the athletes' village and the central events stadium for an international sports event. She was now leading the team drafting the enabling legislation for a national park. Things were not going well, she suspected political duplicity, the team began to fragment, her budget was suddenly reduced and the government department responsible seemed to be marginalising the project. Whenever she asked, she was assured that the national park remained a priority. When she began to think about the questions, Margrit realised how much she feared losing her reputation for getting things done. If she allowed herself to contemplate the loss of her reputation, exciting possibilities opened up. After a great deal more thought, Margrit took a course of action that risked her reputation: she went to the press. It was unprofessional but the resulting popular pressure for the national park was overwhelming, the legislation was fast-tracked and Margrit received much of the popular credit. Having realised that her reputation was less important to her than doing work she cared about, she retired to become the non-executive director of a conservation trust where her expertise and contacts were valued and she could indulge her passion for historic buildings.

Extending my perspective

Looking at the situation as if from someone else's perspective reveals another set of insights. Imagine someone else's perspective to increase your own understanding but recognise that the perspective you imagine is not the same as their 'real' perspective. Again, ask yourself some questions. The point is not to guess what their perspective is but simply to imagine what it might be so that you can enhance your own understanding. You can imagine the perspective of *any* person in or around the messy situation; but where one person, or a group of people, seems particularly difficult, it helps to imagine their perspective. Again, give yourself some time, space and a notepad to ask yourself these questions:

- Imagining yourself in the other person's shoes, what are that person's concerns in this situation? What are they trying to achieve?

- What do they most hope for in this situation?

- What are they most worried about in this situation?

- What are the constraints on their actions? Where are the pressures on them coming from?

- What do they know about that you do not? Who are they in contact with?

Even this very limited set of questions allows a different perspective on the situation. It is important to undertake these questions without judgement and to recognise that this is only a work of imagination. Doing this exercise often reveals some startling insights about people's behaviour. It will often explain seemingly irrational or difficult behaviour, for example.

Sometimes opportunities to extend one's perspective are serendipitous. Like most Brits, I am most used to world maps that have the UK near the centre with New Zealand tucked into the bottom right-hand corner. During a long wait at Auckland Airport, I found myself entranced by a world map with New Zealand on the centre line. It was quite unlike any map I had seen before. I 'knew' New Zealand as an isolated country in the South Pacific. Here it was in the central Pacific, serving as a hub for a multitude of nations over a vast area of ocean. It was a humbling but exciting experience[11].

Accessing multiple partial views

Perhaps the richest way of extending one's understanding of a mess is to seek a multiplicity of other views by exploring other people's perspectives. Each person has their own perspective, albeit partial, so engaging without judgement with what other people see (and how they interpret a situation), is a powerful way of creating richer understandings, as seen in Figure 2.3.

Figure 2.3 *Students at a painting academy create pictures of Christ's Crucifixion, each interpreting the model in their own way. The Crucifixion is one of the foundation narratives of the Christian faith, invested by Christians with many layers of meaning. One imagines that these many meanings inform the different ways in which the academicians see the Crucifixion. This picture is the frontispiece of part of Veridicus Christianus by Jan David, published in Antwerp in 1603. The illustration is by Theodoor Galle (1517 - 1633).*

In exploring other perspectives, it is helpful to adopt some specific attitudes. Firstly, it is unhelpful to assume any perspective is 'more true' than any other, in the absence of other evidence, because all perspectives are limited. People's perspectives depend on them making the best sense they can of the evidence they see. For example, Jane tells you the dispatches are often late. There are four ways of seeing this as data about the mess:

1   Jane says the dispatches are often late

2   Jane thinks the dispatches are often late

3   It is reasonable to say the dispatches are often late.

4   The dispatches are often late.

The first statement is self-evident data. This is what Jane says. It needs no further justification. Unless there is reason to disbelieve what Jane says, we can reasonably infer that Jane *thinks* the dispatches are often late and that she has *experienced* the dispatches as late on a number of occasions. The first two statements are data about Jane and her perspective. The third statement evaluates the evidence about the dispatches available to Jane, me, and perhaps others. It indicates that, given various experiences and records of them, there is enough evidence of lateness that a reasonable person might make that judgement. The final claim is a little more subtle. It is simply a claim by the speaker that they have decided that the evidence is clear enough that it is appropriate to discard any possibility that the dispatches were not late. Being serious about perspectives entails being clear about what value I attribute to observations, whether my own or others'.

The second helpful attitude is *non-judgement*. There are several reasons for suspending judgement. If I make judgements about what people tell me, I risk discarding or marginalising data before I know whether it is important. Secondly, a bigger picture often reveals ways in which apparent contradictions make sense as aspects of a deeper truth. Richard Feynman, the physicist, put this very succinctly in his Nobel Prize acceptance speech in 1965[12]:

> *[...] sometimes an idea which looks completely paradoxical at first, if analyzed to completion in all detail and in experimental situations, may, in fact, not be paradoxical.*

The third reason for adopting a non-judgemental attitude arises from the *principle of charity*, the philosophical concept that assumes that the other person is telling the truth as they see it and that what they say has a reasonable basis. I suspend disbelief or scepticism in favour of understanding, even if my initial reaction is to disagree or to correct them. This allows me to be open, receptive and free to understand new ideas, including ideas that challenge my own perceptions. It assumes that were I in a similar situation to the person I'm talking to, I would say similar things. The principle of charity is a methodological device. I can engage critically later, after I have sought to understand what is said. The principle of charity enables others to feel respected but it is also a pragmatic approach[13] – an investment in the goodwill of people who may help improve the mess. Finally, I prefer not to be judged. I aspire to treat others as I would wish to be treated myself so I try not to judge them. The principle of charity is also an ethical stance.

The most effective way of exploring other perspectives is to work with others to understand the mess. The success of this strategy depends on an open-minded determination to see everything as legitimate data and to avoid judgement. 'Everything is data' is a good slogan. Judgement and evaluation can be postponed: the aim here is simply to gather as much information as possible about how other people understand the mess and how that informs what they would like to do and what they are doing. Sometimes other perspectives must be gathered indirectly. Some cultures, for example, inhibit people from speaking from their own experience because the view of their boss is paramount. Giving information other than through the boss is construed as disloyal. Other office cultures prohibit expression of concerns or problems. Observations about them emerge tangentially if at all. Interviews, even informal ones, can be intimidating so it may be better to elicit perspectives in informal circumstances or in group discussions. You may have to negotiate permission and boundaries with the person you are talking to or with their boss. Taking notes, or not, may also influence what people are willing to say.

Whatever the circumstances, *active listening* is a powerful tool. In normal conversation, I often don't give the person speaking my whole attention. As they speak, I am formulating a response, comparing their experience to mine, deciding how much validity I will give to what they say and so on. Active listening is the process of giving the speaker my whole attention. The art of active listening starts with the questions you ask[14].

Imagine you are trying to identify someone's main client. You know they deal with Smith and with Jones and are tempted to ask 'Do you mostly work with Smith or with Jones?' The reply will identify whether they work more with Smith or with Jones. Notice however that you did not ask the right question. By asking about Smith and Jones, you precluded the answer about the main client, who happens (in this case) to be Wilberforce. Don't ask questions with either-or answers. These *closed questions* close off many possible answers. The temptation to ask closed questions often stems from a well-meant motive such as establishing that you already know something about the situation. The effect nonetheless is to cut off potentially useful data. Simply ask 'Who is your main client?' Here are some examples of open questions you might ask about a messy situation:

- what are the main issues for you in this situation?

- what is your role in this situation?

- what are you currently doing?

- what would you like to do?

- what are your main concerns or worries in this situation?

The person you are talking to may not see the situation as a mess. They may know much more about the situation than you do and they will almost certainly know more about some aspects of it. Try not to interrupt, offer your own views, agree or disagree. Be guided by your curiosity while allowing the other person to say all they want to say. You may want to add questions to clarify your understanding of what they tell you:

- please tell me a bit more about that

- what happened next?

- how does that happen?

Try to avoid saying 'I understand'. Claiming to understand the other person is a logical nonsense. How can you know what they are trying to say? If you don't know what they are trying to say, you cannot be sure that you have understood correctly. The way around this difficulty is to ask the other person to check your understanding: tell them what you think they have said and ask if you are right. As well as helping to arrive at agreed, shared understanding, checking your understanding also allows the other person to offer more details and clarification.

Finally, you might ask:

- is there anything else that might help me understand more about this situation?

If you ask open questions and give the person your whole attention then they will have the *experience of being listened to*. This will often be a very positive experience. The person will feel they have been helpful, respected, valued and taken seriously. You will have a bigger picture because you have accessed another person's perspective. Even more of the picture will emerge as you reflect on what has been said, noticing new information and ideas.

Be careful about confidentiality. It will help the other person be more open if you are able to tell them their information will be treated in confidence or in a non-attributable way. In practice, especially within organisations, it may not be easy to keep information or opinions confidential. Do not make promises you cannot keep. If someone is reticent about something, do not push. This is especially important in an organisational setting if there are status differences between you.

Perspectives and managing messes

As you deal with a mess, bear in mind that:

- Your view of the situation is necessarily limited by your own preferences, past experience and preferred interpretations.

- It is also limited by your own neurobiology: most of what you 'see' in the world is constructed using mental models created by previous experience, by expectation and by the very, very limited data arriving via your senses.

- If you choose to operate with this awareness, 'knowledge' can only be partial and provisional and is as much to do with you as with the situation you perceive.

- Accepting that perception is limited suggests that you can extend your understanding by:

    o exploring the limitations of your own perspective

    o extending your own perspective by seeking new ways of seeing the world

    o seeking the perspectives of others, recognising that they too are partial and provisional

    o Treating other perspectives with respect and without judgement.

In thinking systemically, I explicitly recognise that a mess includes different viewpoints, different versions of 'the problem', potentially conflicting ideas about its solution and differing knowledge, understanding and ethical positions. If I value these, and learn to accept ambiguity, I can access knowledge and understandings that transcend my own perspective. Taking action to improve the mess will often depend on cooperation and coordination. This is more likely to be forthcoming if knowledge is shared and different understandings and different agendas are respected and legitimised.

Respecting and legitimising other perspectives changes the aims of working with a mess. Reaching compromise agreements in messy situations is both difficult and unlikely to please anybody. A consensus is simply a view that everyone agrees on. It is often seen as the 'gold standard' for agreement but, in a mess, is often only reached when people have to abandon positions that are important to them, trade one principle for another, or when the agreement is fairly trivial and contributes little to resolving the issue. Genuine consensus can be very powerful when it happens but is rare in a mess. In a mess, searching for consensus risks displacing the goal of genuine improvement, creating 'coalitions of the unwilling' or forcing convergence on low-level interventions that change little. In a mess, consensus is often little better than no agreement. Creating consensus about 'the best thing to do' taxes anyone's diplomatic skills and is usually impossible in the complexity of a messy situation. In short, one of the characteristics of a mess is that worthwhile consensus seems unobtainable. Seeking accommodations, on the other hand, creates opportunities for improvements that please some while not displeasing anyone. Accommodations are simply agreements where everyone agrees that the outcome will at least do no harm to their own interests and will do some good for some stakeholders[15] in the situation. Such agreements are much easier to reach than consensus—where everyone has to agree on an action that will do some good for everyone. Accommodations are much larger 'spaces' and are easier to reach, especially when there is acceptance of 'continuous improvement' as a model for addressing the mess. Subsequent improvements can improve the mess for other stakeholders.

HOLISTIC THINKING, PERSPECTIVES AND MESSES

People often confuse systems thinking with holistic thinking but systems thinking attaches importance to other partial views and perspectives thus adding another dimension. Figure 2.4 relates systems thinking to other, perhaps more familiar, thinking styles. Systems thinking is holistic *and* respects multiple perspectives. By contrast, holistic thinking generally takes only one perspective. Ecological thinking is an example of holistic thinking. It takes a more holistic view while retaining the mechanistic qualities of single-perspective thinking. Scientific thinking or mechanistic thinking is reductionist and takes only one perspective. In Figure 2.4, reductionist thinking that acknowledges multiple viewpoints occupies the top-left corner, as in many forms of social science. Different interpretations, coming from different perspectives, co-exist but in a reductionist form.

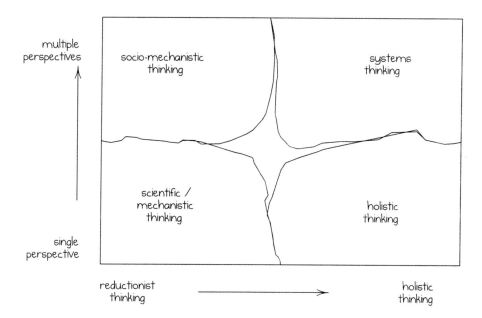

Figure 2.4 *Styles of thinking that incorporate single or multiple perspectives and range from reductionist thinking to holistic thinking.*

Systems thinking does not (or should not) claim superiority to other thinking styles but acknowledges the powers and limitations of each. The skilled systems thinker will move consciously between different thinking styles to gain new insights.

Notes, resources and explorations for Chapter 2

1   *Plato's cave*

In the *Republic* (written around 380 B.C.E.), Plato has Socrates in an imaginary conversation with his brother Glaucon. Socrates argues that people are like prisoners, chained in a cave, seeing only images projected on the cave wall. The images are the only reality the prisoners know. This idea forms part of Plato's discussion of the nature of knowledge and the importance of philosophy.

2   *Stafford Beer*

Stafford Beer (1926 – 2002) was one of those extraordinary men whose contributions range across many disciplines. To claim him as a distinguished cybernetician seems to be a reductionist libel, although he was one of the most distinguished cyberneticians of cybernetics' founding generation. He contributed the Viable System Model to the understanding of how organisations work (or don't work). He was also an artist who taught and practised yoga, a writer, a philosopher and storyteller who spoke several languages, including Latin, Greek and Sanskrit. He described himself as a 'research philosopher', which goes some way towards capturing his written work. He would be better known if his work did not to defy categorisation.

Beer's observation about the disastrous effect of unbalanced reductionist thinking comes from a conversation with Pia Pausch.

Brian Eno, artist, musician, founder member of Roxy Music, and friend of Stafford Beer, has written the foreword to a delightful compendium of Beer's life and ideas edited by David Whittaker.

Beer wrote, among his more serious writings, *The Chronicles of Wizard Prang*. This delightful read is available online.

Beer, Stafford, *The Chronicles of Wizard Prang*, http://www.chroniclesofwizardprang.com

Pausch, P., editor. (2001). *In Conversation with Prof. Dr. Stafford Beer*. Cwarel Isaf Institute. Available at http://www.kybernetik.ch/dwn/Interview_Beer_Bausch.pdf

Whittaker, D., editor. (2009). *Think Before you Think: Social Complexity and Knowledge of Knowing*. Charlbury: Wavestone Press.

3   *Utagawa Kokunimasa's railway engine*

The story about the origins of the engine and the possible propaganda purpose of the print come from:

Kennedy, I. and Treuherz, J. (2008). *The Railway: Art in the Age of Steam*. Kansas City: The Nelson-Atkins Museum of Art.

Including the viewer in considering an artwork is a recent tradition advocated most famously by John Berger. The purposes, assumptions and values of the maker, the viewer and the owner become the critical context for the content of the picture, rather than the art-historical context alone.

Berger, J. (1972). *Ways of Seeing*. London and Harmondsworth: The British Broadcasting Corporation and Penguin Books.

4   *Bill Clinton's 1992 campaign*

The slogan was one of three displayed in the Little Rock, AK campaign headquarters. The others referred to health care and to change rather than more of the same. However, the catchiness of 'The economy, stupid' (usually quoted as 'It's the economy, stupid') caught the popular imagination and sometimes threatened to hijack the campaign, and the presidency, into a single-issue reduction of the issues facing America.

5   *The Enlightenment*

The Enlightenment defines a rather imprecise period of time from the mid-17th century to the end of the 18th century in which science, economics, politics and culture developed rapidly, becoming recognisably 'modern'. It is variously taken to have roots in Descartes' *Discourse on Method* (1637), Newton's *Principia Mathematica* (1687) and the consequent emergence of experimental science. It was characterised by the discussion, publication and increasing democratisation of ideas. The pamphlets, learned societies, salons, coffee houses and debating societies that propagated the ideas privileged skilled argument and may have contributed to the emphasis on dualistic thinking that still characterises science, social, political and economic thinking.

Since the Enlightenment, Physics has been seen as the purest of sciences, formulating universal laws. Over the last 60 years however, Physics has struggled to accommodate ambiguity. Heisenberg's Uncertainty Principle declares the impossibility of knowing both the momentum and position of a particle at any moment. As quantum mechanics developed, it became clear that this was more than an experimental limitation. It seemed to be part of 'the nature of things'. Physics now routinely deals with dualities (both/and) as well as dualisms (either/or), understanding photons both as waves and as particles, for example. Einstein regarded quantum mechanics and its implications with horror and some physicists will cheerfully admit to their failure to understand it.

6   *Sigmund Freud*

Sigmund Freud is as important in the history of ideas as in psychiatry. He pioneered many of the styles of managing psychiatric disorder, and ideas about the nature of humanness, that are common today. These included treating the patient with respect and listening to their story as if it were of value. Freud believed that patients' own stories and their current concerns arise from their own best efforts to deal with distressing childhood experiences. Freud's groundbreaking work was perhaps flawed, however, by his belief that all psychological distress was linked to the patient's childhood experiences of sexuality. The patient, Freud believed, often repressed memories of shameful or distressing childhood sexual experiences. These two beliefs, taken together, sprung a trap for Freud. When patients claimed to have no memory of childhood sexual experience, including experiences of abuse, Freud saw this as 'proof' of repression and thus as proof of sexual abuse – a self-sealing belief. (A similar self-sealing belief triggered a moral panic about 'satanic ritual abuse' in the USA, UK and elsewhere in the 1980s. The vehemence of children's denial, under questioning that was itself potentially abusive, was seen as evidence of the terrifying power abusers had over the children. Almost no evidence was found anywhere of actual abuse during satanic rituals despite widespread and detailed accounts by believers in the phenomenon.)

7   *Selfridges*

Stafford Beer recorded this story in *Decision and Control*. First published in 1966, *Decision and Control* has never been out of print. It is also available in a memorandum marking his 70th birthday and in Whittaker, 2009 (see Note 2 above).

Beer, S. (1997). The Culpabliss Error: a Calculus of Ethics for a Systemic World. *Systems Practice* 10, 4.

Beer, S. (1994). *Decision and Control: The Meaning of Operational Research and Management Cybernetics.* Chichester: John Wiley and Sons.

8   *The Moon*

The earth and the moon can only be understood in relation to each other. Current theories about their co-formation suggest that they formed from a protoplanet. Approximately 4,500 million years ago, a Mars-sized object hit the protoplanet Earth and split off a vast amount of debris. This debris subsequently accreted to form the moon. The maria on the near side of the moon are evidence of the time it took the young molten moon to solidify, relatively protected by the nearby earth from further impacts.

The moon appears to wobble. Its orbit, its axis of rotation and the earth's own rotation allow us to see approximately 59 per cent of the moon's surface over time. This apparent wobble is called *libration*.

9   *The human brain and human knowing*

An accessible account of these ideas about the brain can be found in books by Chris Frith (Professor of Neuropsychology at University College London) and Cordelia Fine (Research Fellow at the University of Melbourne and the Australian National University). Humberto Maturana (formerly professor of Neurosciences at the University of Chile and founder of the Instituto de Formación Matriztica in Chile) has researched, and written extensively about, the biology of knowledge and its implications for human knowing, being and loving. (There is more on Maturana in Note 5 to Chapter 7.)

Fine, Cordelia. (2007). *A Mind of Its Own: How your brain distorts and deceives.* Cambridge: Icon Books.

Frith, C. D. (2007). *Making up the Mind: How the Brain Creates our Mental World.* Oxford: Blackwell Publishing.

Maturana, H. R. and Varela, F. J. (1988). *The Tree of Knowledge: The Biological Roots of Human Understanding.* Boston and London: Shambhala Publications.

Maturana, H. R. and Poerksen, B. (2004). *From Being to Doing: The Origins of the Biology of Cognition.* Heidelberg: Carl-Auer Verlag.

Maturana, H. R. and Verden-Zöller, G. (2008). *The Origin of Humanness in the Biology of Love*. Exeter: Imprint Academic.

10   *Managing my own Complexity*

Chapter 6 discusses this issue more thoroughly.

11   *Maps*

The history of maps is also the history of human visions in various times and places. As a child, I was used to large red areas of the world map signifying the British Empire. More recently, new projections of the globe onto flat maps have sought to correct misleading perspectives created by traditional projections. Some of these break away from the arbitrary north-at-the-top convention that seems to privilege European and North American visions of the world. The Peters projection, created in 1974 by German-born Arno Peters, shows countries so that their relative areas on the map represent their relative areas on the globe. The traditional Mercator (Gerardus Mercator, Flanders, 1512 – 1594) projection conveys the impression that Africa and Greenland are the same size. The Peters projection reveals Africa to be immensely bigger (14 times) than Greenland. Any projection creates distortion but these maps are profoundly unsettling as they challenge the arbitrary assumption that the North-up-South-down Mercator projection is somehow more real. TV's *The West Wing* featured a wonderful discussion of this issue at the White House where the fictional Organization of Cartographers for Social Equality petitioned the use of the Peter's projection map in US schools.

ODT Maps are the official publishers of the Peters map. Their website is at http://odtmaps.com

The West Wing (TV programme) 1999-2006, Season 2, Episode 6, *Somebody's Going to Emergency, Somebody's Going to Jail*, A. Sorkin, T. Schlamme, and J. Wells, producers. Warner Bros.

12   *Richard Feynman*

Richard Feynman was both a Nobel-winning physicist and a man with extraordinary curiosity about all kinds of things. His contributions to quantum electrodynamics came, in part, from his ability to make sense of contradictory ideas. He described this in his Nobel-acceptance lecture.

Feynman, R. P. (1965). *The Development of the Space-Time View of Quantum Electrodynamics*. Stockholm: Nobel Prize for Physics Lecture.

The lecture is also available at the Nobel Prize website.

http://nobelprize.org/nobel_prizes/physics/laureates/1965/feynman-lecture.html

13   *The Principle of Charity*

The *principle of charity* and the associated *principle of humanity* are ideas from philosophy first proposed by Neil Wilson. More recently, it has been described and developed by Donald Davidson.

Davidson, D. (1984). *Inquiries into Truth and Interpretation*. Oxford: Clarendon Press.

Wilson, N. L. (1959). Substances without Substrata. *The Review of Metaphysics*, XII (4 (48)): 521-539.

14   *Active listening*

Active listening arises in a relationship that freely grants the other's legitimacy, and the legitimacy of what they experience and express. Martin Buber (1878 – 1965) explored this deeply in his essay *I and Thou*. David Bohm (1917 – 1992), a quantum physicist, developed some principles for dialogue. Although intended for groups of between 20 and 40 people, the principles capture some of the underlying characteristics of active listening. They include agreement not to decide anything at group level during the meeting; to suspend individual judgements, particularly judgements in the form of assumptions; to endeavour to be open and transparent; and to build on previous contributions. Bohm sets high standards that require everyone to commit to very disciplined behaviour. These ideas nonetheless represent some foundational ideas for facilitative conversation. Patricia Shaw has developed styles of conversation more akin to jazz improvisation than the discipline of Bohm. Nancy Kline's book presents a model of supportive listening in management contexts.

Buber, M. (1937). *I and Thou*. Edinburgh: T & T Clark.

Bohm, D. (2004). *On Dialogue*. 2nd edition. London: Routledge.

Shaw, P. (2002). *Changing Conversations in Organizations: A Complexity Approach to Change*. London: Routledge.

Kline, N. (1999). *Time to Think: Listening to Ignite the Human Mind*. London: Cassell Illustrated.

15   *Stakes, stakeholdings and stakeholders*

A stakeholder is simply someone who has an interest in a situation and is not indifferent to its fate. In traditional analyses, such as those that inform the legal frameworks of most countries, the only legal stakeholders in a company are its shareholders. More recently, management theory has begun to realise that stakeholding in a company extends beyond the traditional four groups of stakeholders (owners, workers, customers and suppliers) to include the local community, government, environmental watchdogs, competitors and others. In systems thinking, this wider sense of stakeholding is used to identify stakeholders in a messy situation. The nature of the stakeholdings will be diverse and potentially conflictual but anyone who is concerned about the situation and its trajectory is a stakeholder.

CHAPTER 3

Drawing rich pictures

… just another way of keeping a diary.

Pablo Picasso (1881 – 1973)

Rich pictures are an ideal starting point for dealing with messy situations[1]. They attempt to capture everything you know about the messy situation without imposing any structure or analysis. Rich pictures launch your 'finding out'. They depict things, ideas, people and connections, indeed everything you perceive to be part of the situation you are concerned with. They also contain representations of more subjective elements of the situation: character, feelings, conflicts and prejudices (literally 'pre-judgements'). A rich picture is just that, a *rich* pictorial representation of the situation in all its messiness.

My sister and I were wondering how best to support our Mum when she had a stroke.

We were facing a problem that appears for many people of our age: *How to look after Mum?* We knew we were dealing with a mess. When my sister raised the issue of planning for her care, Mum had refused to discuss it. Like many older people, Mum was determined not to be a burden on us, not to live with either of us, nor to live in a care home. We wanted to ensure that Mum would receive the care she needed and she was already dependent on others to enable her to remain in the home she loved. I drew Figure 3.1 as my sister and I discussed our concerns.

Mum was 82. You can see her near the centre of the picture with her close companion, Twinkle the cat. She spent most of each day in her armchair, unable to walk without the aid of her walking frame. It was also unclear whether she would return to health or whether the stroke that had left her confused and unable to speak clearly was the start of a terminal decline. This is shown by a 'cloud of uncertainty' hovering over Mum waiting to be resolved into health or permanent incapacity. A number of professional helpers provided Mum's personal care. They were a devoted group of people employed by an agency. The agency took care of the business side of things but didn't take responsibility for maintaining the rota.

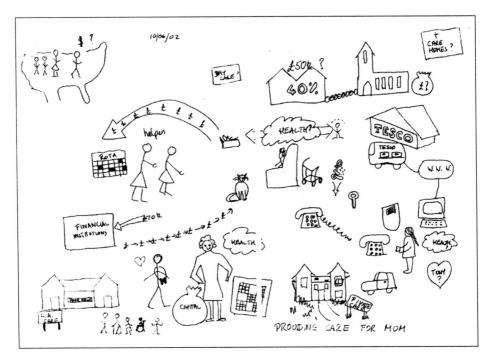

Figure 3.1 *A rich picture I drew with my sister*

My sister, who lived in London, spent a lot of time on the phone ensuring that someone was available each day to get Mum up, to wash and dress her, to make sure she had meals and to make sure she was tucked safely into bed at night. This all cost money and we were unsure whether it was sustainable on Mum's pension. I drew this on the left-hand side of the picture: you can see the rota with gaps in it, the helpers and the stream of money.

We drew some of our other concerns on the right of the picture. A wet pound-sign represents money going down the drain. The key signifies concerns about the security of Mum and her house. Almost everyone in the village seemed to know where the house key was hidden. Arrangements for shopping were a concern. Mum was agitated about money following the stroke so friends were unwilling to take on shopping. I wondered whether internet shopping was a solution. You can see me on the right, thinking about home delivery from Tesco.

My telephone conversations with Mum were incoherent and one-sided. I felt trapped. I had been sucked into the long-hours culture of work and my partner, Tony, had recently had several episodes that seemed to be heart attacks. He was still awaiting a proper diagnosis (another mess!). I visited Mum as often as I could. It was a six-hour round trip each time. You can see our rather unreliable car – I couldn't find time to deal properly with that mess either. You can see my sister at the bottom of the picture. She had chronic health problems at the time and struggled to keep going. She makes beautiful quilts and had just got married. You can see her husband with his birdwatching binoculars. My sister had inherited some money and she was wondering whether she should invest it in an annuity to support Mum. You can see her sack of capital and the possible income stream flowing to Mum (not the cat, as shown) from one of the financial institutions that offer this sort of deal.

Mum refused to consider residential care. We suspected the time was coming when she wouldn't have a choice. There was a local care home run by the County Council with an excellent reputation and a long waiting list. There would be many people with higher priority ahead of Mum in the queue. You can see the County Council home in the bottom left corner with its waiting-list-queue of needy people. We knew much less about private-sector care homes but the national news was reporting their struggle to reach new regulatory standards while remaining affordable. There were public concerns about the quality of the buildings. You can see a private-sector care home in the bottom right of the picture. In the top right corner is Mum's house. We were aware that, in the UK, people usually have to sell their houses to finance long-term care. Mum's house was partly owned by the church. We didn't know how much capital the house represented if Mum were to take that route. We also wondered if the church ran care homes for people in Mum's situation.

In the top left corner, you can see my brother and his family with their then-unknown financial assets and commitments. They live in the USA.

Finally, we were beginning to get reports from the helpers that Mum was making potentially dangerous mistakes. She had put yogurt into the kettle and a metal dish had been found in the microwave. We were also aware that she had been using her panic button almost every night, getting the volunteer neighbours out of bed. Mum could not live on her own much longer.

This was the mess we faced, stretched still further by geography (we both lived several hours away) and relationships with Mum that had been quite complicated over the years. The mess was a set of interconnected small and large issues, some urgent, some less so. The contexts of our own lives were also complicated.

I have recounted the story of the mess we faced for two reasons. Firstly, it shows that a picture is indeed worth a thousand words. A verbal account of the mess was long and fragmented. It would have been all but impossible for my sister and me to hold all these interconnected fragments in our minds as we discussed what we should do. A rich picture gathered all of the mess there in front of us.

Secondly, I will return to this particular mess throughout the book, using it to exemplify some ways of thinking through messes.

DRAWING RICH PICTURES

Many people are wary of drawing their first rich picture. Some object that they cannot draw. The good news is that you don't need to have any artistic talent. Indeed, my experience is that sometimes artistic people get sucked into creating an aesthetically pleasing picture rather than sketching rich, interconnecting visual notes. The good news is that *if you could draw when you were five, then you have all the talent you need* to draw a good rich picture[2].

Creating a rich picture is one of the best ways of experiencing its benefits. As with many systems-thinking ideas, experiential learning is more convincing, more reliable and more fun than simply reading about it. I invite you to draw a rich picture of your own messy situation.

There are very few ways of drawing a bad rich picture and lots of ways of drawing good ones[3]. This is what you do. If you have already identified a messy issue you want to work on, prompted perhaps by the Introduction or by Chapter 1, make it the subject of your picture.

Gathering materials

Start with a large piece of paper and some coloured pens or crayons. Ideally use a sheet of A1 (ANSI D, elephant, double demy) flip-chart (butcher's) paper or failing that, a sheet of unlined A3 (ANSI B, ledger, tabloid). Of course, you can ignore this guidance and work with a ball point on the back of an envelope or on a napkin. These are not ideal for your first rich picture but they are perfectly adequate in an emergency.

Getting started

Then simply represent *everything* you know about the situation. The situation is full of resources for, as well as obstacles to, taking action. A key tip here is to make sure there is plenty of activity in your picture. Don't just draw stick-figure people, show them doing something and show some of their context – where they do it. Include resources, tools, equipment, buildings, ideas, dreams, processes and objects. Use metaphors. Show interconnections[4]. Make it *rich*. My sister and I started by drawing Mum, at the centre of the picture. We drew her in her armchair, which is where she spent most of her time. We next tried to capture her situation by depicting her walking frame, the cat, money going down the drain, her helpers and so on.

Some people get 'white-paper panic'. If you find it difficult to start, just draw a squiggle in the middle of the page. It will break the intimidating power of the empty white paper. Don't do preliminary sketches. The first rich picture will be good enough. You are drawing mainly for your own use; it doesn't have to make sense to anyone else. Don't get hung up about 'getting it right' or using the right symbols.

There are not many ways to get it wrong. Here are some of the very few rules about rich pictures to get you started:

1 Don't structure your rich picture in any way. This means don't draw it as a comic strip; don't structure it with a single over-arching metaphor; don't structure it as a time line or systems diagram (see Chapter 8).

2 Don't use too many words. Words can be used as labels, as exclamations in speech bubbles and in other brief ways but not as sentences and paragraphs that need to be read. (Sometimes I suggest to people that I shouldn't need my reading glasses to discern what is going on.)

3 Don't exclude relevant observations about culture, emotions, and values, including the emotional climate, social roles, and your own values, beliefs and norms, and personal stuff that may 'get in the way'.

4 Include other points of view.

I explain these rules more fully later on. You may want to include ideas for addressing the messy situation. This is fine but you will need to be careful. Treat these ideas as features of the situation. You will be setting a trap for yourself if you allow ideas for dealing with it to structure or dominate your picture of the situation.

As you draw you are likely to find questions and insights coming to mind. Keep a notebook beside you and jot these down; they are important.

A second burst

It takes me about 20 minutes to draw a rich picture. I then seem to come to a halt. At this point, it is helpful to take a break. Walk away and come back.

There are often things I wish to add to the picture. It also helps, especially if you have used flip-chart paper, to hang your rich picture on a wall or door for a few minutes. Hanging your rich picture on a vertical surface moves you from 'drawing mode' into 'viewing mode' and often triggers ideas for further additions.

There are three more rules:

5   Include a representation of yourself[5]

6   Include a title: 'A rich picture of the <a name for your mess> situation'

7   Include a date.

Don't limit your drawing to a depiction of only the problematic elements of the situation. Include resources, goodwill, friendly colleagues and other resources that may be relevant to the situation, without attempting to formulate a solution.

Go for it

I am constantly astonished by people's reluctance to draw their first rich picture. May I politely suggest you give yourself the experience of drawing a rich picture right now? Most of the skill is developed, and most of the value learned, in the process of drawing a rich picture rather than reading about it. I suggest you draw a rich picture of a mess you are involved in. Rich pictures usually work better if the situation is of immediate concern to you. Failing that, news broadcasts are a reliable source of messes to work with and I've suggested a few at the end of the chapter[6]. Use scrap paper and a ball point pen if you don't have other supplies.

Most people find, even if rich pictures don't seem to be their sort of thing, that once they have drawn one, they draw other rich pictures of other messy situations. Users surprise themselves by finding them both useful and empowering.

Finally

Don't assume your rich picture is finished. As new features, possibilities and insights emerge, add them to the rich picture. It can go on evolving until you start to act in the situation. Then the situation changes and becomes a different situation.

THE RICH PICTURE 'RULES'

Most systems-thinking rules can be broken. There is, in any case, something rather odd about setting rules for thinking. Systems-thinking rules usually challenge the systems thinker to greater clarity. Mostly, when I find myself tempted to break the rules, it's because I'm trying to get away with muddled thinking. It's helpful to understand why the rules are there so you can decide whether they are helping or hindering your thinking.

Rule 1: Don't structure your rich picture in any way

Structure can creep into a rich picture in several ways. Remember that a rich picture is a representation of a situation you experience as complex. If you structure it by imposing an organising principle, an interpretation or an analysis on it, you are no longer representing the situation as you experience it. You lose the opportunity for encountering the complexity in all its fullness. You also preclude the possibility of seeing other, possibly more interesting, features later. Metaphors are important in rich pictures but don't let a single metaphor structure your whole picture. It can lead you to miss all the ways in which the situation is *not* like the metaphor. It is inevitable that ideas occur to you as you draw, including 'this is really all about …'. Stop such ideas imposing themselves too strongly on your picture by jotting them down in a note book in the form of a question. Once you've written it down, the idea is much less likely to keeping popping into your mind as though trying to make sure you don't forget it.

Keep asking yourself:

- Is this rich picture telling just one story or is it rich enough to suggest lots of stories about what is going on?

Rule 2: Don't use too many words

I have seen effective rich pictures with lots of words but they are very rare in my experience. More often, lots of words make a rich picture less rich. One of the uses for rich pictures is discerning patterns. Words inhibit your ability to spot patterns. If you use speech bubbles, use what people say rather than your interpretations, unless the bubble is about some general attitude. Examples might be 'Aaagh!', 'Help!', 'Hooray!', 'Oops!' – the sort of exclamations found in comic books. The check for wordiness is to ask:

- Do I have to do a lot of reading to see the relationships between elements in the picture?

Rule 3: Don't exclude relevant observations about culture, emotions and values

Feelings, culture, values, beliefs and norms are not only legitimate but important elements in a rich picture. Some people find it quite easy to record emotions and their own emotional responses to a situation – indeed, they may find it difficult not to express their feelings quite vividly. Others find it difficult to express, or even to recognise, any emotional responses to a situation. Other people are, of course, either somewhere between these two extremes or somewhere else altogether. Neither is good or bad. The point is that if I am to start thinking deeply about a situation, I have to recognise that I, and other people, have emotions even if I am normally unaware of them. They contribute to the complexity of the situation and determine how much energy I have for addressing it. They condition the way I perceive and evaluate the situation. Your own values are also important. They will determine how you are able to respond to the situation.

Rule 4: Include other points of view

This rule is simply a reminder that the 'view from here' is not the only view. Other people know different things, understand different things and have different purposes and priorities. All of these perspectives are part of the messy situation.

Rule 5: Include a representation of yourself

You are part of the messy situation. You became part of it by choosing to think about it and improve it, if not before. You bring your viewpoint and blind spots, your role and stakeholding, your skills and experience and your wish to see an improvement. The situation changes because you are in it, even if you are an external consultant or other non-participant in the mess. If you are a participant, draw yourself doing what you do in the situation.

Rules 6 and 7: Include a title and a date

A title is just enough structure to capture the whole situation without imposing a precise boundary on it. It is helpful not to put a title on your rich picture until you are satisfied that it is 'finished for now'. I often find that my perception of 'the situation' changes as I draw the rich picture and that it needs a different title from the one I would have given it at the outset. One of the features of messy situations is that they evolve, often quickly, through time. This, together with Rule 7 (include a date), helps you to keep track of your evolving understanding of the mess and the evolution of the mess itself.

Temptations

All the rules are only rules because they are useful. Break them if necessary. Nobody is watching to see if you get it right and there are no 'right' rich pictures. Let experience and usefulness be your guide. Be alert to temptations that take the form: 'I won't do it that way because I work better with X'. These are temptations to do things the way you have always done them. You cannot extend your thinking by yielding.

A VERY FEW WAYS IN WHICH RICH PICTURES CAN GO WRONG

There are many ways of drawing rich pictures and, if you follow the rules, you are unlikely to go wrong. Here are three ways in which your picture might be less useful than it could be.

1. The first way to go wrong is to represent the problem instead of the situation. If you are dealing with a mess, it is likely to be deeply embedded in, or have multiple interconnections with, the context. Divorcing the issue from its context risks representing a problem you don't really have, rather than the real but messy problem. There are lots of metaphorical phrases in English that can entice you into this trap. We can talk about 'the nub of the problem'; 'the key issue'; 'the basic problem'; 'the real difficulty' and so on. Representing the problem rather than the situation is a trap and like all traps, once it has sprung, it is hard to escape. The trap seriously limits one's ability to think about the situation in its full complexity. By identifying every problematic feature as stemming from one single interpretation of the problem, you limit your possible ways of dealing with the situation to those that might be answers to this single problem. You have imposed simplicity on the situation, and your rich picture will not reflect the very complexity that makes the situation messy. In contrast, one of the complexities of a messy situation is precisely the difficulty of identifying anything that could be described as the key issue. It is a tangle of interrelated key issues.

The whole point of a rich picture is to represent all you can about the situation. To identify the problem within the picture, or to include only the elements that seem problematic, is to prune out potentially important elements of the complexity.

2. Rich pictures can also 'go wrong' by not being rich enough. If usefulness is the criterion, the most useful rich pictures are the ones that include, or hint at, all the interests and activities going on in the situation. They don't tell a single story, there are lots of stories going on simultaneously. They reveal stories you didn't consciously build into them. How is such a rich picture to be achieved? Use everything you know about the situation. This means taking the trouble to find out as much as possible and talking to as many people as you can. Include interested observers as well as people directly involved in the situation. Lots of people quite unconsciously use visual metaphors in their everyday language. ('Every so often they drop a bombshell on this department'. 'We're swamped with emails'. 'I got nailed to the wall for that'.) Talk to yourself about the situation and you may pick up clues about how to represent features of it in your rich picture. Use the metaphors that people in the situation use. Don't force the images; use the ones that seem to come naturally. There is no library of approved symbols.

Some people draw on a list of symbols for rich pictures. I don't believe such lists are very helpful. I have helped hundreds of people discover rich pictures and no-one has ever needed them. Symbols risk constraining meanings. If you use a symbol to mean something specific then it may cause confusion if not used consistently. For example, a conflict between A and B represented by the conventional crossed-swords symbol is likely to be different to the conflict between B and C in possibly important ways. In the interests of promoting the *rich* rich picture, I advise against standard symbols.

Indicate the connections. Where there are structural entities that have connections and relationships, indicate what they are. There are all sorts of ways of doing this, especially if you ask yourself about the nature of the connection. You can use physical proximity (or distance) or representations of the nature of the connection (hearts, daggers drawn, telephones, hands over ears, walls of silence). Use all the geographical locations if this is relevant.

Some people use computers to draw rich pictures. It rarely works in my view. Some essential quality seems to be missing and the picture is impoverished rather than rich. This quality might be ownership or engagement or perhaps the very act of sitting at a computer keeps the activity at a rational level – it does not allow for the impressions and half-formed awareness to express themselves through the act of making marks directly on paper. A good rich picture needs immediacy and provisionality and that is, as yet, beyond the scope of clip art, or drawing packages.

3. Finally, although the process of drawing a rich picture usually comes to a satisfactory conclusion, it is normally a mistake to consider the picture 'finished'. Imagine instead that it is 'finished for now'. New realisations and observations will crop up and can be added to the picture as you appreciate more and more of the complexity of the situation.

WHY RICH PICTURES?

Systems thinkers typically spend much longer than usual engaging with, and appreciating, the situation of concern. Messes are characterised by lots of interconnection and so any action is likely to have consequences that extend beyond the immediate intervention and to have unintended and unforeseen consequences. Understanding the messy situation as fully as possible is vital if I am to avoid creating worse problems as a result of well-intentioned but badly thought-out actions. Rich pictures are important tools for capturing everything I know about a situation and the interconnected events, people, observations, processes and structures that characterise it.

A rich picture represents the messy situation so that it is there in front of you but the process of drawing is as important as the rich picture itself. As you think about each element, questions, observations, understandings and insights are evoked and can be recorded as notes. The drawing process itself allows you to attend to the details of the messy situation you are trying to manage. You begin to discover the interconnections that make the situation messy.

People are sometimes reluctant to draw a rich picture because they have greater facility with words. They ask, 'Why draw when you're not very good at it?'. This is a valid question. Its answer highlights another benefit of rich pictures.

In order for words to make sense, they must be structured – most usually into sentences and paragraphs. Getting to grips with a messy situation means letting go of thinking that is constrained by structures. Any structure I impose on a mess tends to exclude options for action that don't fit that structure. The structure then prevents me seeing them. For example, if an organisation tends to structure its thinking about poor performance around the lack of skill in its staff, then only actions related to skills development and recruiting new skills will 'appear' as options. Options that relate to lack of resources, lack of clarity about tasks, cumbersome processes or structural obstacles will be invisible. Words structured into something that makes sense will privilege the connections that provide the narrative thread. Connections that are not part of that thread tend to disappear. Words tend to be two dimensional and linear and less able to represent the web-like interconnections perceptible in a mess. Rich pictures don't have a linear order. They are 'random access' rather than linear – the very feature that made DVDs so superior to video tape. Even lists have a structure. There is a built-in sense – in reading them if not in creating them – that makes items at the top more important than those at the bottom.

The second part of the argument for rich pictures rather than words arises from the two, relatively separate, brains humans have. Broadly speaking, the left side of the human brain deals with structures, linear reasoning and words. The right-hand side deals with interconnections, patterns and non-verbal representations. Many other features of human perception, processing, understanding and action are similarly located on one or other side of the brain, almost as if we had two separate brains. Western styles of education tend to develop left-brain skills. One of the consequences of this is that the left brain tends to 'shout down' the right brain, using its greater facility for verbal expression. Interconnections, recognised mainly by the right-hand brain, tend to get overlooked. The right-hand brain is better at images, so drawing rich pictures is a way of accessing the understandings and perceptions of the right-hand brain and its capacity for recognising and understanding interconnectedness[7].

Systems thinking is not primarily about right-brain thinking but, if we are trying to develop skills for holistic thinking, it seems sensible to be holistic in our approach to thinking itself and mobilise all the brain's resources to improve it. If we always think the same way about situations we will tend to get trapped in ways of thinking that are determined by our skills as left-brain verbal thinkers. (For more about traps see Chapter 5.) Messes, with their interconnectedness and non-linear structure, need right-brain as well as left-brain skills.

CONTEXTS FOR DRAWING RICH PICTURES

In what context might one draw a rich picture? This is clearly a good way to start thinking about a mess but there are other ways of using rich pictures as you become more practised. Usually I draw rich pictures for my own use, much as I have explained, but there are other extraordinarily useful ways of using them with other people.

I have seen them used very effectively to make interview notes about a messy situation. The interviewer drew the rich picture very quickly as she asked about the interviewee's mess. She was clearly practised although she didn't seem to be 'artistic' in any particular way. She asked the interviewee's permission to take notes in picture form and drew the rich picture so that the interviewee could see what she was drawing. The interviewee was drawn into the process so that he was saying things like, 'No, not quite like that, more like that' until he was satisfied the interviewer had really understood.

When I teach rich pictures as a way of gathering an holistic idea of a situation, people come back to tell me how they have used rich pictures in their work. One of the most effective uses they report is structuring conversations to explain ideas. Teams pick up complex ideas very quickly from a rich picture. They freely contribute their own ideas and suggestions, adding to the rich picture. The rich picture becomes a 'mediating object' that enriches the conversation[8]. People can contribute their own ideas by disagreeing with the picture rather than with each other and healthy and productive arguments can ensue. Moreover, each new insight and idea can be added to the rich picture. We have done some *ad hoc* experiments and noticed that this process depends on using flip chart paper, felt tipped markers and colours so that everyone can see the picture clearly. People are put off contributing if the picture looks 'finished' or too beautiful and contribute more and better ideas if they add their own contributions, talking as they draw. (This means having a supply of pens available at the meeting and room for people to move about and gather around.)

One of the most exciting systems tasks I have done was with two people concerned that a multi-faceted product-development project in their organisation was fragmenting through lack of communication. Territoriality and acrimony were setting in. We invited people known to be working on the project for an Away Day. I explained the rich-picture rules and asked each person to spend 20 minutes drawing a rich picture of their part of the project, including what was happening, how it was happening, how they saw it fitting in with other parts of the project, the obstacles they faced, their achievements to date and so on. We then put all the rich pictures on the wall and each person explained their rich picture to a partner they didn't normally work with, answered questions and then did the same for the partner's rich picture. We then swapped partners and repeated the process. The conversations were noisy and animated. People were curious and eager to learn about each other's experiences. People added things to their own rich pictures because each time they explained it, new insights emerged supported by the questions their partners asked. At lunch time, people took their colleagues to see rich pictures they had encountered in the morning and, by mid-afternoon, each of 19 people had seen all the rich pictures and asked questions about them. The energy in the room had been massive and self-sustaining. Even though people were tired and almost overwhelmed by the new insights and ideas that were coming up, they kept going. What happened next was a bit like speed-dating. Diaries came out and appointments made to follow up opportunities for cooperation. Two people were nominated to coordinate and to present this to the senior managers as a *fait accompli*.

So I would like to propose this 'art gallery' and 'show and tell' approach as a third context for rich pictures and as one for surfacing different perspectives that can result in huge individual and organisational learning.

Finally, rich pictures can be shared efforts, as was the one I drew with my sister. Provided each person has a pen, or the pen is shared around quickly, this can be an effective way of sharing information and insights. The benefits of shared working get lost quickly if one person becomes 'designated drawer' who draws on behalf of the others. This has the effect of diminishing the visibility of any perspective except the drawer's.

WORKING WITH RICH PICTURES

How can a rich picture be used, once provisionally complete? Much of the usefulness of a rich picture is realised while drawing and so taking notes as you go – about ideas, insights, questions and observations – is important.

Drawing a rich picture can be an intense engagement so it's often helpful to put your picture on a vertical surface to bring yourself out of drawing mode and into viewing mode.

The whole picture

Rich pictures allow you to step back and see the whole situation at once. In doing this, you may notice features of the situation you didn't consciously build into your drawing. For example, is there a discernible 'emotional climate' in your picture? This may be a reflection of your own mood as you thought about the situation and drew the picture. You may want to think about whether you would draw a different picture if, for example, you felt more optimistic about the situation or if you could stop feeling angry with Person X. If you are doing this sort of review, it's important not to be judgemental. You are just exploring whether a different 'emotional filter' would make the situation look different. The emotional climate may also be a reflection of the dominant feelings of the people in the situation. If so, does the rich picture suggest ways of changing this for the better? Remember you are not looking for solutions, only improvements. A key improvement would be one that allowed further potential improvements to emerge. This means that, for example, brightening the gloom with some positive feedback can release people's own energies and enthusiasms for other positive change.

Looking at the relative placement of different bits of the picture can also be revealing. Features you think are central are often placed literally at the centre of a rich picture. Features perceived as peripheral are often placed around the edges or don't show any connections to other features of the picture. Does this reveal anything to you? What would happen if some features had different placements? Are the things that seem peripheral actually more important than you are prepared to acknowledge? Similar questions can be asked about things that are drawn with bold markings while others are wispy.

Rich pictures suggest new lines of inquiry into the messy situation. Avoid the temptation to articulate what you cannot do and focus instead on what you can do. Ask yourself some questions:

- Which parts of the mess are within your control?

- What resources and allies do you have?

- What questions can you ask?

- What are the good things going on?

- What would you really like to do, if you could do whatever you wanted?

- What would you settle for, if it could possibly be achieved?

- Do you have to engage with this at all? What are your walk-away options?

Make notes about your answers and include relevant features in your rich picture.

Conversations with friends and colleagues

You may want to show your rich picture to colleagues. The way you introduce it is crucial. Don't let anyone think this is a final version or even that 'this is the way it is'. If you indicate that this is no more than *your* sense of the situation, people will be much more accepting. You may have to accept some teasing about such an informal device but if you take it seriously so will they. It's also important that you allow people to criticise your picture: this is the beginning point for discussion. In suggesting alternative representations and interpretations, ideas will emerge. It's useful to record these on sticky notes.

They can then be clustered in groups. It's often useful to think of this process as generating an agenda and the clusters can be around:

- things to discuss

- things to find out about

- new perspectives to bring into the discussion

- things to do.

You will need to be cautious about the last of these. If the situation is a messy one, unconsidered action may have knock-on effects you cannot anticipate at this stage.

Rich pictures as a starting point

A rich picture is a good starting point for deeper exploration of both the mess and possible ways forward. But it can be overwhelmingly complex so it's helpful to have some simpler launch pad without denying the complexity the rich picture represents. One of these is *themes*. Themes are simply names that capture most of the main features of the rich picture. Themes and identifying them are the subject of the next chapter.

SOME HEALTH WARNINGS

Most people find rich pictures fun to draw once they get over the informality and take them seriously. But often they say things like, 'This mess is worse than I thought'. What is the significance of these apparently contradictory experiences? A rich picture undoubtedly draws one's attention to the full situation (sometimes the full horror of the situation) in all its detail and complexity. This is precisely its intention but it can be an awakening to complexity and messiness that has previously been avoided. This can be uncomfortable and potentially overwhelming. It has often been my experience, in working with other people and their messes, that I feel I have nothing to offer against the magnitude and complexity of the issues they are facing and that have surfaced in our rich pictures. On the other hand, it can be empowering to finally see the full extent of the issue, often for the first time. I think this is why, once people have drawn a rich picture, they find them helpful and draw them again in other messy situations. The good news is that, even if the complexity seems overwhelming, systems thinking offers many tools for finding ways of improving the situation that are lasting and do not simply move problems to somewhere else in another form. Even after many years of Systems Practice, I still have to tell myself to trust the process and not to mind feeling overwhelmed and dismayed for a while.

Rich pictures can be very powerful in unexpected ways. Simply put, to those who have not encountered them before, they seem childish and silly. Be careful where you display them. You may unfairly acquire guilt by association and be thought childish and silly.

Rich pictures often express important but politically explosive content. 'Bouffant Bessie', 'Mad Max' or the 'Lone Ranger' may not appreciate your depictions of them in a rich picture and your rich picture may have unintended consequences for your career. Keep rich pictures out of public view.

It is also worth noting that the more senior people are in an organisation, the less likely they are to participate in drawing rich pictures. A shame but true.

Notes, resources and explorations for Chapter 3

1   *Where rich pictures come from*

Rich pictures came into Systems Thinking from Peter Checkland's Soft Systems Methodology. See Note 3 in Chapter 17.

2   *Drawing pictures*

Dan Roam has a nice book on drawing pictures. It is not primarily about *rich* pictures but he has lots of ideas about using informal pictures to explain and explore ideas. He is helpful on how to draw if you really cannot draw or, more likely, you don't have confidence in your drawing skills.

Roam, D. (2008). *The Back of the Napkin: Solving Problems and Selling Ideas with Pictures*. New York: The Penguin Group.

3   *Some other rich pictures*

Here are some more rich pictures. They show different situations in different styles and they don't rely on skilled draftsmanship. They are simply the products of the drawer's determination to represent each situation as completely as possible.

Figure 3.2 *This rich picture, drawn by a project manager, concerns the fragmentation and conflicting priorities of his project. Notice the vivacity of the images. Even without knowing much about the issues, it is possible to discern some of the concerns and experiences he is encountering.*

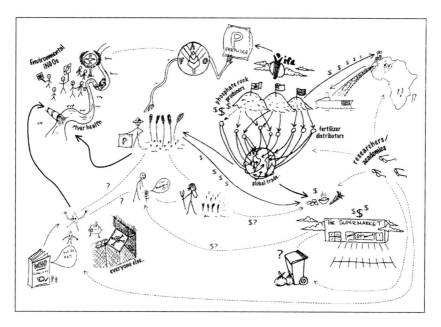

Figure 3.3 This rich picture was drawn by a researcher investigating the sustainability of global phosphorus resources for future food security.

Figure 3.4 A rich picture drawn by a team leader facing potentially major change as the wider organisation adapts to new market conditions. You can see a lot of uncertainty and confusion about how to respond when the strategic direction is still uncertain. Notice the vivid image of the grasping hands on the left of the picture (Want! Give!).

4　　*Aides memoires: things for possible inclusion in a rich picture*

- interfaces and boundaries
- resources
- people
- roles
- organisations, departments, teams
- needs
- obstacles
- conflicts
- alliances
- tools and equipment
- objects

- targets, goals, aspirations
- processes
- progression
- relevant history
- issues
- thoughts and ideas
- concerns, reactions, responses
- dreams
- time
- buildings

5　　*Including yourself in the rich picture*

Since you are not separate from the messy situation, once you choose to engage with it, you need to be in the picture. The presence of the rich-picture drawer is a reminder that a mess is perceived by someone with a perspective.

6　　*Possible topics for practising rich pictures.*

It is much better to pick a topic of your own so use these suggestions as a last resort for practising. Not all of these ideas will seem messy to you.

- funding health care
- the illegal-drugs problem
- teenage knife crime
- transport in a post-peak-oil-production world
- mitigating the effects of climate change
- mitigating climate change
- planning a family wedding
- a family holiday
- domestic violence

7　　*Right-hand brain, left-hand brain*

I recommend Rita Carter's excellent and accessible book for following up how the human brain works. Although now somewhat out of date, it covers much of the still-emerging understanding of the human brain and has a whole chapter on *The Great Divide* between the right and left brains.

Carter, R. (1998). *Mapping the Mind.* London: Weidenfeld & Nicolson.

More recent books that have been part of the renewal of interest in the left and right brains include the following. Both throw interesting new light on the topic and its implications for how humans understand themselves.

Evans, J. and Frankish, K. (2009). *In Two Minds: Dual Processes and Beyond.* Oxford: Oxford University Press.

McGilchrist, Ian. (2010). *The Master and His Emissary: The Divided Brain and the Making of the Western World.* New Haven, CT: Yale University Press.

8   *Mediating Objects*

A mediating object facilitates productive conversations by providing a focus that keeps people's attention on the topic. It also opens up a space for contentious issues by enabling people to disagree with a representation rather than with a person or group of people and by enabling them to say things about the object rather than about the situation itself.

CHAPTER 4

Identifying themes

A name is a label, and as soon as there is a label, the ideas disappear and out comes label-worship and label-bashing, and instead of living by a theme of ideas, people begin dying for labels …

Richard Bach[1] (b. 1936)

How can one think about all the messiness of a complex situation without getting lost in all the detail?

Themes, the subject of this chapter, are a starting point for thinking about the essential messiness without breaking the mess into bits or losing sight of all the detail. Themes provide a 'place to start' for diagrams and other tools, techniques and ideas. Identifying several themes allows me to begin to understand and think about what to do in a messy situation. Themes are a bit like finding a way to pick up a reasonably sized forkful of spaghetti.

A theme is simply a name that seems to capture a significant part of the messy situation.

Themes are most easily identified from a rich picture. A good rich picture will be full of activity, detail and interconnections and will appear to tell a number of stories. One way to identify themes is to identify what those stories are about. It might fit into the sentence:

"This rich picture seems to be telling a story about <theme>."

where <theme> is a one, two or three-word phrase. Remember it is a name, not a description.

If this sentence doesn't work, you might try:

"<Theme> crops up in several places in this situation."

or

"If we could do something about <theme>, it would improve the situation."

The rich picture I showed in Chapter 3 (Figure 3.1) offered several themes. The first theme was very easy to spot.

'This rich picture seems to be telling a story about money.'

If you look at my rich picture you will see 'money' popping up all over it. This was quite a surprise for my sister and me as we contemplated what I had drawn. We had not realised just how many facets of the situation were linked to the theme of money.

It is important, when naming themes, not to fall into the trap of identifying 'the problem'. A theme that captures features that appear in several ways in the situation, or in your picture of it, will enable you to stay holistic in your thinking. Thus 'money' was more useful to us than 'not understanding Mum's finances' would have been. A second trap is to include judgements in your theme. 'Distance', our second theme, was thus more useful than 'long distances'.

A messy situation can usually be thought of in terms of several different themes. It can be useful to identify two or three. There are no 'right' ones or 'wrong' ones. They are simply starting points for thinking more deeply about the situation. When we looked at our rich picture, my sister and I came up with

- money

- distance

- guilt

You can see the money in the rich picture, there are dollar and pound signs everywhere. 'Distance' refers to the effects of geography – our brother in America, my sister and I being some distance apart and both some way from Mum. It also sweeps in some of the issues about the car, about accessing local resources for Mum and the frequent need for telephone calls to people we didn't know and who didn't know us or the situation. 'Guilt' refers to our feeling that we ought to be able to do better for Mum but also a sense of impotence in the face of what appeared to be a limited set of unsatisfactory options. The guilt is probably not obvious to anyone else looking at our rich picture but it was obvious to us as we talked about the situation. Was 'guilt' a judgement? We talked about this and decided that it was simply an observation that appeared in our sense of the whole situation. We were not making any judgements about whether or not we should feel guilty or about whether there was anything to feel guilty about.

Notice that each of our themes was simply a name that picked up, or was at least connected to, a significant proportion of the situation, as represented by the rich picture. A simple name enabled us to avoid treating our mess as if it were a difficulty. We avoided, for example, naming the theme as 'lack of money' or 'how to manage the money'. This might have led us down the path of 'naming the problem' and thus limiting our opportunities to perceive potentially useful approaches.

THE 'RULES' FOR THEMES

The rules for themes are fairly straightforward but well worth observing because it is very easy to default back to treating your mess as if it were a difficulty.

1   Use no more than two or three words to name your theme. It is a name, not a description. This means it should be a noun or noun-phrase.

2   Don't name the problem. This will have the effect of treating your mess as if it were a difficulty.

3   Make no judgements in naming your theme. This too is equivalent to naming the problem.

4   Pick themes that appear in several parts of the situation. The best themes appear in different ways in different areas of the situation. Avoid picking themes that have the effect of chopping the situation up into parts. If you chop a messy situation up into 'zones' it has the effect of naming each zone as a difficulty. Similarly, it is worth checking that each theme reflects more than one perspective.

WHY 'THEMES'?

Themes provide a way of thinking about some of the complexity of a messy situation in a simple way. They are a more holistic way of thinking about a mess than identifying 'the issue' or even 'key problems'. Other techniques in this book support new ways of thinking about messy situations but it can be hard to know where to start. Themes were developed as a way of finding a place to start. Later in the book, themes can be used as trigger ideas for diagrams and as potentially useful starters for thinking about action.

A FEW WAYS IN WHICH THEMES CAN GO WRONG

'Communication' often crops up as a theme. However, for various reasons, it is often not a good launch point for thinking about messes. This is not to say that effective communication is unimportant, but in most messy situations it is tangential to the most effective improvements. Focus on what needs to be communicated. 'Management' can be similarly tangential. It goes without saying that, as you explore ways of improving a situation, they must be well managed. Focus on what would be happening if something were being well managed.

NOTES, RESOURCES AND EXPLORATIONS FOR CHAPTER 4

1   *Richard Bach*

Richard Bach is the American author of the enormously successful *Jonathan Livingston Seagull*, the story of a seagull's love of flying. The sentiments expressed in the quotation seem to me to capture the essence of *themes*, the topic of this chapter.

Bach, R. (1970). *Jonathan Livingston Seagull*. New York: MacMillan.

CHAPTER 5

Escaping mental traps

... but they shall be snares and traps unto you, and scourges in your sides, and thorns in your eyes

Joshua 23.13

Sir Geoffrey Vickers[1] (1894 – 1982) gave a lot of thought to the traps humans get stuck in. He noticed that the design of lobster pots corresponds to the characteristics of lobsters.

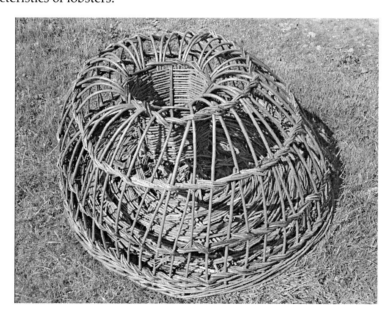

Figure 5.1 *The inkwell lobsterpot is an openwork wicker basket approximately 50 cm high and 75 cm across. It has a strong base that rests on the sea floor, weighted by stones. At the top is a steep-sided funnel that narrows from about 20 cm to 15 cm and is approximately 15 cm long. A strong but light rope, supported by cork floats, allows recovery.*

The traditional 'inkwell' lobster pot (Figure 5.1) has a central steep-sided hole at the top ending in a drop into the basket. The lobster pot is baited with mackerel or salted white fish. The omnivorous lobster smells the tasty bait and finds the hole by climbing the wicker sides of the pot. It makes its way through the hole and drops into the pot where it consumes the bait. The lobster pot exploits the lobster's characteristics and behaviour – walking along the sea floor, finding food, and its liking for particular fishy foodstuffs. It is easy for the lobster to get into the pot but its curved chitin carapace bends in the wrong direction for getting out.

Lobsters get trapped by being lobsters. The lobster's back, which has many advantages for the lobster, is as much a vulnerability as its need to eat, when it is confronted by a baited lobsterpot. Vickers observed that humans become trapped not because they are ignorant or stupid but by their particular human characteristics, including the things they are good at. Human vulnerability to trapped thinking arises from the way we think and, often, from the very things we excel at.

'Trap' is an illuminating metaphor, often expressed spontaneously when options seem limited. In this chapter, I want to explore the idea of mental traps, how they work and, more importantly, how to avoid and escape them. I also want to explore how being trapped can be as much about my own characteristics as it is about the messy situation I am facing. In exploring this metaphor, and the experience of being 'trapped' or 'stuck', I find everyone's thinking is potentially vulnerable to traps, that messy situations often conceal traps and that getting stuck is part of the experience of messy situations. Humans have some significant advantages over lobsters. Humans can learn to recognise that their thinking has become trapped and then to work out how to escape. Better still, they can learn to recognise traps and avoid them.

Messes set traps for those who choose to engage with them. They are a feature of the complexity I experience. Every potential escape route seems to run into uncertainty, lack of resources, other people's unwillingness and so on. This is in the nature of messy situations. It seems wise to acknowledge that I may be trapped.

Even if all my options are blocked, I can explore the possibility – indeed I can make the provisional assumption – that by changing my thinking I can escape from the trap. A lobster cannot change its shape but, as a human, I can change my thinking. By changing how I think about the mess, I regain my ability to make progress. This is a strong claim, so I invite you to suspend disbelief for a while to see if this strategy – thinking about your thinking – offers a way forward. Clarifying your thinking makes new options for action evident.

In his cult classic *Zen and the Art of Motorcycle Maintenance*[2], Robert Pirsig distinguishes between traps set by the environment and traps set by ourselves. However, it seems to me that escaping a trap is more important than how it was set, so in this chapter I identify some traps that seem to lie in wait for those who dare to engage with messy situations and I offer some ideas for escaping and avoiding them. Figure 5.2 assembles these traps.

A systems map of significant thinking traps

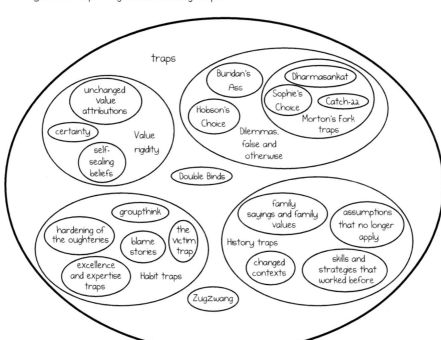

Figure 5.2 *A selection of traps that lie in wait for the systems thinker engaging with a messy situation.*

HISTORY TRAPS

Individuals and organisations are vulnerable to getting trapped by their history. Our individual and collective histories embed ideas and assumptions that may have been valid for different times and different circumstances but trap our thinking if they remain unchallenged. The trick is to learn from the traps we have fallen into. The sayings and beliefs of families, teachers and friends who formed our own core beliefs, the things we have learned ourselves and the solutions that worked before – all may be traps in the adult circumstances of a decade or two later.

When I was young, I lived in a series of cheap apartments and quickly picked up home-improvement skills to better my circumstances. Now, I often assume I will do home-improvements myself, even when getting a professional to do it would be better and more efficient. I even limit my perception of what is possible. In recent family discussions about a new kitchen, I found myself considering only minor improvements that I could complete in a few weekends. Once I spotted that professional builders were an option, I came up with a much better solution, relocating the kitchen to another part of the house. Choices that worked well when I was an impoverished student – and still work well for minor repairs and improvements – work less well when I have other options, a busy work schedule and a family. I get trapped by my history.

More seriously, family and other relationships become traps when we fail to account for the processes of growing up and aging. For example, Florence's parents talk to her as if she were a child, castigating her for her 'immature attitude', even though she is in her mid-30s. But it is hard to demonstrate a mature attitude if you are treated as a child. Resentment is inevitable in such a trap. The assumptions they made about Florence twenty years ago now trap her parents too. Assumptions that no longer apply undermine a satisfactory adult relationship.

A response to feeling trapped in a messy situation is to ask, 'What have I learned in the past that may be limiting my thinking?' and 'What am I assuming?'

Organisations also fall into history traps. A new high school was just completing its fourth year of operation. Each year, with each new intake of students, the staff complement had been increased until faculty numbered around 50. The principal, a talented leader who had inspired the high standards and caring ethos of the school, became concerned that she was 'out of the loop' and people were not telling her things she felt she should know. There were growing resentments in the staff room, particularly directed at new staff. Those who had been around when the school started, including the principal, had enjoyed the intimacy of a small faculty and the pioneering spirit that had inspired them in the first year. They were trapped by memories of their collective past and were struggling to accept that growth and maturity required new ways of doing things, a new leadership style and openness to new staff and their ideas.

HABIT TRAPS

Habit traps are closely related to history traps and can bind us to immobility. They are more challenging to spot and, perhaps, more uncomfortable to address. You may not recognise the following examples but, if you feel trapped, I invite you to consider the possibility that your thinking habits have trapped you. Here are some examples of habit traps.

Hardening of the oughteries

Children brought up with strong guidelines for personal behaviour often build the language of moral imperatives into their thinking. Thus *must, ought* and *should* become part of their mental software – 'I must get this finished today'; 'I ought to visit Aunt Agatha'; 'I should lose weight.' These formulations become traps in a number of ways. Firstly, they blur the distinction between doing (or not doing) something and the consequences. Framed as *must, ought* or *should* statements they disguise themselves as truths rather than as decisions. A decision on the best use of resources such as time, energy, money and enthusiasm, or even a decision to postpone a decision, clears a lot of unnecessary complexity. Framing a *must, ought* or *should* thought as a decision, will reveal more options. For example, instead of 'I ought to finish the work tonight' try 'If I finish the work tonight, I can be more relaxed at the beach tomorrow. What shall I do?'. Secondly, *must, ought* and *should* thoughts are distracting. If this happens, try writing them down for later attention. Thirdly, *must, ought* and *should* sap morale and enthusiasm. It is hard to be enthusiastic about something I 'ought' to do. Focus instead on the benefits of doing it. 'It will be good for everyone if I confront Suresh' is more motivating than 'I ought to confront Suresh'. The language of *must, should* and *ought* evokes the role of a child who has done, or may be about to do, something wrong – not a good role for thinking clearly, performing well or enjoying a challenge. Finally, and most destructively of all, *must, ought* and *should* are stressors. They stimulate anxiety reactions in the body that neither improve performance nor enhance thinking. Ultimately, the continual anxiety creates exhaustion. None of this helps in dealing with messy situations.

Experiment with noticing *must, ought* and *should* thinking. Turn each thought into a decision. Breaking the habit is easier if you do this as soon you notice the thought.

The victim trap

Sometimes it seems that the whole universe is conspiring against me. The evidence for this hypothesis can seem particularly strong when I am trying to deal with a messy situation. Whether it is true is beside the point. It is simply unhelpful to think that way. *Victim thinking* is a trap because it disguises my options, demotivates me from finding better options and saps my enthusiasm for improving the situation. Candace Pert[3], the distinguished research pharmacologist, describes how emotions profoundly influence every cell in our bodies. Peptides released by anxiety and demotivation act like low-level toxins, risking ill-health. Feeling like a victim is a genuinely self-reinforcing trap.

The good news is that enthusiasm, motivation and commitment release peptides that improve our capacity to learn, to solve puzzles, to take action and to feel good. Indeed, as techniques develop to treat depression, chronic fatigue syndrome (myalgic encephalomyelitis) and chronic pain, evidence is accumulating that focusing on positive thoughts and feelings (including faking them if necessary) may set the patient on a sustainable path to alleviation[4].

Feeling gloomy is a natural response to disappointing and unpleasant circumstances. Denying this, and the gloominess, is to be less than human. But choosing to stay with gloominess, victimhood, self-recrimination and feelings of powerlessness is disabling. There are always choices. In the context of managing messy situations, choosing to do something, or even to walk away, is the first step to acquiring enthusiasm and energy for improving the situation.

Blame Stories

When things go wrong it is tempting to ask who is to blame. Blame seems to offer an explanation and to make sense of disasters, failures, accidents and inconvenience. But blame, and the stories we tell ourselves about who is to blame, are traps when dealing with a mess. There are at least three ways the trap can close. First, blame stories put you straight in line for the victim trap: 'It was my mother'; 'You made me so angry'; 'The suppliers let us down'. These blame stories place me in the role of someone else's victim. They allow me to shrug off responsibility for what has happened and dissipate any energy for changing things for the better. Even if the blame stories are true, they are disabling and *focus on the past*. Understanding the histories of the mess, from a variety of different perspectives, enables learning from past mistakes and past successes. Allocating blame serves little purpose in improving the situation. Finally, blame stories are dead-end thinking. They tend to end with the equivalent of 'she is a bad, stupid, incompetent, evil person'. Such thinking, however strong the evidence, closes any avenues to improving the situation.

I am not saying here that no-one is ever to blame for anything but I am claiming that the allocation of blame rarely does anything to improve the situation. Consider the following story. Viktor had been promising Liza he would fill in their garden pond ever since baby Peter had learned to walk. Viktor went out for some groceries, leaving Liza and 5-year old Peter playing in the garden. Liza was distracted, for no more than five minutes, by a phone call. When she looked from the window, she saw Peter face down in the pond. Despite her own and the paramedics' efforts to revive him, Peter was pronounced dead. Amazingly, neither parent chose to blame the other even though, to the outsider's eye, there were grounds for mutual recrimination. Liza and Viktor seemed to recognise that blame, on either side, would destroy their relationship, piling another tragedy onto their already grievous loss.

On a larger scale, Nelson Mandela had plenty to blame white South Africa for. He had spent 27 years in prison for his anti-apartheid activism. Elected President of South Africa in 1994, he established reconciliation as the route to national reconstruction and renewal. He recognised that, while many black people had suffered terrible injustice, tragedy and hurt, South Africa had no future if blame and recrimination were to hijack the nation's energies. In 1995, South Africa hosted the Rugby World Cup. Mandela urged the whole of South Africa to support the Springboks as their national team. The overwhelmingly white Springboks won a remarkable victory over New Zealand in the final. In a symbolic gesture that was to have an immense public impact, Mandela wore a Springbok shirt with the number of its Afrikaner captain when he presented the team with the World Cup[5].

Blame is an easy trap to fall into but, in messy situations, it blocks progress towards improvement. The truth, or otherwise, of who is to blame is less important than retaining important relationships. Short-term anger, fear and hurt are natural but take up 'mental bandwidth'. One way to deal with this is to acknowledge to myself what has happened using sentences with only three elements: I or We followed by a verb phrase and then an object for the verb. The resulting sentence should describe the present situation.

I feel hurt	*not*	You hurt me
We lost the contract	*not*	Jim's behaviour lost us the contract
I am angry	*not*	He makes me angry

This way of formulating responses to difficult situations carries the seeds of improvement and points to the future: taking steps to heal the hurt, finding new contracts and dealing with my anger. It places responsibility on the person – *I* – or people – *we* – who can improve the situation. Punishing those who are to blame may improve things in limited cases. Blame on its own is *never* enough to improve the circumstances.

A more constructive approach is to work on the basis that most people do their best at what appears to them to be the best thing to do. Whether or not this is true and whether or not I actually believe it, this approach opens up many more options for improving the situation. This is the very pragmatic *principle of charity*[6]. It recognises that I cannot change other people, or the past, but that I *can* change present and future circumstances.

Groupthink

Groups fall into the *groupthink* trap when preserving the group, or individuals' relationships with it, is placed ahead of the purpose of the group. The term, coined by William H. Whyte in *Fortune* magazine in the early 1950s, describes the situation when the group subtly suppresses open discussion, new ideas and dissent in favour of preserving the coherence of the group. The group may then begin to converge on consensus that bears little relationship to its purpose or to the demands imposed by the environment. Challenge is disallowed and the group's original purpose gets lost as the group diverts its energy to keeping 'safe'. Eventually, it begins to perceive external threats and even become paranoid, acquiring a sense that the group alone has privileged knowledge and that the rest of the world must be kept at bay. Outsiders are seen as 'the enemy'. The group then takes decisions that any individual member would consider too risky. The group ignores awkward facts as the group makes this *risky shift*. Religious cults exemplify groupthink but any group, particularly high-performing groups, can fall into the groupthink trap. Significant features of the spectacular banking crisis in 2008-10 can be attributed to groupthink. *Cognitive dissonance*, the coexistence of conflicting versions of reality, went unrecognised in favour of misplaced confidence in the banking sector.

The trap shuts as individuals begin to value the security, sense of purpose and 'success' the group gives them and to ignore symptoms of trouble. Indeed members are reluctant to do or say anything that challenges the coherence of the group. When individuals value, and wish to remain part of, a group, there is a potential groupthink trap. Shared loyalty to a leader can also generate groupthink. Any group that works well together is at risk. Shared assumptions and values, rapid communication in which each knows what is being said before it is voiced give a sense of well-being and focus, and that the group is on a roll.

Groups can protect themselves against groupthink by asking: 'Are we fulfilling the purposes of the group?' and 'Do our activities make sense in terms of our task?'

Excellence and expertise traps

Trapped or blocked thinking is not evidence of culpability. Each of us has vulnerabilities, often as the flipside of our talents, strengths and skills. When I challenge clients to notice their own traps, they report getting trapped by:

- the desire for excellence, trapping them into impossibly huge commitments when 'good-enough' would be good enough

- assuming that every problem is one that matches their expertise: engineers tend to see problems as engineering problems, psychologists see problems as psychological ones, IT people see problems as 'mainly' about IT systems, and so on. As a systems thinker, I tend to see all problems as systems problems – a trap I have to watch out for.

Organisations also set traps for themselves. Like individuals, they get trapped by what they are good at. A large multinational organisation established its international reputation by pioneering a radically new product. It was the market leader for nearly 40 years but recently competitors have started to deliver similar products more cheaply. The organisation asked itself some sharp questions. Inquiries found that the organisation bought in little expertise, internal recruitment was the norm and new product development always started from scratch. The organisation had fallen into a trap set by its long history of success. It was hard to conceptualise change because of the prevailing belief that, 'we are the only people who can do this well enough for our customers'.

Asking 'What am I good at?', 'Which of my skills do I believe to be relevant to dealing with this situation?', 'Are they the right skills?' and 'What other skills are available?' creates opportunities for checking that skills and past experience are not blocking my thinking. The Zen idea of *shoshin* or *beginner's mind*[7] is helpful here. It refers to the openness, enthusiasm and lack of preconceptions that beginners bring to a new activity. Retaining *shoshin* as skills develop allows learning and improvement to continue. This, in turn, allows the practitioner to transcend normal limitations on excellence.

DOUBLE BINDS

An organisation adopted a 'decentralisation' change programme[8]. Staff were encouraged to take more responsibility for their own work and decisions. But, at the same time, managers constantly checked up on them, made suggestions and monitored progress. In some cases, staff were even reprimanded when they did not do the task the way their manager thought it should be done, even when the task was completed satisfactorily. Staff found themselves trapped by a *double bind* where successfully taking responsibility for how they completed a task inevitably incurred the displeasure of their manager who would have done it some other way.

A double bind is a communication trap in which the victim receives conflicting messages so that a successful response to one message is a failure to respond to the other with the additional twist that the contradiction cannot be confronted and resolved. This 'twist' doubles the bind and makes the trap more difficult to escape than the simpler 'mixed messages' trap. The inability to confront and resolve the double bind often arises because the disapproval messages are conveyed by informal or undiscussable means such as body language, tone of voice or emotional demeanour ('mixed messages, mixed media'). (Notice that Florence's relationship with her parents, described above, contains a typical double bind.)

Gregory Bateson[9] drew attention to the double bind's location in a relationship that the victim must preserve. Parent-child and boss-worker relationships are typical locations for the double bind. Inequality in power or the need to preserve a relationship means that the double bind is often not consciously recognised by the unhappy victim because there is no single trauma to confront. Bateson noted that double binds can trigger unexpected responses as the victim simultaneously tries to behave in two mutually contradictory ways. Double binds can be subtle. 'I would like you to decide what we do for Christmas' is a double-bind statement when the victim already knows that the hidden message is 'but I will be upset if you decide on something I don't like'. Other double binds tighten through distorted understandings of, for example, love ('you ought to love me'), or play ('Show Granny how you play').

Escaping from a double bind is not easy. It is set to be escape-proof, often unconsciously, by the person who sets it. As with many traps, escape begins with recognising that one is trapped. Once the trap is recognised there are choices to be made. The most significant choice is *exit*[10]. Exit is simply the choice between staying in the relationship with the double bind or leaving. Robert felt trapped by his circumstances. He worked for a company that was well-known for its employee welfare programmes and its friendliness. He felt lucky to have got a job there, especially since the company took a lot of trouble to accommodate his special needs. When a new boss was appointed to his department, the atmosphere changed. Robert continued to lead his team, to get new business and to meet his targets but, at his monthly one-to-ones with the new boss, the message was: 'You are not good enough but I won't sack you because I know you will find it difficult to get another job'. Robert was in the double bind of mixed messages and feeling grateful. When, through the help and support of a business-network group, Robert finally recognised the trap, he decided to exit the situation. He risked the insecurity of unemployment in favour of happiness and job satisfaction. The cost of getting out of a double bind can be high – but so is the cost of staying in it.

Feeling trapped in a mess may mean a double bind is in operation. They are particularly hard to spot. I have tried several approaches over the years but, by the nature of double binds, none guarantees success and exit can be costly and painful. However, the following approach seems to work well if someone seems trapped in a mess. Spotting the double bind is the first step. I ask:

- Are you clear about what you are being asked to do?

- Is it clear what 'success' would look like in doing what you are asked to do?

- What happens when you succeed?

It is puzzling when success in doing what I am asked to do causes displeasure or even attracts punishment. The questions address the puzzlement and reveal hidden mixed messages. It is sometimes possible to address the mixed messages directly by questioning the person setting the trap (the *voice* option). Asking non-confrontational questions such as 'How will you recognise that I am succeeding?', 'How will you know if I am doing this well?', or 'What do you need from me?' may enable them to recognise their own conflicting needs.

Even asking neutral questions may be impossible. The person setting the trap may have too much power or they may be unwilling to confront their own conflicting needs. Take care in asking the questions, recognising that it is not your responsibility to help the trap-setter resolve the contradictions impelling them to use the double bind. If the double bind arises from conflicting needs in the trap-setter, they may experience *any* questions as confrontational or threatening.

Exit might involve calling the other's bluff, going over their head to a higher authority or leaving the situation altogether. The double-bind trap is, to some extent, released when the victim finally becomes aware of the choice. The costs of staying in the relationship are often high, the costs of exit may include guilt, regret or insecurity. A damaged relationship with the trap-setter is inevitable. Their bluff has been called. They now face an uncomfortable decision about whether to resolve their own contradictions or to shift responsibility to another victim. Deciding on exit requires the escapee's courage. It is unusual to find another option in a double bind. As usual, a full review of the situation comes first. I ask myself:

- What are the benefits of exiting from this double-bind relationship?

- What are the costs of exiting from this double-bind relationship?

- What are the costs of loyalty to this double-bind relationship?

- What are the benefits of loyalty to this double-bind relationship?

Having established an inventory of costs and benefits, I next ask

- What sources of support, help and information are available to me?

This is an important question because exit from a double bind is a big and uncomfortable decision. So only when I have resources in place do I ask myself:

- Do I have the courage to take an uncomfortable decision?

If the answer is *No*, more resources are needed. There can be no final *No* because, having spotted the double bind, deciding not to decide is a decision to stay in the double-bind relationship. If the answer is *Yes*, I can ask myself:

- What forms of exit are available to me?

DILEMMAS, FALSE AND OTHERWISE

The history of ideas provides all sorts of names for the dilemmas humans experience. A dilemma is simply a decision offering only two options, usually both unattractive. Education in the Western tradition of dualistic and reductionist thinking habituates people to the idea of dilemmas. This means that decisions appear to be two-option choices.

The happiest form of dilemma is Buridan's ass[11]. The ass, caught between a pile of hay and a pail of water, cannot choose which to try first and dies of both hunger and thirst. Choosing between two attractive options is easier if it is transformed into a choice between disappointment and pleasure. Decide that Option A will be 'heads' and Option B will be 'tails' and toss a coin. If the options really are equally attractive, your decision is made. If you have a previously unrecognised preference for one option, the disappointment or relief of the coin's 'answer' will tell you what to do.

Unpleasant choices are more difficult. In no-win situations such as Morton's Fork[12], one either has to choose between two unattractive *options* or has to choose between two equally unpleasant *outcomes*. Morton's Fork itself comes from the declaration by Henry VIII's Lord Chancellor who argued, in 1487, that if the English nobility lived lives of luxury then they could afford new taxes. If, on the other hand, they lived abstemious lives then they must surely have sufficient savings to pay more tax. They were caught both ways. The well-known *Catch-22* is an example of this form of Morton's Fork. Yossarian, the hero of Joseph Heller's World War II novel, can avoid flying combat missions if he is insane. But Catch-22 of the rule book says that requesting a sanity evaluation is proof he is sane (since no sane person would want to fly). Either way Yossarian will find himself flying combat missions. *Sophie's Choice*, this time from William Styron's novel of the same name, is an extreme version of the unpleasant-options form of Morton's Fork. Sophie, a Polish woman arrested by the Nazis, is taken to Auschwitz with her children. On her first night, she is forced to choose which of her children will be gassed immediately and which 'spared' for a life in the camp. Sophie's choice is one that leaves her forever feeling guilty and mourning her precious child. A Sophie's Choice has recently come to mean a tragic choice that, though forced, leaves the victim guilty and distressed. Similar Morton's Forks come about when, as in some US states, death-row prisoners choose how they wish to be executed.

Dharmasankat is a Sanskrit word evoking a sense of 'troubled duty' or 'problematic duty'. It is a form of Morton's Fork where either option compromises one's ethical or moral principles. On a global scale it often appears in the form of a strategy conundrum such as, 'Do we leave these oppressed people undefended in the face of serious assault or do we make war on their oppressors?' Both options carry enormous ethical and moral implications[13].

Hobson's Choice appears to be a choice but is really a take-it-or leave-it offer like Henry Ford's offer to car buyers – 'any colour you like as long as it's black.'[14] Thomas Hobson (1544 – 1631) owned a Cambridge livery stable and was determined that each horse be used in strict rotation. His customers had the choice of the next horse in line or nothing.

Reductionist thinking can be a trap when we face the complexity of a messy situation. *False dilemmas* are another trap set by reductionist thinking. Not all the examples quoted above are *false* dilemmas: much depends on context. But the trap set by reductionist thinking is to assume there are only two choices when there might be many more. Many of us are so attuned to either-or thinking, true-or-false thinking and right-or-wrong thinking that it is hard to break out of the trap. One of the key ideas in classical philosophy is Aristotle's *Law of the Excluded Middle* which says very clearly that a statement is either true or false. It cannot simultaneously be both. I am not foolhardy enough to take on Aristotle[15] but in a mess, the truth of a statement, in any absolute sense, is usually uncertain or contested and may be less important than how it is interpreted. The drive to find the truth may become a trap. Working one's way out of a trap may involve adopting both-and thinking, suspending judgement, and searching for third, fourth and fifth ways – not necessarily in the middle.

Albert Einstein (1879 – 1955) observed that:

> *The significant problems we face cannot be solved by the same level of thinking that created them.*

In systems-thinking terms, Einstein's observation suggests that we look at the *context*. Considering the context reveals previously-invisible options. The trap works only when we limit our range of options.

Ask yourself:

- 'Am I trapped by dualistic thinking that limits the range of options I can see?' and 'Does a wider picture that includes the context of my choices and actions allow me to find more options and a way out of this trap?'.

ACTION TRAPS

Zugzwang

Zugzwang is a position in chess where the player is obliged to move but the only moves available worsen his position (a Sophie's-Choice move). A loose translation from the German is 'compulsion to move'. I use the idea of Zugzwang to mean a trap that closes when, particularly in a messy situation, the internal impulse to do something – anything – overrides the more sensible strategy of thinking through the consequences of one's actions. Western traditions and organisations tend to assume that nothing is happening if there is no action whereas Eastern traditions recognise the value of thinking. (Try sitting alone and thinking in a European or American office – very soon someone will notice you are 'not doing anything'.) Thus, Zugzwang is a culturally set trap. It encourages its victims to be decisive, take action and damn the consequences. Although delay may have costs, the unthinking action hero is likely to make a mess worse rather than better.

The 'quick fix' trap

A nasty, but surprisingly common, trap can spring shut when a mess is treated as though it were a difficulty. Action to address the problem seems to achieve initial success but, after a delay, negative consequences begin to appear. At this point, it is tempting to re-double efforts to deal with the problem and again there is initial success. This trap should be suspected when you find yourself running harder and harder to maintain success. Recognising this experience as symptomatic of a mess is the first step to escape[16].

VALUE RIGIDITY

In *Zen and the Art of Motorcycle Maintenance*, Robert Pirsig's hero discusses the South Indian monkey trap[17]. The trapper drills a small hole in a coconut, places a ball of rice inside and chains the coconut to a stake. The monkey smells the rice and inserts his hand to grasp the rice. But now he is trapped. His fist with the ball of rice is now too big to pass through the hole. He is trapped only because he does not let go of the rice. *He cannot see that freedom without rice is more valuable than capture with it.*

Pirsig calls this trap *Value Rigidity*. The trap springs when the victim attributes inappropriate value to facts or goals. In the case of the monkey, the normally high value he places on rice needs re-evaluation in this life-threatening situation. We want to say to the monkey, 'Let go of the rice. The rice is not important right now.' Value rigidity skews the value we attach to facts. Escape is available to the monkey but the rigidity of his valuation of the rice prevents him seeing the most important fact – that he can be free as soon as he lets the rice go. Changed circumstances demand reappraised values.

I include Pirsig's story because clients tell me value rigidity is one of the most frequent traps they find themselves in. Once spotted, however, it is one of the easiest traps to escape. They can very quickly list the values that trap them and their organisations. Most discover that the mess they are working on locks them in at least one value-rigidity trap. Value rigidity can make it hard to learn new facts and to recognise important facts right in front of you because you pre-select facts as important, or not, in line with your values. In a messy situation, the trap often takes the form of 'a diagnosis' or 'a solution' that you believe to be at the heart of the mess. This is why letting go of both diagnosis and solution is more effective in dealing with messes. We get caught more firmly by our certainties than by our uncertainties. Beliefs, analyses or hunches can immobilise us far more effectively than preparedness to live with ambiguity and uncertainty. This is the territory of *self-sealing beliefs*. Self-sealing beliefs cause us to notice only the evidence that confirms our pre-existing beliefs – a kind of personal group-think.

If you experience stuckness in a messy situation, you are likely to be already trapped by values. Escape the trap by stopping what you are doing. Ask yourself:

- What do I take to be important in this situation?

- Where am I trying to get to?

- What becomes available if I no longer attribute importance or value in this way?

A STRATEGY FOR TRAPS

Falling into thinking traps happens to everyone, not just the ignorant, stupid and foolhardy. The shadow of our particular skills, perspectives and expertise hides the traps we are most vulnerable to.

Ideally, of course, I hope never to get caught but complacency almost guarantees trouble. Being aware that thinking traps exist is the best defence. Self-knowledge, alertness and learning from experience reduce vulnerability. It may be some time before I notice I am in a trap. The symptoms are subtle and often appear as features of the situation, rather than as outcomes of my engagement with it. Perhaps the best strategy is to check the possibility regularly and frequently. Once I recognise I have become stuck, it may be necessary to backtrack mentally to the point just before the trap closed, revising decisions or lines of inquiry into the mess. The key skill for getting out of the mess is to change my thinking. A different level of holism or reductionism, a different perspective, a change in my assumptions and revaluing the relevance of my skills and understandings to the situation, may release the trap.

NOTES, RESOURCES AND EXPLORATIONS FOR CHAPTER 5

1   *Sir Geoffrey Vickers*

Sir Geoffrey Vickers was a remarkable and thoughtful man. He was a soldier in both World Wars, winning the Victoria Cross for his front-line bravery in the trenches. He became a lawyer specialising in international finance. After military service in World War II, when he was in charge of economic intelligence for the British Government, he was instrumental in setting up Britain's National Coal Board. It took over the ownership of all the mines in the UK and the employment of 750,000 miners whose welfare, training and safety improved dramatically under his supervision. He served in many public bodies including the Medical Research Council, the Mental Health Research Fund and the Society for General Systems Research.

When he retired, he reflected on his experiences in public life and wrote a number of books exploring judgement and policy-making. He pioneered the application of systems thinking to human activities. This book stands in the tradition he founded and owes a great deal to his thinking.

His discussion of traps comes from *Freedom in a Rocking Boat*. You can read more about Geoffrey Vickers and his work in Ramage and Shipp.

Vickers, G. (1965). *The Art of Judgment: a study of policy making*. Thousand Oaks, CA: Sage Publications.

Vickers, G. (1972). *Freedom in a Rocking Boat*. Harmondsworth: Penguin.

Ramage, M. & Shipp, K. (2009). *Systems Thinkers*. New York: Springer.

2   *Robert Pirsig's 'Zen and the Art of Motorcycle Maintenance'*

Pirsig's cult novel defies categorisation and much of it still puzzles me. However, I return to it regularly and find new insights each time. The book is part story of a journey, part autobiographical reflection by the narrator, part psychological mystery, part secular sermon, part reflections on motorcycle maintenance and part philosophical exploration. Chapter 26 has some interesting reflections on traps the author has fallen into as he maintains his motorbike. If you don't mind not understanding all of it at the first reading, the book has wonderful reflections on thinking about thinking – right on the edge. Originally published in 1974, the book reappeared as a 25th anniversary edition.

Pirsig, R. M. (1999). *Zen and the Art of Motorcycle Maintenance: an Inquiry into Values*. London: Vintage.

3   *Candace Pert*

Pert's book describes her findings about the biochemical basis of emotions. Every part of the body experiences emotions through the effects of peptides that circulate throughout the system. Her book is accessible to the non-expert and explores the scientific and human implications of the new understanding of emotions. The implications of her work for our understanding of the world – and of the epistemologies that support our understanding – are huge.

Pert, C. (1997). *Molecules of Emotion: Why You Feel the Way You Feel*. New York: Simon & Schuster.

4   *Positive thoughts*

Positive Thinking extends from the idea that positive thoughts attract money, sexual partners and fabulous jobs to the more mundane but relatively well-substantiated idea that mood, health and mental capacity are interconnected.

Cognitive Behavioural Therapy (CBT) challenges unhelpful thoughts. It works to identify, and then seeks to manage, thought patterns that trap the subject in unfavourable habits or circumstances. There is increasing evidence that CBT can be effective in treating depression, eating disorders, substance abuse and related disorders by noticing, and then challenging, unhelpful ideas and beliefs.

Neuro-linguistic programming (NLP) is much more controversial as a therapy but is widely used for building confidence and for coaching clients at risk of undermining their own intentions with unhelpful negative thoughts. Again, there is some evidence that this can be helpful but 'wishing things better' carries risks where positive thought and intention are insufficient.

Insensitive encouragement of positive thinking can reinforce feelings of inadequacy. It can contribute to a particularly cruel double bind when the victim is blamed for their own failure to recover because they were 'not positive enough'.

5   *Rugby, South Africa and the end of apartheid*

This story is told in Clint Eastwood's magnificent 2009 film *Invictus* (Warner Bros.), which is not just for rugby fans.

6   *The Principle of Charity*

See Note 13 of Chapter 2.

7   *In the beginner's mind there are many possibilities, in the expert's mind there are few*

The title of this note comes from Shunryu Suzuki's book *Zen Mind: Beginner's Mind*. Shunryu Suzuki (1904 -1971) was the first abbot of the Zen Buddhist monastery in California and was hugely influential in establishing Zen Buddhism in the United States. Beginner's mind is a potent idea in many Zen practices of The Way from flower arranging (*kado*), to martial arts (*budo*), calligraphy (*shodo*) and business.

Whether or not you are interested in archery, Prof. Herrigel's 1948 book is a fascinating account of a European's attempt to achieve beginner's mind in the practice of *kyudo* (the way of archery) in the early 1930s.

Herrigel, E., Trans. Hull, R. F. C. (2004). *Zen in the Art of Archery: Training the Mind and Body to Become One* (new ed.). Harmondsworth: Penguin.

Suzuki, S. (1973). *Zen Mind: Beginner's Mind*. Trumbull, CT: Weatherhill Inc.

8   *Decentralisation*

Decentralisation is one of many management fads that have passed through
organisations in the last few decades. Each such fad contains a good idea
but they often lack any attention to context. They are, in H. L. Mencken's
terms, simple solutions unmatched to the complexity of the situation. (See the
quotation in Chapter 1.)

Decentralisation is related to *Empowerment*, the idea that employees can take
responsibility for deciding how to complete a task. Decentralisation and
Empowerment only work well when managers understand and assent to their
underlying philosophy and are willing to let go of control. Targets undermine
employee empowerment.

9   *Double Binds*

Gregory Bateson identified six components in a double bind. These are:

* the situation involves two or more people, one of whom is the 'victim'
  and others 'superior'

* repeated experience, making the double bind an habitual expectation
  for the victim

* a primary injunction with a reward (implied or explicit) for
  compliance or a punishment (implied or explicit) for non-compliance:
  rewards and punishments can include the awarding or withholding of
  approval, love, or promotion prospects. Abandonment is the extreme
  form of punishment for a child (or even some adults)

* a secondary injunction, commonly communicated by non-verbal
  means such as tone of voice, body language or meaningful action
  which, in a more abstract form than the primary injunction, contradicts
  the primary injunction (Bateson allows for the possibility that one
  parent may, at a more abstract level, negate the primary injunction of
  the other parent)

* a tertiary injunction that prevents the victim 'leaving the field'

* the complete set of conditions becomes unnecessary when the victim
  has internalised the double bind.

The most accessible account of Bateson's work is in:

Bateson, G. (1972). *Steps to an Ecology of Mind: Collected Essays in Anthropology,
Psychiatry, Evolution, and Epistemology.* Chicago: University Of Chicago Press.

10   *Exit*

Exit, in the sense I have used it in this chapter, derives from a concept explored in
Hirschman's *Exit, Voice and Loyalty.* Hirschman applies the idea to a free-market
consumer facing a choice as the quality of goods declines. They choose whether
to maintain *loyalty, voice* their dissatisfaction or to *exit,* shopping elsewhere or
not at all. From the perspective of the seller, exit is simply a warning that all is
not well. *Voice* is a much stronger signal that may provoke the seller into change
and improvement. Extending these ideas to a relationship, an individual or
organisation has the same choices in an unsatisfactory relationship.

Hirschman, A. O. (1970). *Exit, Voice and Loyalty: Responses to Decline in Firms,
Organizations and States.* Cambridge, MA: Harvard University Press.

11 *Buridan's Ass*

Buridan's Ass was named to satirise Jean Buridan (France, approx. 1300 to after 1358), the moral philosopher. It refers to a discussion in Aristotle's *On the Heavens* (*De Caelo*) in which a man is positioned equidistant from food and drink and, being both hungry and thirsty, has no basis for choosing which to consume first. Buridan's moral philosophy advocates choosing for the greater good and it is this idea that is satirised as a choice that would only arise for an ass. Buridan's ass also connects to systems ideas as an example of *unstable equilibrium*. If the ass were only slightly closer to one option than the other, the equilibrium would be destroyed and his choice made.

12 *Morton's Fork dilemmas*

First published in 1961, Heller's classic is still in print. Like *Catch-22*, William Styron's *Sophie's Choice* is considered one of the great twentieth century novels. It was filmed by Alan J. Pakula in 1982 (Universal Pictures). Meryl Streep won an Oscar for her portrayal of Sophie.

Heller, J. (1961). *Catch-22*. New York: Simon & Schuster.
Styron, W. (1979). *Sophie's Choice*. New York: Random House.

13 *Morality and Ethics*

The terms *moral* and *ethical* are often – inaccurately – used interchangeably. Morality refers to the 'rules and norms accepted by a group of people or a culture' and is thus a codification of what is accepted as right or wrong. To be moral is to behave in conformity with accepted norms of what is 'right'. Ethics is the branch of philosophy that studies the sources of moral standards. By extension, ethical behaviour is an outcome of thoughtful decisions about the rightness of one's actions and their consequences. In messy situations, complexity frequently renders the application of moral rules problematic. Thus, ethics becomes an immediate concern of systems thinking in the context of messy situations.

14 *Any colour you like as long as it's black*

This restricted choice came about in 1913 when Ford introduced the moving conveyor belt to his Detroit car plant. Other colours had been available previously but the conveyor limited paint drying time and black dried quickest.

15 *Socrates, Plato and Aristotle*

These three Greek philosophers laid the foundations of Western philosophy by providing the 'software' of Western thinking, and particularly its preference for reductionist and dualistic thinking. Aristotle discusses the excluded middle in *De Interpretatione* and in *Metaphysics* (Book 3)

16 *The quick fix trap*

The underlying mechanism for this sort of trap is discussed on this book's website.

17 *The monkey trap*

Pirsig's discussion of the monkey trap appears in Chapter 26 of *Zen and the Art of Motorcycle Maintenance*. See Note 2 above.

CHAPTER 6

Managing my own complexity

*To transform the world, we must begin with ourselves; and what is
important in beginning with ourselves is the intention. The intention
must be to understand ourselves, and not to leave it to others to
transform themselves. This is our responsibility, yours and mine;
because, however small may be the world we live in, if we can
bring about a radically different point of view in our own existence,
then perhaps we shall affect the world at large.*

J. Krishnamurti (1895 – 1986)[1]

Most people assume that their perspective on the world is reasonably
objective – that they see the world pretty much as it is. In this chapter, I
explore the limitations of this view in trying to deal with a mess. The chapter
includes an exercise that people have found helpful when they try to escape the
limitations of their own perspective.

Many management books present diagrams something like Figure 6.1. Indeed,
I suspect most people think about management in this way. The diagram
shows someone looking at, and then acting on, a complex and messy situation.
The wobbly blob whose boundaries I take to be rather vague, irregular and
changeable, represents a messy situation. The circle represents a person
trying to manage the situation. The regularity of the shape contrasts with the
blobbiness of the situation. The regularity of the person's shape suggests that,
unlike the situation, the person is uncomplicated and fully describable. The
regularity of the shape also suggests that the person is uniquely rational and
has a clear agenda about any action he or she might choose to take.

I find diagrams like Figure 6.1 somewhat unsatisfactory. They don't really
represent my experience of trying to manage messy situations. My first reaction
is that this person is nothing like me. My experience of engaging with complex
situations is that I don't feel very rational. Initially, I feel confused, puzzled and
sometimes even overwhelmed by the situation. I fear it might be impossible
ever to understand the situation enough to do something useful within it. Given
the complexity, unknowability and uncertainty of a messy situation, this is an
understandable reaction. I have agendas. I want to deal with the mess. I fear
some outcomes and hope for others. None of this seems to have much to do
with rationality.

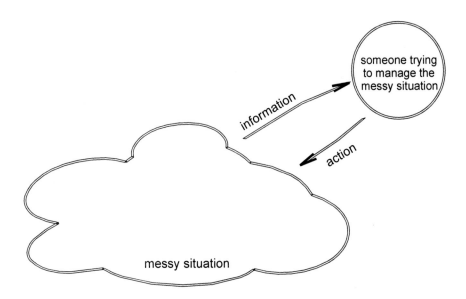

Figure 6.1 *A common way of thinking about someone managing a situation (messy or otherwise). This way of thinking about the relationship between the person and the situation they are managing is limiting in a number of ways.*

I also wonder whether the location of the systems thinker outside the complex situation is appropriate. I imagine that, like me, most people experience themselves as being *within* the complexity they are trying to deal with. When I juggle the day-to-day realities of work, home, family and the messy situations they, and clients, present, I am *in* the situation – a part of it. I am not a disengaged outsider who has the advantage of a dispassionate view. In most of my engagements with complexity, I am a stakeholder as well as someone trying to make sense of it all. I am part of the situation and, perhaps, part of the problem. Even when I engage with someone else's complex situation, perhaps in a support or consultancy role, I get drawn into the complexity, even if only through fascination with the task. Only rarely would I choose to represent myself as located outside the situation.

The only element of Figure 6.1 that seems 'real' is the wobbly blob mess.

WHAT'S WRONG WITH COMPLEXITY?

Before moving on to looking at my own complexity, I want to explore a common misunderstanding. I invite you to consider the following question for a few moments:

- What is your immediate reaction to the idea of 'a complex situation'? What are the images that come to mind?

I ask this question because many people unconsciously believe that 'complexity is bad'. They immediately identify *complex* with *problematic*. Perceiving something to be complex is usually a response to experiencing it as difficult to understand or taking a lot of words to describe. Sometimes the word *complex* is used as if it were synonymous with *problematic*. This leads on to the notion that dealing with complexity necessarily means *simplifying* complexity. Systems thinking is not about simplifying complexity but about simplifying one's *thinking* about complexity.

Short term brain activity can only deal with approximately seven concepts at once[2], and so anything more complicated than this is difficult to think about rigorously. But 'problematic to think about' should not be confused with problematic *per se*.

In fact, I would like to celebrate complexity. For me, the world is interesting and beautiful *because* it is complex. I don't understand it, so I can wonder at it. I perceive it as being capable of almost infinite variety and exhibiting a density of interconnectedness beyond human comprehension.

The variety and interconnectedness of the human organism and the human brain allow people to survive and thrive in a variety of environments, including those generated by human activity. This interconnectedness makes the human organism, and its relationship to its environment, problematic to understand but not problematic in itself – quite the reverse.

Variety and interconnectedness enable me to deal with the world. Ross Ashby, one of the founding fathers of cybernetics, recognised their importance in adapting to circumstance and proposed his now famous Law of Requisite Variety[3]. An informal statement of this law, attributed to Ashby, is

> If you can describe complexity, then it's not complex any more.

This observation captures the implications of the law very neatly. To describe variety and interconnectedness in something, I need at least as much variety and interconnectedness myself, otherwise I could not perceive or describe the complexity. Extending this argument, I have to have variety and interconnectedness myself to manage variety and interconnectedness. By extension again, to adapt and survive I must be capable of at least as much variety as the environment I must respond to. This brings us to the way the law is more formally understood.

When a system, such as a human being, is exposed to perturbations in its environment, it may have a number of responses. These responses lead to a number of possible outcomes. Of all the possible outcomes, only some will be 'acceptable' in terms of the system's purpose or survival. This is as true of organisations, baggage-handling systems, telephone-enquiry systems and other purposefully-interconnected systems as it is of humans and their society. In practice, the Law of Requisite Variety says that, in order to fulfil its purposes and survive, the system must be capable of a greater variety of responses than the variety of perturbations in the environment. The fewer the number of acceptable outcomes, then the more the variety of possible responses must exceed the variety of perturbations. The system then has *requisite variety* – the variety it requires to survive and fulfil its purpose.

This is why I want to celebrate complexity. The very human variety that can be so infuriatingly difficult to understand is the variety that enables the human-person system to survive in an environment that also exhibits astonishing variety. Returning to the context of systems thinking, and the significance of bringing all my human variety to situations I perceive as complex, I need to be capable of variety in my thinking, actions and emotions to respond appropriately to the complexity I perceive in the messy situation. This is what Ashby meant by *requisite variety*.

While I bring requisite variety to the task of improving a messy situation, I find myself asking, 'How can I be sure I am not contributing to the process that keeps the mess in place?' and 'How can I be sure that some of my variety of actions, thinking and emotions is not getting in the way of improving the situation?' I am thinking here of my confusions, prejudices, preferences, entanglements and blind spots. These too are manifestations of my variety and, unless I can account for them in some way, they can make the situation even more difficult to understand than it was before. I need awareness of how I interact with situations that I am trying to improve. This means I have to be aware of how I see the situation (my perspective[4]); how I understand the situation; how I distinguish systems within it; how I communicate my understandings to other stakeholders; how I act in it; how I see and recognise the outcomes; and how I evaluate the outcomes. I explore these issues in the next sections of this chapter.

THE SYSTEMS THINKER'S COMPLEXITY

My experience of managing messes is more like Figure 6.2 than Figure 6.1. I picture myself as being surrounded by a cloud of 'stuff'. This stuff includes all the elements that make up my perspective – my ideas and attitudes, my thoughts, my assumptions and so on. The boundary of the cloud is rather vague and it changes. I have shown two loops of experience, reflection and interpretation. This reminds me that I'm perfectly capable of holding two contradictory interpretations at the same time. Moreover, I have no clear view through the cloud. My ideas, interpretations, emotions and attitudes are filters that limit and condition my perception of the 'real world'. They don't just obscure my view, they *are* my view.

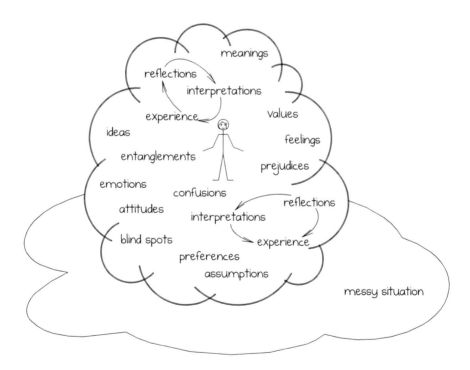

Figure 6.2 *A representation of my experience of engaging with a situation. This is a personal view – my experience. I could have included other items in the 'cloud' that surrounds me and conditions my perception of the 'real world'.*

ACCOUNTING FOR YOUR OWN COMPLEXITY

When astronomers photograph objects beyond our own solar system they first take 'darks' and 'flats'. These are photographs of a black field (with the lens cap on for example) and plain white sheet. These allow the astronomer to see errors generated by the imaging system itself. These errors can then be electronically 'processed out' to give much clearer images of the objects. Modern telescopes and imaging systems are immensely sophisticated and imaging errors creep in at every stage of image gathering. Dust, electronic noise and 'holes' in the light-detecting array mean that images can be quite murky. 'Hot' pixels in the imaging array can generate bright spots. Without darks and flats the astronomer is 'trapped' behind the murkiness, unable to distinguish between stars and imaging artefacts. Subtracting the image represented by the flats and darks gives bright clear photographs of the galaxies, nebulae and star clusters.

The exercise below is equivalent to 'taking darks and flats'. It gives you a much clearer sense of how your own complexity changes the way you see a messy situation. It does not remove the complexity of your 'cloud of stuff' but it does allow you to subtract some of it. Many people experience this exercise as positively 'eye opening'.

The exercise consists of answering some questions about your messy situation[5]. I suggest you allow approximately 20 quiet minutes with a pen and a pad and that you agree with yourself not to discuss your notes directly with anyone. This encourages you to be honest. The more honest you can be, the more helpful this exercise is likely to be. You do not need to answer every single question, nor attempt an exhaustive answer in each case. The 20-minute suggestion should be your guide. However, if you feel tempted to skip a question, ask yourself whether by doing so you are allowing yourself to dodge some awkward issue. The awkward issues are often the sticking points and may be precisely the issues that need thoughtful attention.

Sitting comfortably and thinking about the messy situation you are facing, make notes in response to the following questions.

Identifying your own stakeholdings

The first task is to identify your stake in the situation. Such a stake might arise in a number of ways. Stakes may be formal ones that are open and discussable (better performance in the area you manage, etc.) or they may be more informal and personal ones (such as reputation).

    1   Do you have any roles in this situation?

- o   identify your formal roles (e.g. Project Leader, parent, investor, shareholders' representative, protester, etc.) and any other roles recognised by other people

- o   identify your informal roles (e.g. the person representing the minority view, the office pessimist, the innovation champion, etc.)

2   What do you have to gain in this situation?

3   What do you have to lose in this situation?

4   What outcomes are likely to maximise the chances of you getting what you want?

5   What outcomes are likely to minimise the chances of an outcome you would not want?

Next, your indirect stakes:

6   Do you have a stake through some other person or other people? Perhaps you share similar values, value their support, have aspirations for them or empathies with them. Perhaps there is someone you do not like very much. Whether or not this is an appropriate consideration, recognising it will help you to account for your own perspective.

7   Do you have any stakes in this situation through ideological preferences?
For example, do you favour environmentally responsible outcomes? or deregulation? or family-friendly hours? Do you have an allegiance to a group that espouses a particular position?

8   Do you have any stakes arising from your identity?
For example, do you want to remain popular, gain the respect of a potential customer, be seen as the calm mediator?, etc.

Mapping your capability to act

9   What is your responsibility in this situation?

10 What capability for action do you have? Do you have the power to take decisions, control resources or influence others?

11 How likely are any of the outcomes you listed for Questions 4 and 5 above if you don't take action? How likely are any of these outcomes if you do take action?

Identifying your thinking about the situation

The next task is to identify your thinking about the situation. Although in systems-thinking terms it is rarely a good idea to identify 'core issues' or 'key problems' in a messy situation (see Chapter 1), most people make some initial judgement about what these are. It's easier to take an open view if you are aware of what pre-judgements you are making. Recognising pre-judgements allows you to set them aside as you take a more systemic approach.

12 What do you believe to be the key issues?

13 Which issues seem particularly clear to you?

14 Which issues within the mess seem obscure, confusing or unknown?

15 What explanations for the mess, or parts of it, appeal to you most?

16 What ideas about dealing with the mess, or parts of it, appeal to you most?

17 Do you have any 'if only ...' feelings about the situation?
    These are the thoughts that express themselves in words like 'If only Martin had not left the company...'; 'If only I could talk to Shiplap about this ...'; 'If only I had not told the boss that ...'

18 Who are the key people or agencies responsible for the situation?

19 Who is to blame?
    Stories we tell ourselves about who is to blame are rarely helpful but blaming is a common habit and it is important to recognise and account for it (see *Blame stories* in Chapter 5).

20 Who should be sorting it out?
    Must, ought and *should* are thought patterns that can easily be a trap (see *Hardening of the oughteries* in Chapter 5). If you are thinking this way, you may also limit your ability to see ways to improve the situation. In either case, it is important to notice if you are thinking this way.

Identifying your feelings about the situation

The next task is to identify your feelings about the situation. There are a few things to bear in mind as you think about the questions:

- It's easy to censor feelings, especially in a professional context. The censorship arises from the idea that emotions have no place in rational discussions or from, for example, the desire to avoid passing judgement on someone else's behaviour or attitudes.

- In much of what we do in the professional context, we prefer to be seen as rational, objective and impartial. Emotions are irrational and subjective. This does not mean that they can be ignored, however. They may limit what is feasible or acceptable and, unless we manage our own feelings, they can steer our actions in ways we may not recognise and cannot account for.

- Feelings are not necessarily politically correct either. While political correctness can challenge us to examine the basis of our feelings, gut reactions are generally not guided by intellectual principles. Get past this censor as much as you can.

- Another block to recognising feelings is the idea that the feelings have to be justified in some way. You don't have to do this in this context. You should simply record the emotions that are there. Be as specific as you can about what you feel.

Here are the questions:

21 What are your feelings about this situation? Are you, for example, angry? cynical? amused? amazed? scared? optimistic? impatient?

22 Do you have any feelings on behalf of any of the other people involved (compassion, empathy, approval, frustration, pride, worry, etc.)?

23 Do you feel it's not fair? (Be specific about what's not fair. Not fair to whom?)
Fairness is a deeply ingrained value. Even small children are determined in expressing their sense of fairness, or lack of it. Unless we are explicit, a sense of unfairness can turn into impotent resentment that blocks the ability to take assertive action.

Recording your impressions of the context

Next, record your impressions of the phenomena that gave rise to this messy situation. Include, as necessary:

24 The social arrangements

25 The political or management arrangements

26 The behaviours

27 The culture.

Recording your initial views about what to do

Finally, record your initial views about what should be done to improve this situation. Do not worry if these are based on gut reactions and do not worry about feasibility at this stage. This is not planning, it is simply noticing what your initial thoughts and gut reactions are.

28 What ideas do you have about what should be done or about what should be explored?
    Your ideas may be more, or less, feasible, or more or less long-term. Use the language that first springs to mind, even if it's in the form of, for example, 'A and B need their heads banging together', or even something politically incorrect. (Unacceptable or 'politically incorrect' attitudes can only be dealt with if we are aware of, and can examine, our prejudices.) In particular, if you have any ideas that take the form 'X must ...', 'X should ...', or 'X ought to ...', record them because these word forms usually disguise some judgement about someone's culpability.

And finally ...

At this point, take a break. Put your notes to one side and then come back to address a final question.

29 Are there any patterns in your responses?

THE CLOUD THAT COMES BETWIXT

People often experience this exercise as demanding. It can be both challenging and revealing. It has the potential to reveal, with uncomfortable clarity, that situations we experience as messy don't have a completely autonomous existence 'out there'. They are intimately linked to ourselves and our role in the situation. This often means that we have to examine our own role and accept that we do not have access to an objective view of the situation – and never can have. I am not separate from my perspective. I cannot be separated from my history, my rich accumulation of experience, my tendency to view situations in habitual ways and my own history of successes and failures in dealing with the world.

Everything we see, hear, smell, taste and feel is filtered through our own perspective. Whenever we look at the world, what we see is determined almost completely by our 'cloud of stuff'. This astonishing idea is well-founded in neurological studies and means that *epistemology*, the study of how we know about the world, becomes a live topic rather than an abstract area of philosophy. Epistemology is especially important in messy situations where other people may see the situation in very different ways. Chapter 7 addresses epistemological issues that arise in messy situations.

As well as revealing how much your vision of a mess is influenced by your own issues, the exercise can reveal ideas for shifting your perspective slightly. Your notes will provide much material for reflection. I offer no particular procedure for reflecting on your notes, only an invitation to consider whether some of what you take for granted can be seen differently. I suggest you make notes on what you have learned from the exercise and what it reveals about the messy situation you are considering. If you have a rich picture (see Chapter 3), you may want to add to it.

The exercise does not, of course, produce a comprehensive catalogue of your cloud and the complexity you bring to a messy situation, but I hope it will help to challenge the assumptions that may obscure more fruitful ways of seeing the messy situation.

This entire discussion means that the systems thinker has a choice about how to see the world. I can choose the 'common sense' but limited view that assumes the world is pretty much as I see it. Alternatively, accepting responsibility for my own role in creating my view can open up other possibilities. I can choose to see the world differently by challenging my own assumptions – my own perspective. I can also accept other people's perspectives as adding to and enhancing my own. Other people's perspectives are limited too but they will see features I cannot see, allowing for the gathering of multiple partial views (see Chapter 2) to create a much richer picture of the situation. The cloud may limit my view but, because each person is unique, it has gaps in it that no-one else has. These gaps allow me to see things other people do not see. My perspective, like everyone else's, is a privileged one. No-one else can see exactly what I see.

Notes, resources and explorations for Chapter 6

1   *Krishnamurti*

Jiddu Krishnamurti was an Indian spiritual teacher. Rejecting his early adoption by the Theosophical Society, he drew on Indian spiritual traditions (he was born a Brahmin), psychology and theories of social action. He believed that the key to social change was change in the individual and urged people to find out for themselves the causes of social evils. His numerous books, writings and talks (preserved in recordings) continue to have a profound influence on his admirers.

This quotation seems to capture the essential idea that often change comes about when we think differently about our situation.

2   *The Magical Number Seven*

G. A. Miller's classic paper on the number of concepts the human brain can think about simultaneously makes sobering reading, implying as it does how limited is our capacity for dealing with complexity. It reminds me that the temptation to think about the world *as if it were simple* will be very strong. I try instead to find simple ways of thinking about the world.

The implication of Miller's work is that the number of separate but interconnected entities I can think about is only three because there are three interconnections as well as the three entities. (Four entities have six possible interconnections, totalling 10: three too many to think about all at once.)

Miller, G. A. (1956). The Magical Number Seven, Plus or Minus Two: Some Limits on Our Capacity for Processing Information. *The Psychological Review* 63: 81-97.

3   *The Law of Requisite Variety*

W. Ross Ashby (1903 – 1972) was one of the founders of cybernetics, a discipline that shares much common ground with systems thinking. He was a psychiatrist by training but the searching questions he asked about the functioning of the normal brain, and the principles to be followed in restoring the sick brain to normality, led him far beyond the boundaries of his profession. Ashby saw the brain as immensely complex at a time when its core functions were assumed to be essentially simple. In his second book, *An Introduction to Cybernetics*, he explored his ideas using the concept of variety. This book has had a profound effect on several generations of cyberneticians and systems thinkers. The formal statement of his Law of Requisite Variety ("only variety can destroy variety") gives no clue to its usefulness and applicability to information theory, data compression, management, control theory, cryptography, robotics, thermodynamics and many other fields.

Ashby, W. R. (1956). *An Introduction to Cybernetics*. London: Chapman and Hall.

4   *Perspective*

See Chapter 2.

5   *Suggestions for topics*

If you do not have a messy situation of your own, there are some suggestions in Note 6 at the end of Chapter 3.

Part 2: Understanding messy situations

Part 2 is about 'understandascopes'. As pictured here by Michael Leunig, understandascopes are tools for looking at complex situations so they begin to make sense to the observer. They are 'constructed', by the observer, from systems-thinking ideas and concepts.

Messy situations are bewildering because of their extent and their many components and interconnections. Before deciding on actions for improvement, it is important to explore the mess thoroughly. Well-chosen, efficient and effective interventions will not cause unintended consequences. Part 2 offers ideas and approaches for exploring messy situations through understandascopes 'built' from systems-thinking ideas.

The structure of Part 2

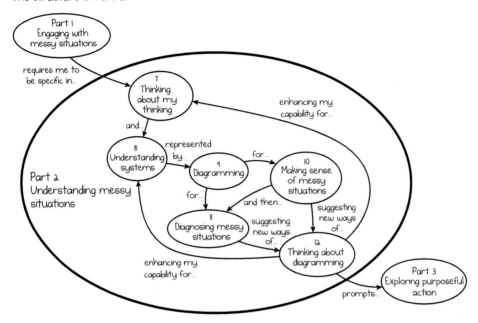

Part 2 starts by exploring the relationship between the mess and the person attempting to deal with it (Chapter 7). It then uses ideas associated with a system (Chapter 8) to derive some understandascopes in the form of diagrams (Chapter 9), diagrams for making sense of messy situations (Chapter 10) and for diagnosing what goes wrong (or right) in them (Chapter 11). Chapter 12 is an invitation to think of diagramming as a way of thinking as much as a tool. Diagramming develops skills for thinking differently by seeing the world systemically rather than simply using diagrams as tools.

CHAPTER 7

Thinking about my thinking

Thinking is the crest of deep physical turbulence rushing from a point of original unity at the beginning of the universe. It is a product of the same motility and physical processes that created galaxies. When one thinks clearly about thinking, one is present at the first instant of time.

Edgar Allan Poe[1] (1809 – 1849)

I only decide about my Universe. [...] My Universe is my eyes and my ears. Anything else is hearsay.

Douglas Adams, *The Restaurant at the End of the Universe* (1980)

This chapter is a bit more theoretical than the others. But, in the spirit of Boltzmann's dictum[2] that 'there is nothing so practical as a good theory', it is nonetheless intended to be of practical use.

In the Introduction, I explained that systems thinking is much more than a set of tools and techniques, however useful those might be. This chapter has some ideas for reflection and perhaps for incorporation into your own understanding and thinking. Systems thinking is fundamentally about *thinking*. In this chapter, I consider *thinking about your thinking, knowing about your knowing* and *understanding your understanding*. This is traditionally the domain of *epistemology*, the branch of philosophy that deals with how we know about the world.

In Chapter 6, I explored the idea that we are not separate from our perspective. We do not have access to an objective view because none of us is separate from our histories, our accumulated experience, our own interests and our habitual ways of observing. We each make sense of the world in terms of what we already know and believe about the world. This way of understanding what we know and how we know it is *constructivism* – the idea that we construct reality in our minds by making sense of what we perceive[3]. 'Making sense' depends upon our circumstances and upon who we are.

Common sense tells me that my experience and understanding are limited. I am 173 cm in height. That limits my view of the world. It may not matter much that I cannot see what my house looks like from above but there will be things going on in the roof that I may not notice until they impinge on areas that I can experience.

More significantly, my understanding of other people's experiences is very limited. You might tell me about your experience but, however good your description, I cannot share your experience. I can only construct my own mental representation of what your experience might be like. But the limitations on my understanding of the world are even more fundamental than this.

In recent years, the philosophical study of epistemology has been touched by developments in the physiological sciences, especially psychology and neurobiology. Epistemology traditionally argues from first principles. Experimental psychology has discovered and explored the huge gap between perception and demonstrable facts. Neurobiological insights offer direct evidence relevant to some of the key questions about what we can know. Neither psychological nor neurobiological findings have penetrated to the heart of traditional epistemology but they have profound implications for how one might think about, and know about, messy situations.

The new insights indicate that human (and animal) brains have so little demonstrable access to the outside world, that there is insufficient data to form any clear picture of the world[4]. This implies that my mental models not only *interpret* my perceptions but *generate* them as well. Data reaching my brain from the outside world triggers my perceptions but does not form them. I am inside an autopoietic ('self-producing') interior world. My perceptions of the world are not *caused* by anything in the world.

This does not mean I can 'make up' any world I wish for. I am 'structurally coupled' to my environment. *Structural coupling* is an ongoing process, in continuous development and reinforcement, that coordinates my thinking, knowing and understanding – and my whole body – with my environment. My environment changes me and I change it through the linkages of structural coupling. We co-evolve through time on a trajectory of reciprocally triggered change. Structural coupling means that my thinking, knowing and understanding connect to the exterior world, but are not caused by it. They change in response to my experience of the exterior world but the exterior world does not directly cause the changes. What I think, know and understand may correspond very little to what exists in the outside world – but how would anyone know?

At first sight, this seems to be nonsense, flying in the face of all that is obvious about experience. But Humberto Maturana, the Chilean neurobiologist whose work is central to this new understanding of cognition[5], starts by accepting, very directly, what is obvious from experience. He notes that a table 'is there' only in the sense that the observer can see it and touch it. The table is distinguished by an observer with a body whose bodily perceptions give rise to the idea of a table. The body is at the centre of the processes of cognition. I can see a table only because my human body has evolved to perceive tables. These ideas directly challenge scientific method and its insistence on observer-independent knowledge.

My mental image of the world is a model. It is a partial representation based on partial knowledge. So, when I think I am thinking about the world I am actually thinking about my model of the world. This model of the world is built up in a way that is itself a model. So I am using a model, built by a model, to represent the world I think I see. The Australian cartoonist Michael Leunig captures the idea well in Figure 7.1.

Figure 7.1 Leunig's cartoons often seem to capture important epistemic insights. In this cartoon, the character seems to be walking a path of his own making. It determines what he sees and where he goes and yet it is a product of his own mind.

This has important implications. The model that represents the world tells me what I see and tells me what *to* see. The model both limits what I see and reinforces itself. When I think about the world, I am thinking about my own thinking; I have no direct cognitive access to the world at all.

Many people find these ideas unsettling when they first meet them. They seem to defy common sense. They raise the question of how real the so-called real world really is.

People often assume the brain is very similar to a computer. Both have a similarly large proportion of 'processors' operating on internally generated signals. But there is an important and absolutely fundamental difference. The computer does not create its own meanings. The computer has no capacity for deciding, for example, which paintings in the National Gallery are its favourites. I do. I have a history of interacting with external stimuli that generate new ways of interacting with further stimuli and the internal structure of my brain changes as a result. The computer's ways of dealing with data are not the result of its own self-production. The way the computer works remains the same, whether it is processing pictures from the National Gallery or whether it is processing letters of the alphabet. The rules that relate input to output are constant over time. This is not the case for a human (or any other animal).

LIVING IN EPISTEMIC AWARENESS

These emerging insights have some important consequences for the way we think about, know and understand the world. A few of them are set out in this section. Epistemic awareness is simply an awareness that how I think, know and understand the world depends on me as much as it depends upon the world.

No external reality to appeal to

The most striking consequence of these findings is that there is no appeal to an external reality by which we can judge how true anything is. All our knowing is circular. Maturana gives an illustrative analogy:

> *Imagine pilots sitting in the cockpit and flying a plane in complete darkness. They have no immediate access to the external world nor do they need it, they act on the basis of measurement values and indicators, employing their instruments when the values change or particular combinations of values emerge. They establish sensorimotor correlations in order to keep the relevant values within specified limits. When the plane has landed, friends and colleagues may appear who have observed the plane arrive, and congratulate the pilots on their successful and admirable landing in thick fog and dangerous storms. The pilots are confused and ask: "What storm? What fog? What are you talking about? We just handled our instruments!" You see: What happened outside the plane was*

*irrelevant and without meaning to the operational dynamics inside
the plane.*

Maturana and Poerksen[5], 2004

Knowledge is not independent of the body

Western traditions of thinking, knowing and understanding aim for objectivity.
This is an explicit epistemological stance that is 'observer independent'.
Working within this tradition, it is taken for granted that a knowable,
transcendent world exists and we should try to attain knowledge of it that is
universal and transcends the individual observer. It is an *a priori* stance – one
that takes the existence of a knowable world for granted *even before we know
about it* – and it is a disembodied knowledge. The individual human body and
its role in acquiring knowledge are deemed irrelevant to the knowledge itself.
The new cognitive sciences (and some postmodern philosophical thinking[6])
bring the body, and the way it experiences the world, back to the centre of the
picture.

*And, as a matter of fact it cannot be otherwise as the observer
disappears as his or her bodyhood disappears.*

Maturana, 2004

Everything that is said is said by an observer

Knowledge that can never be independent of the body implies that everything
that is said is said by an observer. Thus claims such as 'Fred is avaricious'
cannot be a truth claim – an utterance that claims to be 'true' – because it is said
by someone. The claim only has validity as 'I have experienced Fred's behaviour
and I believe him to be avaricious'.

When we agree with a statement, we are agreeing with the language. I don't
have direct access to the speaker's understanding, or even to what they intend
to say. I can only agree with *my understanding* of the language of the statement.
This means that statements of agreement such as 'I understand what you
mean' are literally nonsensical. I do not have any access to what you mean
so how can I claim that I understand what you mean? I may be tempted to
think I understand you but my sense of recognition is triggered by your words
and only makes sense to me *in terms of my own experience* rather than yours.
Does this mean that I am isolated in my own experience with no possibility of
understanding other people?

Again experience is the starting point for a response. When I have a good
conversation with someone, I do not experience myself as isolated from them.
In many ways, my sense of a 'good' conversation comes from a sense of mutual

understanding and connection. This happens when conversational partners are attentive and respectful of each other. They do not cut each other off with statements such as 'I understand'. Instead, there is a willingness to listen to the other person's descriptions of their experience, taking the other as a *legitimate other* – a person whose experience and understanding is as legitimate, meaningful and rich as one's own. Statements such as 'you are wrong' are discarded in favour of offering attentive attempts to understand, followed by alternative observations and interpretations that encourage the other to change their mind while, at the same time, offering a willingness to change one's own mind.

Why am I writing this?

At the beginning of the chapter, I described it as 'a bit more theoretical' than the other chapters in the book. There are two main reasons for including this chapter. The first is that I am an 'observer' and so whatever I say, about systems thinking or anything else, is said *as an observer*. If you find anything in this book that is valuable and makes sense to you, then it is because it triggers something in you that is coherent with your experience, with your needs and with your way of making sense. I write this book because I believe that my account of what has been useful to me – and to the clients, students and colleagues I work with – may be of use to you, the reader. But nothing I write will *cause* your interest or learning. It may *trigger* changes in the way you think about or do things but, essentially, I can do no more than invite you to try ideas and to create experiences that may support you in making sense of your world and, more particularly, the messy situations you engage with.

The second reason for including this chapter is to suggest some 'stances' and ways of approaching messy situations. These are helpful, whether or not one chooses to engage with the implications of recent cognitive science. The helpfulness comes from recognising that, in messy situations, it is hard to know whether or not I can be certain about all the things I need to know and whether indeed there are important features of the mess about which I have no inkling.

"Willingness to give up beliefs is the beginning of wisdom"

A willingness to give up beliefs in the face of new evidence is the beginning of wisdom according to Humberto Maturana. He was not the first person to make this claim.

> *When the facts change, I change my mind. What do you do, sir?*
> J. M. Keynes, the economist, (when accused of changing his position on monetary policy during the Great Depression)

Of course, knowing that most of what I'm aware of is actually generated within my own brain does not mean I can make up any version of reality I choose. But it does mean I have to recognise that my knowledge of, and understanding of, the world is partial and provisional. It also depends to a significant extent on the way that I have constructed representations as my personal history has unfolded. The theme of internal representations comes up repeatedly in systems thinking and in this section I want to suggest a number of attitudes and or mental stances that will be helpful in dealing with messy situations.

Some of the mental attitudes that I try to maintain are:

- being open and sensitive to all kinds of 'knowing' about a situation: not just so-called factual information but impressions, intuitions and hunches, including other people's

- being willing and able to see the situation from many different points of view in addition to my own

- being as open as I can be to seeing the situation and not letting my theories, presuppositions and assumptions tell me how I ought to see it

- not taking terms of reference, boundaries or constraints too seriously; I try to assume they may not be as rigid as they seem to be; and I try to find out how other people see them

- being wary of *any* 'solution' to a complex question (including my own solutions)

- enjoying diversity and complexity in a situation; resisting the temptation to discard inconvenient bits of information; paying more, rather than less, attention to awkward facts, impressions or ideas

- not minding too much if there are areas of uncertainty in my understanding, or bits of information I don't have; being sceptical about the facts I *do* have.

Maintaining these stances isn't necessarily easy, even with practice, so here are some suggestions about things you can actually do when you are looking at a messy situation that concerns you in some way. Practising these will help you to develop the open, inquiring style that can make systems thinking so exciting.

Make sure you include in your thinking about the situation:

- its preceding history and its wider context

- information about how people (including you) involved in the situation think and feel about it; and the hunches, intuitions and suspicions they, and you, have about it

- information about the dynamics (procedures, flows, communications, feelings) of the situation as well as the structure (roles, organisation framework, boundaries, materials, components) and how the process and structure fit together

- information about how the situation appears to other people, including those around the situation as well as those directly involved

- attention to what is *not* going on and what is *not* present.

All of these items can be included in a rich picture of the messy situation[7].

EPISTEMIC AWARENESS

Neither discussions about perspectives, nor the insights of philosophy, can tell me how true my internal representations of the world are, but neurological studies seem to suggest the outside world is unknowable as it is. This idea pervades this book. Epistemology becomes a central concern. This contrasts sharply with many other approaches to management, even systems thinking, that never address epistemology: these approaches assume the world is 'out there' and more-or-less as it appears.

Recognising that the world is unknowable presents me with a choice. How do I make sense of day-to-day observations and events that seem to emerge from it? Once I become aware of this unknowability I am confronted with – and need to make – my own choice. Options seem to cluster around three main poles.

- The first of these is to act as though the world is more-or-less as I see it, and to ignore the incompleteness of my viewpoints and my representations. This is equivalent to saying 'there is no epistemological issue about the way I see the world'.

- The second is to decide that the world is more-or-less as I see it but to recognise that my viewpoint is limited and the view-from-here may be misleading because it is only partial – there is no view of the roof, to use my previous metaphor. This stance accepts that I must be careful to explore the world as fully as I can because I cannot see everything and may be misled.

- The third pole is to take on fully the implications of the world's unknowability. This stance demands that I be always aware that I will never know the world and must therefore always be trying to account for my own role in my perceptions of the world. Consciously making the choice between these poles, and all the variants in between, is an act of *epistemic awareness*.

The choice one makes has profound implications for one's ranges of thought and action.

As humans we each find ourselves with a unique perspective – one that no-one else shares – and this enables us to each make our own unique contribution to understanding an issue holistically. But we also have to[8] accept that our viewpoint is only ever a 'view from here' (a perspective) or even a 'view from inside here' (a perspective that takes account of some of the new insights about cognition). I have no direct access to a reality that is independent of my way of looking at things. And this is true however much I set my own desires and interests to one side in an attempt to be objective.

Whatever stance I choose to adopt, being aware of the epistemological issues increases my range of options-for-action. It means that I can change the issue I perceive by changing the way I think about it. This isn't the same as saying I can see the situation in whatever way I choose. If I understand some of the things that influence how I see the situation, then I can take steps to reduce the limitations of my view. I can also extend the range of possibilities I might see through alternative perspectives.

Notes, resources and explorations for Chapter 7

1   *Edgar Allan Poe's 'Eureka'*

Edgar Allan Poe believed *Eureka* was the high point of his career. It is a poetic prose essay on cosmology, written from an intuitive understanding. It contains some remarkable scientific insights – well before their time – including the beginnings of the universe from a tiny particle of matter, the paradox of a dark sky in an infinite universe, general relativity, the equivalence of mass and energy and the structure of the atom. Copies of the essay can be found online.

I am not sure I would claim as much as Poe does, but I include the quote in the belief that thinking about my thinking can change some of my own experience of reality.

2   *Ludwig Boltzmann*

Ludwig Boltzmann (1844 –1906) was an Austrian physicist who made enormous contributions to the understanding of thermodynamics. He was one of the advocates for the then-controversial atomic theory. His observation that 'there is nothing so practical as a good theory' is often attributed to Kurt Lewin. Ludwig Boltzmann also pioneered a statistical approach to entropy, a concept that has since proved important to complexity science and information theory, as well as to thermodynamics.

Lewin, K. (1951). *Field Theory in Social Science*. New York: Harper and Row. (p. 169)

3   *Constructivism*

Constructivism has a history that can be traced back to classical Greek philosophy. The term was coined by Piaget, the great theorist of developmental psychology, in 1967. Its central contention is that meaning and knowledge are always a human construction. This means that the discovery of 'truth' about the world outside the mind can only be claimed if one already has an idea of what that truth is. Social constructivism has achieved tremendous importance in the social sciences where claims to 'know' have been critiqued on the basis that knowing has class, gender and race biases that limit its validity. Knowledge, including scientific knowledge, is thus 'relative'. Science's claims to objectivity, constructivism says, depend on validity criteria that are only available to scientists. Indeed, one can see examples of this where, for example, indigenous peoples' knowledge of medicinal plants is denied validity but is nonetheless used by the drugs industry to develop patentable pharmaceutical compounds. In constructivism, attributing validity to knowledge is a political (and often economic) act.

Constructivism claims to be liberatory because it allows oppressed or excluded groups to challenge the knowledge and expertise of a dominant group. However, the technical language of dominant groups often limits the power of such challenges.

Constructivism is a huge topic with many strands of interpretation as well as many applications. Constructivist approaches have had an impact on all the social sciences, as well as education, literature, science and medicine.

4   *Too little information to form a picture*

The retina receives approximately 10 billion bits per second, only a small proportion of the information available in the human environment. The optic nerve at the back of the eye has approximately 1 million connections with a total capacity of 6 million bits per second. Of these, only around 10,000 make it to the visual cortex of the brain. After further processing, only 100 bits per second make it to the brain centres that create conscious perception. If our brains depended only on information from the outside to form perception, it would be like watching a television with a ten by ten pixel array and screen-refresh only once per second. Our conscious brain receives only one in 100 million of the bits of visual information available to the eye. More about this in:

Raichle, M. E. (2010). The Brain's Dark Energy. *Scientific American*, 302, 28-33.

5   *Santiago School of Cognition*

The School is not a school as such but a recent tradition of understanding that has emerged from the work of Humberto Maturana (b. 1928), sometimes known as Humberto Maturana Romasin, and Francisco Varela (1946 – 2001). Their work on the relationship between external stimuli and behaviour is, in some senses, fairly straightforward neurobiology but they applied their findings to exploring the implications for their own cognitive processes. The implications prove to be far-reaching although difficult to understand. The difficulty arises, in large part, from the difficulties of writing about their findings in languages predicated on a subject-object relationship between observer and observed – the very epistemology they challenge.

The implications of this work reach into many areas of activity, including managing messes and cannot all be included here. Indeed, I fear I am unable to do the work any justice at all in this chapter's summary. Far better accounts are to be found elsewhere including in the famous *Autopoiesis and Cognition* from 1979; a popular book, *The Tree of Life*; and perhaps most accessibly in Bernhard Poerksen's interview with Humberto Maturana, *From Being to Doing*.

Although Maturana insists he is a biologist, his work is seen as one of the foundational elements of second-order cybernetics. The concept of autopoiesis, self-organisation, has been a key starting point in some strands of social theory and complexity science as well as biology.

Maturana, H. R. & Varela, F. J. (1980). *Autopoiesis and Cognition: the realization of the living*. Dordrecht: Reidel. (This is a revised version of the original report on Maturana's neurobiological work published in 1970.)

Maturana, H. R. & Varela, F. J. (1988). *The Tree of Knowledge: The Biological Roots of Human Understanding*. Boston and London: Shambhala Publications.

Maturana, H. R. & Poerksen, B. (2004). *From Being to Doing: The Origins of the Biology of Cognition*. Heidelberg: Carl-Auer Verlag.

Humberto Maturana's webpage can be found at http://www.matriztica.cl
The site is in Spanish but has links to a wide variety of videos, blogs and chat rooms.

A useful directory of key terms in second-order cybernetics can be found at http://www.imprint.co.uk/thesaurus/

6   *Foucault and the body*

The body has returned from its relatively invisible position in philosophy through the work of Michel Foucault (1926 –1984). He identified the body as being on the receiving end of coercive social and institutional power through schools, hospitals and prisons, where it passes under the 'gaze' of a relatively few experts. Such 'surveillance', in Foucault's terms, controls people's lives because such institutions define what is normal, ensuring that self-surveillance enforces institutionally-approved behaviour.

Foucault, M. (1975). *Discipline and Punish: The Birth of the Prison*. New York: Random House.

7   *Rich Pictures*

See Chapter 3.

8   *Do I have to?*

Why, after all the foregoing discussion, do I 'have to' accept the limitations of my own viewpoint? I admit to the coercive language and accept that each person has a choice. Nonetheless, if I assume that the world is more-or-less as I see it, then I accept the validity of scientific knowledge and cannot admit ambiguity. I will find, by my own 'rules,' that I have to accept the limitations of my own stance in order to maintain the objectivity I espouse. I prefer to start by acknowledging that I have no direct access to any reality that is independent of my own looking.

CHAPTER 8

Understanding systems

I do not believe in things. I believe only in their relationships.
Georges Braque[1] (1882 – 1963)

If you try and take a cat apart to see how it works, the first thing you have on your hands is a non-working cat.
Douglas Adams[2] (1952 – 2001)

This chapter puts the system into systems thinking. It builds on your own understanding of a system to create some powerful tools for thinking about messy situations. The idea of a system becomes an understandascope through which you can look at messy situations to discern simple structures for thinking about the mess.

WHAT IS A SYSTEM?

If you are following an experiential-learning approach to this book, I invite you to ask yourself the following questions. You may be surprised by how much you already know about the amazing idea that we call 'system'.

- What does the word *system* mean to you?

- What are the characteristics of a system?

When systems-thinking professionals gather over drinks late at night they often express regret that systems-thinking pioneers didn't come up with a better word than *system*. It is a word in common use and so, they say, the 'more sophisticated' technical meaning gets confused with the common-usage meaning. Why, they lament, did the founding spirits of the systems movement not use a new word such as *holon*, the Greek word for a whole? I find myself dissenting from this view. The common-usage sense of *system* carries as much meaning as the technical sense. When I ask people what they understand by a system, even complete beginners come up with ideas which, taken together, have all the senses that 'experts' have in mind when they talk about systems.

Most groups come up with some or all of the following ideas when asked about a system:

- systems are collections of things connected to each other

- systems do something

- systems have subsystems assembled in hierarchies

- the whole is greater than the sum of the parts.

This list, derived from common-usage understandings, is almost complete. A working definition, acceptable to most experts, might be:

> *A system is a collection of elements connected together to form a purposive whole with properties that differ from those of its component parts.*

The trouble with definitions of this kind is that 'every word in it except the articles, the preposition and the conjunction is richly ambiguous'[3]. If I accept the challenge implicit in this observation, I can illuminate the idea of system by discussing each key idea in the definition.

A collection

The *collection* of elements the definition refers to is not just a random assemblage – each element plays its part in the system. The system changes when one or more of the components is changed or removed or if other components are added. Thus, a physical system like a wrist watch (or the cat of Douglas Adams's observation above) changes, and may cease to be a system, when essential elements are changed. By contrast, a heap remains a heap – and a partial set of watch components remains a partial set – and does no more or less than heaps do when the set of component elements changes.

Elements

Elements covers a broad set of entities including ideas, concepts, activities, phenomena, organisations, processes and data, as well a physical objects.

Connections

Connections may be similarly diverse. In the case of physical systems with physical components, the components may interact directly or by pipes, wires or connecting rods through which materials, energy or data flow. Connections may also be conceptual, including cause and effect (A causes B), time sequencing (B follows A), contingency (whether B happens depends on A happening) and many others. Influence (A influences B) is always one of the connections between components of a system. This is a manifestation of the observation that adding, removing or changing a component changes the whole system. Each component connects to at least one other component while others may connect to many more components. Components may thus link into chains or into webs of interconnection. Tools arising from connections come up in Chapters 9 to 12.

Purpose

Systems are *purposive* – an observer observes an apparent purpose[4]. In the case of designed systems, the system's purpose informs its structure, its workings and what it does. Other systems are capable of having purpose attributed to them.

In other words, a system does not need to have a purpose intended by a designer. It just needs to *appear* to have a purpose[5] to fulfil the definition of a system. There is more about this odd criterion in *Systems as doing something, having purpose and emergence* below.

A whole

A *whole* is simply something that seems to make sense as a single entity, even when, as a system, it is an assembly of components. This definition is a useful one, despite its apparent circularity. 'Seeming to make sense' is a powerful criterion in a messy situation. So, for example, a wrist watch makes sense (and qualifies as a system) in a way that half a watch does not. There is no word to describe 'half a watch' and this too indicates that half a watch is not a systemic 'whole'.

The sum of the parts

Aristotle (384 – 322 B.C.E.) was, perhaps, the first to notice that 'the totality is not, as it were, a mere heap, the whole is something besides the parts' (*Metaphysics*, Book 8, Chapter 6) and this is a fundamental quality of a system[6].

By connecting its component parts in a particular way, the system acquires qualities that simply do not exist if one of the parts is changed or connected differently. This quality is called *emergence*. Thus, watch components only become a watch, and acquire emergent time-keeping properties, when assembled in the right way.

The *properties* of the component parts often give no clue about the emergent properties of the whole. For example, oxygen is a colourless, odourless gas. Many quite stable materials become extremely flammable in an oxygen environment. Hydrogen is a 'lighter-than-air' gas that lifts balloons, embrittles exposed metals and burns with an invisible flame when ignited in oxygen. Hydrogen and oxygen combine chemically to form water, a colourless liquid that is essential to life, is refreshing to drink, dissolves salts of all kinds and flows musically along rills and over waterfalls. The properties of water, so different from the properties of hydrogen and oxygen, emerge when hydrogen and oxygen combine to form water.

THE PROPERTIES OF SYSTEMS

Messy situations, like systems, have multiple entities and multiple interconnections. The idea of a system can be a mental tool for creating a more orderly appreciation of a mess. If I think of a mess with its multiple elements and interconnections through the idea of system, I can begin to disentangle the elements from each other and begin to disentangle my appreciation of the mess. The properties of systems offer some tools for looking at a messy situation through the 'system' understandascope.

A system has some fundamental features, which are shown in Figure 8.1. Most notably:

- It has a *boundary* that defines the system as separate from its environment.

- It has an *environment* that is not part of the system but which influences the system and which the system influences.

- It has *subsystems*: systems within the system boundary that are part of the system and contribute to its purpose.

- Its subsystems have their own subsystems and the system itself is part of a larger system so that it is part of a *hierarchical structure*.

- Each subsystem has a specific *relationship* to other subsystems such that any change to a subsystem, or its relationship to other subsystems, changes the behaviour of the system as a whole.

- It has *purpose*, either by design or by attribution.

- It shows *emergence*, a property that makes the system different from a mere collection of the same parts.

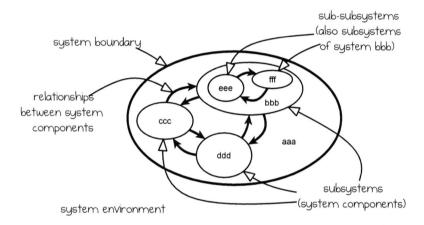

Figure 8.1 *The component parts of a system. The black-tipped arrows are part of the diagram and represent here 'connections between subsystems' in a very general sense. The white-tipped arrows are explanatory annotations and are not features of the system.*

Figure 8.2 shows an example of a system – the local postal-services system, seen from the perspective of a local resident. The system boundary separates the system from its environment. The environment has elements that are relevant to the postal system but not part of it. The postal system has a hierarchy of subsystems, sub-subsystems and sub-sub-subsystems.

The map shows the postal system from the perspective of a domestic customer who receives and sends things through the system and so the inferred purpose is to provide sending-and-receiving mail services for the domestic customer. The subsystems, brought together in a coherent whole, provide the local postal infrastructure.

A systems map of the local postal service

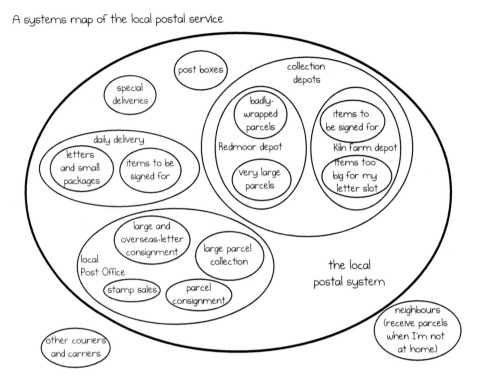

Figure 8.2 *A systems map of my local postal system. For a customer, the key features are local. (How an international postal service works is irrelevant to me.) It includes local and special deliveries and depots where items can be collected if normal delivery is impossible. Occasionally I use other couriers and carriers but they are not formally part of the postal system. Neighbours play an important role in receiving packages when I am out.*

Each of the properties we have just identified – boundary, emergence, purpose, subsystems, relationship, system environment and system hierarchy – provides tools for thinking about messy situations and each is explored in the sections below. But first, an important question.

Do systems exist?

The language of systems assumes that systems are 'real': that they exist in the real world. While this may be true for a watch, it is less obviously so for an assembly of processes such as an airport's baggage-handling system. The system is an assembly of activities such as baggage drop, labelling, security checks, loading and unloading, scanning, transfers between aircraft and baggage reclaim as well as processes such as bag tracking that may happen thousands of kilometres from the bag itself. These activities happen but does the system 'exist' or is it simply a way of understanding that these activities work together to create a baggage-handling whole? This is an open question. The existence of such activities, including many of the same processes in large airports all over the world, suggests that the systems exist. If, however, we ask whether baggage-handling systems include processes for handling bags deemed a security risk or processes for handling accompanied pets, then the boundaries of the system become less clear and answers start to depend on what perspective one is taking.

The question is essentially a decision about how to think. In many contexts, such as engineering or other areas associated with physical artefacts, it is reasonable to work on the basis that systems exist in some verifiable way[7]. In others, the *idea* of a system, used as an understandascope, gives a much richer appreciation of the situation. The idea of a system becomes a way of looking at the world. This latter position, the one taken in this book, looks for the properties of a system in, for example, a messy situation, and identifies clusters of entities, people, ideas or phenomena and then *chooses to see* the cluster as a system. Neither approach is right or wrong. The big difference comes from *noticing that there is a choice*. When I deal with a mess, the issue has less to do with the truth of whether any particular system exists than with how I might think most effectively about the mess.

System boundary and system environment

As humans who name the things we observe in their environment, we get into the habit of assuming that the boundaries we place around the systems we name are also fixed. So, for example, in many organisations, teams or departments provide the organisational structure. People refer to Team X or the Marketing Department as if they were things one could see. But even in rigidly structured organisations, people from one department talk to those in another and information, both formal and informal, moves around the organisation so that getting things done often involves reliance on networks. Organisational restructuring often disrupts the informal networks that facilitate easy relationships between departments and teams, slowing business and inhibiting work flows. Conversations around the water cooler often inform strategic decisions by providing important background information. All this suggests that organisational structures limit thinking. An example from energy-supply shows how this can happen.

In the 1970s, the UK electricity industry was a state-owned monopoly. Efficiency and sales were the dominant factors in generating revenue. Fuel, distribution and waste-heat disposal were its principal costs. The industry was proud of its performance as an electricity generator and, as technology improved, it strove to increase its electricity-generation efficiency and its market share still further. Elsewhere in Europe, notably in Scandinavia, the Netherlands and Germany, different thinking was beginning to prevail. Power stations in these countries began selling waste heat from the electricity-generation process to local communities for home heating. Waste-heat generation is an inevitable consequence of electricity generation, whether fossil fuels or nuclear fuels are involved and the UK landscape is dotted with the huge cooling towers that dump the heat into the environment. In mainland Europe, waste-heat output became a revenue opportunity, rather than an unavoidable cost. Cogeneration of heat and electricity slightly decreases the efficiency of electricity production but massively increases overall fuel-use efficiency from around 30 per cent to nearly 80 per cent. Electricity demand dropped as homes moved from electricity to waste heat for their heating but waste-heat sales became a major new source of revenue, more than balancing lost electricity sales. Electricity generators now saw themselves as part of the energy-supply system rather than the electricity-supply system. In systems terms, the electricity generators of mainland Europe had seen beyond their electricity-generation system to a wider system that included their other main energy output, transforming the heat output from a waste product to a revenue-generating product. Figure 8.3 shows this boundary shift. Doing the wrong thing righter trapped the UK into higher energy costs while mainland Europe made massive savings in their fuel costs and greatly reduced their CO_2 footprint.

Systems maps for electricity production and cogeneration

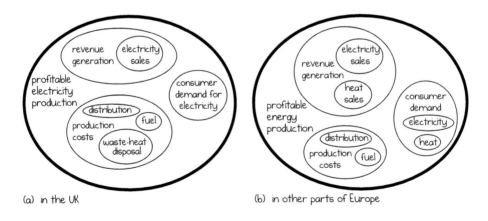

(a) in the UK   (b) in other parts of Europe

Figure 8.3 *By changing the boundary of the revenue-generation system to include waste heat, some European electricity generators opened a new market and transformed themselves from electricity producers to energy producers.*

There are two immediate ways of challenging boundary assumptions. The first is to shift your focus from structures to processes and activities, and the second is to widen your view. Thinking about your messy situation, ask yourself:

- Am I taking boundaries for granted?
  (Such an assumption often takes the form of attributing 'thing-like' status to entities that are not things as such. Such entities may be departments, accepted practices, 'systems' and groupings of processes or technologies.)

- What processes or activities are happening in the situation?
  How do these processes and activities connect, if at all?
  Does the situation have systems of processes and activities operating within it?
  (Looking for process-based systems usually provides an alternative understanding of the situation that overlays the more usual structure-based view.)

- What comes into view when I look at the context of something that I take to be a system?
  (The system influences entities in its environment and they influence the system. Perhaps I should include them as part of a larger system?)

In answering all these questions, treat the idea of a system as an understandascope. The importance of this idea is that it sets you free from the need to discover the 'right' system. There is no right system when you use the idea of a system in this way. Two mediaeval stone cutters do exactly the same job. One believes himself to be in the business of cutting stones – part of a stone-cutting system. The other believes himself to be in the business of building a cathedral – part of a cathedral-building system. Asking which is right is meaningless – they both are. They see different boundaries. The immediacy of his task sets the first man's boundaries. The second man sets his boundary wider and, as a result, sees a wider, and possibly more meaningful, purpose in his stonecutting. Changing the boundaries changes the view.

A large company producing multi-media products was committed to meeting the needs of customers with disabilities as well as it met the needs of non-disabled customers. To this end, its Equal Access Team tailored the mass-produced products to the needs of customers with special needs. As the company acquired a reputation for its products' accessibility, demand grew and the Equal Access Team strove to keep up with demand. Despite improving their efficiency, they could not keep up. Their leader took on the challenge of confronting the company with the need to change the boundaries. He challenged the company to see accessibility as part of the whole process rather than the special task of one team outside the boundaries of mainline production. Accessibility became part of the production process for all the company's products. Designers, producers and marketers now saw accessibility as part of the process rather than an add-on. It created a new commitment to accessibility from people working on every stage of production. Accessibility was now inside the boundaries of the production process. The quality of service provided for customers with special needs improved as designers began to understand needs better and equal-access specialists began to understand the design process better.

Setting boundaries presents choices. There are no right answers to questions about the correct place for a boundary. In any situation, there are a number of satisfactory ways of setting a boundary, recognisable by their ability to help us make sense of the situation. In Figure 8.4, photos (a) and (c) make sense in ways that photo (b) does not and in many ways the art of setting boundaries around the systems we perceive is akin to the art of composing a good photograph. The practice – lots of practice – of experimenting with boundaries and making judgements about where to place them, illuminates new understandings of a situation. Systems maps, discussed later in this chapter, represent boundary judgements and the systems the boundaries define.

Figure 8.4 Three ways of setting a boundary on a photograph. A photograph provides a useful metaphor for setting a system boundary. Photo (b) does not make sense because it does not depict a 'whole'.

Structure, hierarchy and connectedness

Systems occupy a place in a hierarchy of systems and subsystems and a wider system environment. For example, looking at the rich picture I described in Chapter 3, through the understandascope of 'system,' I perceive a care-home system, a care-at-home system, a finance system, a shopping system and fragments of other systems. The finance system includes subsystems such as my sister's finances, my mother's income and her capital. These systems are the mental images of the system by which I then thought about the messy situation. Each subsystem is itself a system and provides a structure independent of any other connections between elements in the system. This means that each subsystem connects to the system above it in the hierarchy by a connection we can label 'is part of'. I could now look for features of the messy situation in these terms. So the 'County-Council care-homes sub-system' and the 'private-sector care-homes subsystem' connect to the 'care-homes system' by being part of that system. The nested structure of systems helps me think more efficiently about complex and messy situations because it allows me to think simply without attempting to simplify the situation itself, perhaps by ignoring details that may be important. The systems I perceive through the system understandascope act as 'containers' for the details. I can examine the details if I need to but they are hidden, not lost, within the system while I am thinking about other features of the mess.

Exploring the deepest subsystems of detail has led to the extraordinary success of science since the Enlightenment of the 18th Century. So, for example, we understand a great deal about trees by examining the cell structure of their leaves, heartwood and bark, by observing how water and nutrient molecules migrate through the cells, by observing the interactions of molecules and sunlight that energise the tree's life processes and in many other detailed ways. More recently, there has been a resurgence of interest in holism – understanding that arises from moving up the system hierarchy that we use to frame our notion of 'tree'. This places the tree in the context of the wider habitat and brings other plants, animals, soil, atmosphere and water into focus. Systems thinking develops an ability to identify *systems of interest* – systems that have sense-making potential – somewhere in this hierarchy of nested systems. Systems thinkers move their attention up and down the hierarchy, engaging with the trees at many system levels to attain the understanding they need.

Systems as doing something, having purpose and emergence

The idea of a system that does something and has a purpose, whether designed or attributed, provides a powerful way of understanding some of the complexity within a messy situation. 'Snappy Systems' is a technique for breaking out of taken-for-granted understandings of what something is or does. Snappy Systems is simply a rapid (hence 'snappy') way of generating a list of different ways of seeing something as a system with a purpose. Snappy Systems works well even if only one person is making the list but it works even better with a group of people contributing ideas. This is an example of how it works:

I have a compost bin outside my kitchen door. Vegetable waste from the
kitchen, small amounts of leftover cooked food, shredded newspaper and
chicken poo go in and, after several months of activity by the resident worms,
I can take out clean, non-smelly garden compost to enrich the soil. Phase 1 of
Snappy Systems is simply to list all the systems you can think of, as fast and
uncritically as you can, that describe the compost bin, by using the form 'A
compost bin is a system to <do something>'. Write down every item of your list,
even if it seems silly or irrelevant. Here is part of my list.

A compost bin is:

- a system to dispose of vegetable waste
- a system to create garden compost
- a system to save money
- a system to live sustainably
- a system to get something for nothing
- a system to improve soil structure
- a system to save energy
- a system to reduce the volume of garbage
- a system to reduce guilt about wasted food
- a system to make the garbage less gooey
- a system to provide a congenial environment for worms
- a system to cut down the number of garbage bags we use
- a system to recycle plant minerals.

This list was generated very quickly and without censoring anything. The only
rule is to use verbs – action words – to define the system in terms of what it
does. All the items suggest different ways of seeing the compost bin.

Phase 2 of Snappy Systems has two list-building stages. Firstly, list as many
compost-bin stakeholders as possible. A stakeholder is anyone who might have
a stake in – any reason for caring about – my compost bin. Again, working fast
and without self-censorship is the key. My stakeholder list includes:

- me
- the garbage collectors

- the City Council

- the garden shop

- the worms in the compost bin

- the neighbours

- my family

- the worms in the garden

- flies.

Next, pick one of the stakeholders: it doesn't really matter which one but it may work better if their stake is rather different from your own. In this case, I would choose the City Council or the worms in preference to my family since the compost bin is a family enterprise and family stakes are similar to mine. Now repeat the Phase 1 process of listing systems but this time, do it from the perspective of your chosen stakeholder. Here is part of my list constructed from what I take to be the perspective of the City Council.

- a system to reduce the volume of garbage

- a system to minimise the smell of garbage

- a system to increase the combustible value of garbage

- a system to make garbage collection more pleasant

- a system to make garbage less tempting to foxes

- a system to reduce fly nuisance around garbage

- a system to make garbage drier.

I don't need to understand fully the Council's perspective on compost heaps in order to generate a much richer understanding of the wider context of my compost bin.

Phase 3 of Snappy Systems – Sinister Systems – is optional but especially useful for exploring why things go wrong. This time the ideas-storm concentrates on systems causing things to go wrong. In other words, each system in the list has the 'purpose' of creating unwanted effects. My compost bin rarely goes wrong but here are some of my sinister systems.

- a system to create a smell by the back door

- a system to attract flies

- a system to create nasty brown liquids

- a system to complicate vegetable-waste disposal

- a system to accumulate more compost than we need

Sinister Systems suggests the existence of systems I do not want and invites me to explore how they work and how to sabotage them in messy situations. It also alerts me to some possible unintended consequences of systems I identify.

Using Snappy Systems, and its variants, I begin to discern interlocking systems within the messy situation; the mess begins to acquire a structure. The idea that a system does something is closely allied to its purpose[8]. 'Doing something' can be used as another way to clarify a messy situation by identifying systems within it. A system *transforms* something. The transformation it performs is the 'doing something' and is a key characteristic of the system. The system takes something in one state and transforms it into another state. This simple statement creates a tool, the ITO model[9], which challenges the user to be very clear and simple about what the transformation is. The ITO – Input, Transformation and Output – model is simply a diagram of a system transforming an Input into an Output. It is sometimes called an *input-output diagram*, although that term is less precise. The input is something in one state or condition. The output is the same thing in a different state or condition, transformed by the system. Figure 8.5 shows the generic ITO model and, below it, a 'toasting system' that transforms bread into toasted bread.

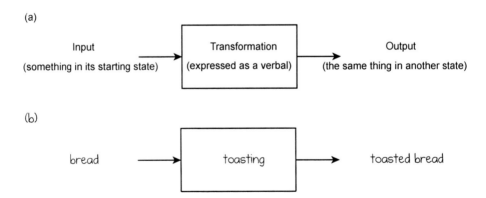

(a)

Input
(something in its starting state)

Transformation
(expressed as a verbal)

Output
(the same thing in another state)

(b)

bread

toasting

toasted bread

Figure 8.5 *A generalised ITO model of a transformation (a) where the state of an input (I) is transformed into another state (O) by the transformation (T). In a specific example of the ITO model (b), the bread in one state (untoasted) is transformed into toasted bread by the transformation. This allows me to identify the transformation as 'toasting'.*

The ITO model forces me to think clearly about two issues: 'What is really happening here?' and 'What essential transformation is needed here?' The model itself may appear trivial or overly simple but simplicity challenges my muddled responses to a messy situation.

Newcomers to the model are often tempted to think of inputs as 'ingredients' or process inputs. The ITO model is not a process model and so, for example, 'bread and electricity' is not an appropriate input for this model. It is important to stick to the specification of 'something in its starting state' for the input and 'the same thing in another state' as the output in order to identify the transformation. The forced simplicity may mean I need several ITO models to disentangle what is going on – another way in which the model forces clear thinking. For example, from my own experience, 'dealing with email' could be messy and suggested the need for a system that deals with email. When I tried to identify the inputs and outputs I noticed there were several different processes so that 'dealing with email' seemed too vague. I came up with several ITO models:

Input	Transformation	Output
incoming emails unread	reading	incoming emails read
incoming emails unanswered	answering	incoming emails answered
outgoing emails unwritten	writing	outgoing emails written
outgoing emails unsent	sending	outgoing emails sent
read emails unsorted	sorting	read emails sorted
old emails undeleted	deleting	old emails deleted

Some people deal easily with email but, like many other people, I found that dealing with email was an overwhelmingly messy task that took time and energy. Using the ITO model, I discovered that the most demanding task was answering the incoming emails that needed responses. I devised a system for dealing with the read-only emails in the morning and responding to other emails later in the day, after I have had time to think about them. Deleting old emails was another task I found irksome, partly because, I realised, I am never sure when emails are truly finished with. I dealt with the issue by changing a system boundary. I now deal with old emails as part of my system for weekly computer back-up. I cannot claim that emails are no longer a problem but I achieved a major improvement and I expend much less time and worry on 'dealing with emails'.

Some transformations specified in an ITO model do not help very much. For example, *dealing with, managing, organising, coordinating, resolving* and several other verb-forms are too vague to clarify very much. The ITO model works best when the transformation is *active*. Ask, 'What would I see happening if I were to see this transformation in action?' and 'What gets changed?' A suite of activity-based transformations will be more useful than a vague, generic term like *organising*. Thus:

Input	Transformation	Output
office unorganised	organising	office organised

becomes:

Input	Transformation	Output
documents not filed	filing	documents filed
dates noted on sticky notes	calendaring	dates entered in calendar
tasks on scrap paper	task-listing	tasks on things-to-do list
invitations received	responding	invitations responded to
tasks unscheduled	scheduling	tasks scheduled

Part of the power of the ITO model comes from its attention to *what* the transformation is rather than *how* it happens. This enables an escape from the trap of existing, but inadequate, processes to focus on the essential transformation. In the email example, I transcended my unsatisfactory experience of ploughing through my emails one-by-one by creating new processes that achieved the same essential transformations in a more satisfactory way.

Two adjectives

Before moving on from the properties of systems, I want to make an important distinction between two adjectives, *systemic* and *systematic*. People often confuse the two and assume, mistakenly, that systems thinking is about being systematic.

Systematic means *orderly, methodical and according to some system*. It often, for example, means taking a planned, step-by-step approach. 'He had a systematic approach to housework'. Systemic refers to the whole system. It often refers, for example to the whole body so that a systemic disease, such as flu, is one that afflicts the whole body as opposed to a non-systemic disease, such as a cold which is primarily an ear, nose and throat infection. By extension, in systems thinking, systemic is often used to characterise approaches that take a sceptical view of boundaries, taking account of a much wider picture and attending to relationships within and around an entity. Thus, a systemic approach to a problem will look beyond the problem to consider its context. Systems thinking may sometimes be systematic but is always systemic.

SYSTEMS MAPS

Systems maps show the structure of systems that I choose to make sense of a situation. Figures 8.2 and 8.3 show systems maps. Systems maps show the boundary; the hierarchy of subsystems; and the system environment for a system of interest. They are essentially a snapshot. They carry no more information than a structured list but I can interpret them much more easily. Like any map, they represent only some features of the situation. They are helpful at the early stages of dealing with a messy situation because they enable me to clarify my thinking about the situation, to experiment with the boundaries I choose to work with and to focus at the right level in a hierarchy of systems. Systems maps are composed of labelled blobs and a title. They show systems and subsystems that belong together and to each other. They show no other interconnections.

Getting started

You will need a supply of large paper and marker pens or soft crayons that will make a bold mark easily. You will need several sheets so scrap paper is ideal. Sticky notes can also be helpful.

It may not be easy to discern where to start. 'Themes' and lists are helpful. An item from a Snappy-Systems list may also provide a starting point for a systems map. I usually start with a theme. This is simply a one or two-word noun-phrase label that fits a sentence like, 'There is a lot about <theme> going on in this situation.' Chapter 4 describes how to identify a theme. In the messy situation I described in Chapter 3, we identified 'money' as one of the themes. I next list all the things in the situation that relate to the theme. The things may be people, ideas, processes, organisations, artefacts or any other kind of entity. If you have a rich picture of the situation, it will be a powerful resource for this process. I then start drawing a map putting things that seem to belong together in systems and subsystems. Constructing the list using sticky notes makes this easier. By writing each item on a separate note, I can move the notes around to create a prototype systems map on a wall or table-top. The list from my own messy situation (described in Chapter 3) was:

- my sister Viola's capital

- money to pay helpers

- financial institutions offering annuities

- Mum's capital

- Mum's income

- Mum's daily expenses

- capital tied up in the house.

It was not a complete list but it was a good start. I clustered things that seemed to represent 'Mum's resources' and worked from there. As I drew a subsystem called *Mum's resources*, I asked myself 'What else belongs in this subsystem?' and added some items not on the list. I asked similar questions about each subsystem and about the system itself. I did not use all the items on the list but it helped me start. After several false starts and six or seven drafts, each adding something to our understanding, I ended up with the systems map shown in Figure 8.6. It was an important breakthrough. For the first time, my sister and I had a clear picture of Mum's financial situation and what we should be planning for. It also alerted us to things we were less certain about – Mum received interest from several savings accounts and we were not sure where they were, how much money was in each account and whether they were the best accounts for Mum's needs and circumstances.

A systems map of Mum's present and future finances

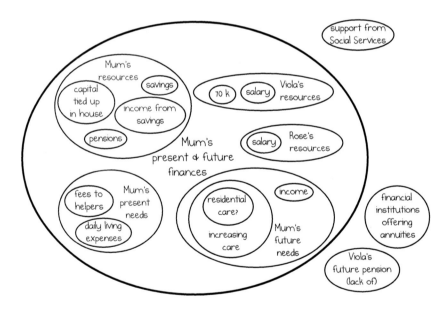

Figure 8.6 *A systems map I drew when my sister, Viola, and I were considering how best to support and care for Mum. The map drew on our identification of 'money' as one of the themes of the messy situation we faced and enabled us to understand the broad picture as well as the details of Mum's, and our own, financial circumstances.*

The map enabled us to have a conversation that might otherwise have been difficult. It was a 'mediating object' in the sense that we could say things about the map that were less easy to say about the situation[10]. Viola had recently inherited some money and was wondering whether she should invest it on Mum's behalf. We included it in the systems map. It was immediately clear that we should postpone any decision about investing in an annuity for Mum until we had a much clearer idea of Mum's own resources. Finding out about Mum's resources became an 'important next task'. We made a provisional decision to hope that Mum could continue to meet her needs from her own resources, for the foreseeable future; to hope that revenue from selling the house would finance any care-home fees, should they be needed; and that, if necessary, we would contribute from our own salaries if that money were finally exhausted. This latter decision was a bit 'up in the air' but gradually settled into a more grounded plan over the next few weeks as we learned more about Mum's resources.

Rules

1   Blob lines represent boundaries

2   Every system and subsystem has a name

3   Systems that have important influences on the main system are shown outside the main system boundary

4   Blobs within the system boundary are subsystems; they may themselves have subsystems

5   Blobs may overlap only if some components are seen as common to both subsystems

6   A title identifying the main system is essential.

Guidelines

- Only one 'main' system – the system-of-interest – is included in the map. It has a bold outline.

- Use blobs rather than boxes. Boxes tend to imply clearly-defined systems. Such systems are rare in systems maps because the purpose of drawing a systems map is to create boundaries for poorly defined systems.

- Do not use overlaps more often than necessary. Although they are allowed by the rules, I almost never use them. When I am tempted, it is usually because my thinking is less clear than it could be. I prefer to rethink what I'm trying to draw.

- Ensure that subsystems within any system are all of the same type. For example, a systems map of a bike that includes a braking system, a power system, a steering system and a suspension system should not also include a subsystem of 'aluminium components'.

- Blob size is independent of the size or importance of the system it represents. It makes sense, however to ensure that important systems are centrally placed. Readers of your systems map may also infer that small blobs are unimportant systems.

- When grouping subsystems within a system, ask yourself, 'What else belongs in this system?'

- Don't overcrowd the systems map. Clear space creates room for last-minute additions and the map will be easier to read.

- Aim for no more than nine subsystems at any level within a system (see The Magical Number Seven in Chapter 6). If you find yourself wanting more than this, try grouping them into a subsystem.

- Aim for no more than four systemic levels in one systems map. If you need more, select a suitable subsystem and draw a systems map in which it is the system of interest. When drawing subsystems within systems within systems, try to avoid an onion-ring effect. You can see hints of an onion ring in Figure 8.6 where the 'residential care?' blob is close to the boundaries of its parent and grandparent systems.

- Most of the benefit of a systems map is realised in the drawing rather than the final product. Take notes about insights, questions, ideas and possible alternative maps. Redrafting is, in many ways, the whole point of drawing a systems map. Each 'failed' map clarifies your understanding of the messy situation.

- Expect the task to be challenging! Be of good cheer. The effort is usually worth it and, if not, it is good practice for the day when it *will* be worth the effort.

There is no single 'correct' systems map for any situation. It is a bit like cutting into a fruitcake – not all the elements of the cake will be visible in every slice. It is usually possible to produce several useful maps for any particular messy situation. Notice too that a systems map, like a snapshot, represents a particular perspective. My map of local postal services in Figure 8.2 is from the perspective of a customer-resident. Someone working for the post office might have drawn a completely different map with subsystems representing collecting mail from post boxes, sorting, international transport, transport between cities, delivery and so on.

Be clear about whether your systems map is about activities or processes. Systems maps can represent either but get muddled if you confuse the two. Activities or processes can be hard to 'see' sometimes but as your understanding of a situation develops, a systems map of an organisation is usually far more revealing if the systems represent activities (product development, product design, product manufacture, marketing, selling, customer care, etc.) rather than departments. Purpose does not feature very strongly in systems maps.

I have learned not to add a title until I am close to finishing my systems map. Usually, my finished map is not the one I thought I was drawing when I started. The title should match the map!

SEARCHING FOR SYSTEM

The idea of a system allows me to simplify my thinking about a messy situation without pretending that the complexity of the situation is simpler than it is. Thinking about some of the features of a messy situation as though they were systems simplifies my thinking by providing a framework that accommodates the complexity without losing the details. You can use the properties of a system to structure your thinking about a mess. To recap:

1   Use ideas of structure, hierarchy and boundary to draw systems maps.
    Look for things that seem to belong together or do something together. Alternatively start from a 'theme' (see Chapter 4). Make boundary judgements as you go but be prepared to start again as you change your mind. Re-drafting is a sign that you are developing your thinking and creating more understanding as you experiment with boundaries.

2   Identify purposive activity within the mess. Ask *Whose purpose?* and use Snappy Systems to explore alternative, and possibly contradictory, interpretations of purpose from your own, and other peoples', perspectives. Notice that purpose is inseparable from

perspective. Use Sinister Systems to explore possible unintended consequences of activities and entities in the messy situation.

3   Identify transformations. Are they desirable transformations? Whose needs do they meet? What is entailed in the systems that do the transformations?

4   Make clear notes of all the insights, questions and ideas that emerge from this exploration. Be prepared for surprises as you search for elements of systemicity in the mess. You will discover things about the mess, about your own thinking about it and about other ways of seeing the situation. I cannot tell you what to look out for or where you will get to. Almost everyone who looks at their mess through the understandascope of systems gains delightful insights. You may be disappointed, however. The search for system may not work for you at this time. Don't worry. Try another set of ideas from another chapter.

USING THE IDEA OF SYSTEM IN MESSY SITUATIONS

There is, as always, only so much you can learn from reading. Here is the challenge:

Have a go at drawing a systems map. Start from a rich picture (see Chapter 3) (or a similar holistic representation of your messy situation) and use a theme as a starting point (see Chapter 4). If you don't have either, just jump in. Keep redrafting until you are happy with it and make notes as you go.

Create Snappy-Systems lists of some of the key systems you identify and explore them from other perspectives. Identify some of the key transformations. Create ITO models for them. Include existing and wanted transformations, existing but unwanted transformations and transformations that might exist in an improved situation.

Notes, resources and explorations for Chapter 8

1   *Georges Braque*

Alongside Picasso, Georges Braque was the co-founder of Cubism and became one of the great artists of the twentieth century. Cubism so outraged the public that he and Picasso were repeatedly questioned about their art. This quotation is a response to one of those questions. Systems thinking is not, of course, related to Cubism but it too privileges relationships as much as things.

2   *A non-working cat*

This passage refers to emergence, which is a key systems idea and characteristic. Life itself is an emergent property of a properly assembled cat. The passage comes from *Dirk Gently's Holistic Detective Agency*. Prof Richard Dawkins quoted this passage in his eulogy for Douglas Adams after Adams died, aged 49, in 2001.

3   *Rich ambiguity*

This delightful quote comes from Checkland and Holwell, writing about the difficulty of testing claims made in everyday language.

Checkland, P. & Holwell, S. (1998). Action research: Its Nature and Validity. *Systemic Practice and Action Research, 11*(1), 9-21.

4   *Purposive and purposeful*

Purposeful is an adjective meaning 'having a definite purpose' or 'being determined in pursuit of a purpose'. Being purposeful is usually taken to be a property of the entity deemed to be purposeful.

Purposive is an adjective meaning 'showing signs of conscious intention'. In other words, an observer attributes purposiveness by interpreting the signs as indicating purpose. Purposiveness arises in the interaction between the entity and the observer.

5   *The solar system*

Is the solar system a system? If we take a system to be purposive, rather than purposeful, then we can answer *Yes* along with many scientists and philosophers from Pythagoras (c. 570 – c. 495 B.C.E) to Johannes Kepler (1571 – 1630). It *appears* to have the purpose of keeping the planets in orderly orbits around the sun. The purpose of the solar system was believed to be to create the music of the spheres – 'the ceaseless round of circling planets singing on their way' – audible only to God but discernible in the harmonious proportions of the planets' orbits. In the *Divine Comedy*, Dante Alighieri's (1265 – 1321) Virgil ascends through the seven spheres of heaven, each with its patron planet, and hears the music of the spheres. Johannes Kepler developed the Laws of Planetary Motion that describe the motions of the planets in their orbits around the sun, in his search for the *musica universalis*.

6   *The etymology of 'system'*

The first use of the word 'system' in English seems to have been by John Selden (1584 – 1654), scholar and jurist. In his argument that the paying of tithes was a civil duty, rather than a religious one, he used the word to mean the whole creation, the whole universe. It is in this sense that Alexander Pope (1688 – 1744) used it in his *Essay on Man*.

> Who sees with equal eye, as God of all,
> A hero perish, or a sparrow fall,
> Atoms or systems into ruin hurl'd,
> And now a bubble burst, and now a world.

Alexander Pope, *Essay on Man*, Epistle I

Selden seems to have borrowed the word from Late Latin, *systema*, where it meant an arrangement, derived from the Greek *systema* 'standing together'. In early Greek, the word carried little sense of internal organisation and could mean *crowd*. Later, following Plato writing about pleasure and knowledge in *Philebus*, Aristotle writing about city governance in *Politics* and Euclid (around 300 B.C.E.), writing about geometry in *Elements*, it acquired a sense of 'standing together in an organised way'. Thermodynamics adopted the concept of system whence it diffused into other science disciplines. It attained its current usage as a generalised concept when Ludwig von Bertalanffy (1901 – 1972), the biologist, adopted it in 1945 as the basis for General Systems Theory (GST) – *models, principles, and laws that apply to generalized systems or their subclasses, irrespective of their particular kind, the nature of their component elements, and the relation or 'forces' between them.*

von Bertalanffy, L. (1945). Zu einer allgemeinen Systemlehre. *Blätter für deutsche Philosophie 3-4.*

7   *Systems in the physical world*

Systems Science distinguishes between closed systems and open systems. Materials cannot leave or enter a closed system. Its interactions with its environment are limited to information and energy. By contrast, open systems are open to matter as well.

Science uses the idea of a system to describe coherent entities in the physical world, such as human and animal organisms, planets and human artefacts. Life forms, which adapt to changes in their environment, have recently been studied through the lens of complex adaptive systems (CAS). In complex adaptive systems, large numbers of elements interact according to simple rules and show emergent behaviours that are adapted to the environment. From my study window, I can see hundreds of starlings creating complex and beautiful patterns in the sky. It is as if they are obeying simple rules that govern how close and how far from other birds they are 'allowed to fly'. Despite the simplicity of the rules, the swirling mass of birds adapts to air currents, the presence of birds other than starlings and the fading evening light without any directing 'squadron leader'. Each individual bird is responding only to the rules and the position and velocities of neighbouring birds. The generic CAS in Figure 8.7 shows the positive (change promoting) feedback and the negative (stabilising) feedback that creates the emergent behaviour. Every bird in the flock receives positive and negative feedback and regulates its flight accordingly. Small changes quickly propagate through the flock giving the impression that the birds respond to a single guiding intelligence. In the 1980s, CAS theory opened up new lines of inquiry in information systems, psychology, economics, anthropology, sociology and many other areas.

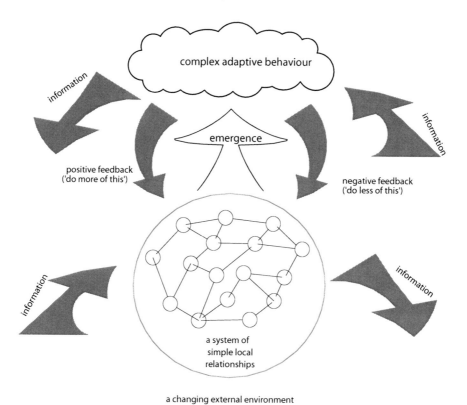

Figure 8.7 *A complex adaptive system shown here as a system of simple local relationships with emergent, complex, adaptive behaviour. The components of the system receive information about each other, and the environment, and feedback about their emergent behaviour. The feedback may be positive – encouraging the system to do more of something as the system adapts to its changing environment – or negative – encouraging the system to do less of a behaviour that does not meet its survival needs in the changing environment.*

8   *Beer on purpose*

Stafford Beer (see Note 2 in Chapter 2) asserted that 'the purpose of a system is what it does' (POSIWID). This gets us past the difficulty that sometimes the designed purpose is not realised or the system does something that was not intended. POSIWID is an elegantly simple formulation but I am not convinced. While Beer's intention is to simplify the issue of purpose, I think he over-simplifies: few real systems do only one thing. What they do can be interpreted in different ways from different perspectives. The POSIWID formulation makes a system's purpose a property of the system and thus independent of the observer. It thus makes the observer – the person who attributes purpose – invisible. I find it more consistent, and in the end less confusing, to be explicit that an observer *attributes* purpose to a system. In the sense that I am using 'purpose' in this chapter, I observe what a system does, or might do, and declare that to be its purpose.

Beer, S. (2002). What is Cybernetics? *Kybernetes*, 31(2), 209-219.

9   *The origins of the ITO model*
        See Note 3 in Chapter 17.

10   *Mediating Objects*
        See Note 8 in Chapter 3.

CHAPTER 9

Diagramming

> *Experts – people who know no more than you do but use diagrams.*
> Andy Capp, in Reg Smythe's *Andy Capp* comic strip[1]

This chapter focuses on the processes of drawing, thinking about and using diagrams. The processes – diagramming – rather than the objects – diagrams – are its focus of attention. Messes have multiple interconnections: everything seems to connect to everything else. Systems thinking is about interconnection. Diagrams can represent the complex webs of interconnection between entities, ideas, phenomena and variables so they are ideal tools for getting to grips with messy situations.

Many kinds of interconnection appear in a mess: cause-and-effect, influence, 'belonging-to' and 'being part of', dependency and many others. These provide the basis for a suite of diagrams – collectively called *systems diagrams*[2] – that map the often-dense interconnections. Systems diagrams – with the exception of systems maps (see Chapter 8) – are *not* primarily diagrams of systems. Systems diagrams are *systemic* because they include relationships as well as entities. It is often possible to identify parts of systems diagrams as representing systems but this is not their primary purpose.

Diagramming is not a methodology. It does not tell me what to do. In diagramming, the systems thinker organises their thinking about a messy situation rather than attempting to discover 'truth'. Thus, many of the benefits of diagramming emerge from the diagramming process, rather than from the finished diagram. Diagramming helps me to 'see' the messy situation differently, to diagnose messes that seem not to respond to treatment, and to think about improving the situation. I discover clarity through a conversation between me and the diagram I am drawing – rather like talking to a clear-headed friend. The conversation ranges across me, my diagram, the 'rules' for that diagram and the mess itself. Figure 9.1 shows this conversation as a system of mutual influences. With practice, I learn to 'see' webs of interconnection in a messy situation – without necessarily drawing the diagrams. Diagramming builds my capacity for seeing the world systemically.

An influence diagram of my diagramming practice

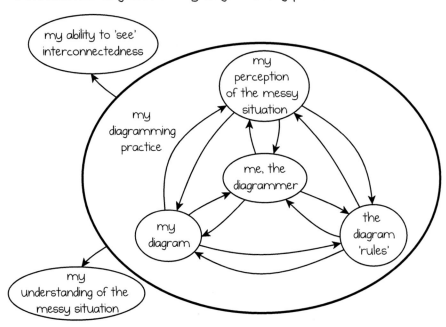

Figure 9.1 *An influence diagram of my diagramming practice. In an influence diagram, arrows mean 'influences'. I have identified the mutual influences in a 'conversation' – between me, the diagram I am drawing, the diagramming 'rules' and the messy situation – as a system because they seem to represent a whole: my diagramming practice. The system has the emergent properties of improving my understanding of the messy situation and, in the longer term, improving my ability to see the web of interconnections in the world.*

Diagrams come in many forms, but in systems thinking I can think of them as *models*. All models are partial representations. They do not show everything. Maps of metropolitan transport networks, for example, do not show distances or compass bearings. They simply show the relationship between stations connected by the railway lines. Systems diagrams are similarly partial; they only show some of the features of the situation. Like a slice through a fruit cake, I may not see all the ingredients (cherries, peel, sultanas, etc.) but I shall begin to see beyond the surface characteristics to the essence of the cake.

Architectural models transcend 'reality' to represent structures that exist only as concepts. Thus, a plan of a house not yet constructed, or a diagram of the social relationships within a neighbourhood, is still a model. The same is true of systems diagrams. In each case, there can be many different perceptions of the 'reality' the diagram captures. No one conception is more real than any other, although people often believe their own is the only possible conception and assume that it is shared by everyone else. So, to be comparable and readable, diagrams modelling messy situations follow agreed conventions, selecting those features of most interest in a situation, and showing the relationships between them.

USING DIAGRAMS

Diagramming has four benefits:

- clarifying the messy situation as you draft and re-draft the diagrams

- creating a focus for productive conversations

- presenting complex ideas in a simple and easily understood form

- building your ability to perceive important interconnections.

Clarifying the messy situation

Drawing diagrams to clarify a messy situation is the first and most obvious use for a diagram. Diagramming for understanding and clarification is a messy business, starting as it does from confusion and messiness. It involves lots of half-formed ideas, lots of crossing out, lots of fresh starts and lots of scrap paper. Don't be afraid of getting it wrong. It is inevitable. In fact, getting it wrong enables me to see *where* I got it wrong and then to draw it again, but better. Would-be systems diagrammers will need lots of paper. I collect one-side-only waste paper from office printers and photocopiers.

Iterative drafting is faster, more effective and more efficient when I draw diagrams by hand. Something about computer-drawing seems to snag diagrams in ways that make the outcome slower and less satisfactory. I encourage beginners – in fact almost everyone – to use hand drawing to create their diagrams-for-clarifying and to use a computer only to draw diagrams for presentation.

Keep all your drafts, numbering them if it seems appropriate. Date the final version, if not all of them. Take notes of ideas and questions as they arise. Notes-on-the-side represent your developing understanding of the situation.

It is often hard to know where to start. If you have a rich picture (Chapter 3), you may have identified themes (Chapter 4) within it. You can start any diagram by attempting to diagram the theme. For example, I identified 'money' as one of the themes of my rich picture (Figure 3.1). My next diagram was a systems map around the theme of money that evolved into a systems map of 'Mum's present and future resources' (Figure 8.6).

Diagrams have 'rules'. Rules are a way of testing and refining your thinking. Breaking the rules is, of course, permissible but the temptation to break them often comes from trying to avoid one's own confusions. Be wary of giving in. Some rules are concerned with the conventions of a particular diagram type. These rules often determine what arrows mean, for example.

Creating hybrid diagrams is another temptation and again, it usually arises when one's thinking is still unclear. My suggestion is to accept the challenge of sticking to the conventions. To extend my metaphor of the diagram as 'clear-headed friend', the 'rules' provide the clear-headedness. Draw two diagrams of different types rather than one that muddles two sets of conventions. Some of my most important diagramming insights have come from sternly facing down the temptation to invent a new type of diagram. But, on the other hand, it is always helpful to privilege enhanced understanding over blind adherence to the rules.

Diagrams need titles – not least so that you know what type of diagram it is and how to interpret it. The latter is not always obvious when you come back later. Add the title only when you know what your diagram is about – usually only apparent after you have drawn it. Many times, I have started a diagram believing I am drawing, for example, a diagram of UVW, only to find, when it is finished, that it is actually a diagram of XYZ. All part of the un-muddling process.

How do you know when the diagram is complete? Each diagram has its own set of rules for ensuring completeness but, in broad terms, a completed diagram is only ever 'completed for now'. There is a quality of obviousness about a complete diagram. It hangs together as if it were inevitable or obvious. This does not mean it was inevitable or obvious. Really useful diagrams arise from thorough exploration, careful observation, and rigorous understanding of the situation. Only hindsight makes it seem obvious.

Creating a focus for productive conversations

Teams pick up ideas very quickly when presented with a large diagram. Diagrams make excellent 'mediating objects' for small teams working through complex ideas. People argue with the diagram, not each other, and stay focused on getting the diagram right and building shared views.

Drawing the diagram by hand on a large sheet of paper, and providing felt-tipped pens, frees team members to alter or add to it. Small diagrams or ones that look finished discourage contributions. People contribute more and better ideas if they feel they can change the diagram. This can be uncomfortable when you have laboured for hours the night before to get it right but, if they have contributed to the ideas and diagram, the team will own a common commitment. As friends and colleagues become used to diagrams, the discussions can take place as they develop a diagram together.

Deeper engagement comes from drawing diagrams together as a joint enterprise. Diagramming in groups is challenging. It quickly reveals the diversity of perspectives so that they can be discussed, widening the perspective of each diagrammer. Once the tensions of surfacing different perspectives resolves, diagrammers can then incorporate a wider range of knowledge and understanding, producing a richer diagram and expanding everyone's mental models of the situation.

Presenting complex ideas in a simple and easily understood form

Diagrams are an efficient way to present complex ideas when the audience is receptive. Unskilled readers often dodge diagrams in reports so a diagram in an unfamiliar format may not communicate effectively. For example, people typically interpret arrows as meaning 'leads to' or a similarly vague or time-sequenced interpretation. However, in a presentation, where the presenter can explain the diagram, diagrams communicate very efficiently. Systems thinkers consider their audience, and the context, in deciding whether to use diagrams for presenting an idea.

Converting hand-drawn diagrams to presentation-quality for a presentation or report can be problematic. Scanning neat hand-drawing is one option, although hand lettering undoubtedly retains an informal appearance. Diagramming software is another solution, although many packages – including some of the most famous ones – produce very poor systems diagrams. Curved arrows seem to be the problem. The best ones allow you to move blobs and words with any attached arrows following. A digital camera is a useful item in meetings that produce diagrams. Photograph the diagrams for re-drafting, circulating or for actioning outcomes.

Building your ability to perceive important interconnections

As people develop their systems-diagramming skills, they begin to 'see' systemic interconnection in the world. It is as if they see fragments of diagrams without drawing them. This builds their ability to think systemically and become even better at managing messy situations.

Diagrams are a brilliant way of building systems thinking into everyday thinking skills. The following chapters present a number of diagrams. Most people begin with only one or two diagram types. Be aware of all the types of diagrams available but become good at just a few before you engage with more. Try not to choose. Engage with each diagram type once and wait for an opportunity. Then practise by drawing the appropriate diagram, with this book beside you. Let the situation decide. Eventually your diagramming skills become an interaction between you, the situation you are trying to manage, the diagram type and your goals. Whichever diagrams become your own specialities, let the *process* of diagramming be the means of understanding the situation better and a means to develop your own systems-thinking skills.

DIAGRAM TYPES AND PURPOSES

In the chapters that follow, I describe diagrams that most effectively deal with messy situations and develop systems-thinking skills. I have excluded many types[3] because they are not as systemic as those itemised in the systems map in Figure 9.2. I drew this diagram to convey the general shape of the next two chapters.

A systems map of diagrams referred to in the book

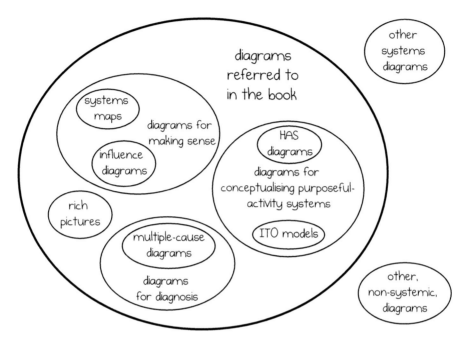

Figure 9.2 *A systems map of diagrams included in the book. Rich pictures were discussed in Chapter 3, systems maps and ITO models in Chapter 8. Diagrams for making sense and diagrams for diagnosis appear in Chapters 10 and 11. Finally, human-activity system diagrams appear in Chapter 14. I drew this diagram when I was planning the general shape of the next few chapters.*

NOTES, EXPLORATIONS AND RESOURCES FOR CHAPTER 9

1   *Andy Capp*

Andy Capp was syndicated all over the world, always appearing with his flat cap pulled over his eyes. He was the creation of Reg Smythe, first appearing in the *Daily Mirror* (UK national daily newspaper) in 1957. Andy is a stereotypical working class Northerner, racing pigeons, playing darts, football and snooker, and getting drunk. He is chronically unemployed although his wife, Florrie, works hard as a charwoman. Andy himself is unmotivated and cynical about anyone doing better than himself. Despite the stereotyping, Andy was greatly loved – not least by Northern working-class men. He appeared regularly from 1957 and continues even though his creator died in 1998. A statue in Hartlepool commemorates Andy.

2   *Systems diagrams – a muddle of names*

In this book, I use the term *systems diagram* in a generic sense to mean *a diagram that is systemic* (i.e. one that incorporates systemic ideas such as boundary, interconnections, purpose, etc.). It does not indicate a *diagram of a system* (or *systems*). A better name would be *systemic diagrams* but it is probably better to stick with a widely used convention and note the potential for misunderstanding.

Many people confuse *systems diagrams* with *systems maps* (see Chapter 8). A systems map is one particular type of systems digram. Other systems-thinking traditions use *systems diagram* to mean a very specific form of diagram.

3   *Other diagram forms*

There are many forms of 'business diagrams' that are useful in thinking about and communicating ideas, but which are not included in this book. Some of these are:

- Force-field diagrams for identifying and evaluating the forces acting to promote and inhibit change.
- Gantt Charts and PERT Charts for analysing the task schedules and the time it will take to complete a project and which events determine the critical paths.
- Organisational charts (organograms) for showing the structure of an organisation.
- Flow charts for showing the flow of work, data or materials through a process.

CHAPTER 10

Making sense of messy situations

It's not the money. It's not the fame. It's the influence.

Clay Aiken (b. 1978)[1]

INTRODUCTION

A common response to a messy situation is that 'it doesn't make sense'. Making sense of at least part of the mess provides a foundation for taking action for improvement. The diagram described in this chapter makes sense of messy situations, most usefully at the early stages of exploring the mess. Influence diagrams add another dimension to systems maps by exploring how bits of the mess influence one another. More precisely, they explore entities like ideas, people, components and activities and their influences on each other.

INFLUENCE DIAGRAMS

Influence diagrams express the idea that one thing influences another, perhaps many others, in a messy situation. The immediate experience is often that everything seems to influence everything else. Influence diagrams go straight to the experience of complexity.

Influence diagrams have blobs, words, arrows and a title. The blobs of an influence diagram indicate 'things' and labels identify each one. The arrow means 'influences'. Figure 10.1 shows the essential grammar of an influence diagram. In many diagrams, it is easy to assume and misread arrows as meaning 'is followed by', 'leads to', etc. But in an influence diagram, the arrow has one meaning only: 'influences'. Theoretically, the blob boundary indicates a system but it is usual to interpret each blob in the looser sense of being a *thing*.

'Thing' includes artefacts, technologies, people, concepts, phenomena – in fact almost anything to which I can attribute the capacity to influence[2].

Figure 10.1 An influence diagram meaning 'A influences B'.

Choosing an influence diagram

When do you use an influence diagram?

Influence diagrams reveal interconnections in the messy situation through the understandascope of influence. Often in a messy situation, it seems as though everything influences everything else. An influence diagram reveals exactly what influences what by distinguishing between direct and indirect influences. An influence diagram is a snapshot showing where I believe the influences to be.

Influence diagrams make sense of messy situations so they often help early in your engagement with a mess. They may for example, be the next step after capturing the situation in a rich picture. Sometimes, I draw one as an alternative to a systems map – another form of sense-making diagram – sometimes as a supplement to a systems map. They are helpful partly because I do not need to be specific about what sort of influence I am dealing with.

Mostly, in my experience, it is simply a matter of trying to draw an influence diagram and seeing if it helps. If it does not help within 20 minutes or so, I usually abandon it and try something else.

There is no approved order for drawing diagrams so, if influence diagrams turn out not to be your sort of thing, or they are not quite the right thing on a particular day, or for a particular mess, then nothing is lost by trying something else.

Making sense with an influence diagram

Influence diagrams are 'sense making' tools for early in the encounter with a mess or, as described here, for making sense of unease or puzzlement.

In our discussions about Mum's future care needs (see Chapter 4 for the background story), my sister and I became aware of the delicacy of making decisions on someone else's behalf. I later drew an influence diagram to make sense of my unease. Figure 10.2 shows the first element I drew. I did not choose it with any great thought: it simply expressed an influence I saw in the situation. It expresses the idea that Mum's mental capabilities influence her ability to make decisions.

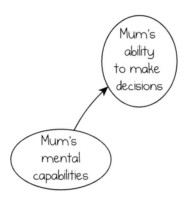

Figure 10.2 *The first 'sentence' in an influence diagram I drew as I tried to understand the issues surrounding making decisions on Mum's behalf.*

Having made a start, I identified something that influenced Mum's mental capabilities – her health. I took this as a catch-all term indicating her vulnerability to further strokes, the possibility she might recover somewhat and other debilitating events or illness that might befall her.

I asked a key influence-diagramming question of the 'Mum's mental capabilities' blob: 'What else does this influence?' I added 'Mum's ability to express herself'. That, in turn, led me to add 'our perception of Mum's wishes'. I then asked, 'What else influences this?' and added an arrow from 'Mum's ability to make decisions'. These two questions build the influence diagram backwards and forwards from each blob.

I now had an influence diagram that looked like Figure 10.3. I confess to having tidied it up a little in the interests of clarity. My diagram already had some crossings out as I experimented with different wording to capture the essence of the influences I saw.

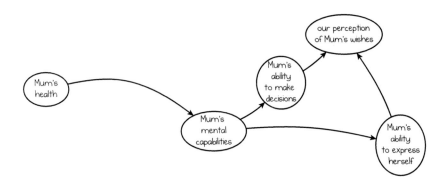

Figure 10.3 *My next steps in constructing the influence diagram. I used the questions,'What else does this influence?' and 'What else influences this?' to add additional blobs to my diagram.*

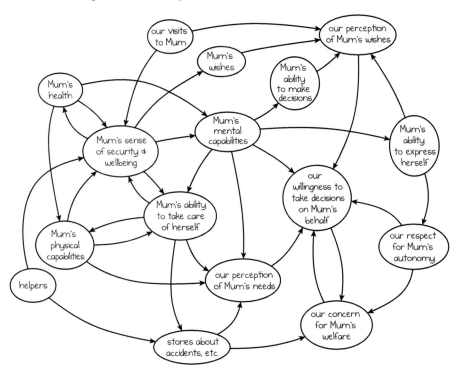

Figure 10.4 *The influence diagram I drew as I explored my uneasiness about making decisions on Mum's behalf. The diagram required several drafts before arriving at this version; early drafts had lots of crossing out. The diagram reassured me that I would be able to make appropriate decisions, when the time came, without usurping Mum's autonomy.*

Figure 10.4 is the diagram I eventually settled for. It had helped me make sense of my uneasiness. I try not to decide a diagram is 'final' but a time comes, of course, when it is sensible to stop. You may wish to read your way through it, remembering that the only interpretation of an arrow in an influence diagram is 'influences'. Don't worry if you cannot understand it all.

Notice that I have used curved lines for the arrows. The human eye follows curved lines more easily than it follows intersecting straight lines. In this particular influence diagram, there is no central feature, nor does the diagram read from left to right, or top to bottom. There is no particular argument in this diagram; it simply represents influences I perceive in the situation. Sometimes direction or centrality emerge as important features but it helps not to force either, particularly when you are trying to make sense of a messy situation.

As I drew the diagram, I resisted the temptation to draw everything influencing everything else. I drew arrows only where strong clear influences connected the blobs. I asked myself, with each arrow, whether the influence was reasonably direct and understandable. If not, I added an intervening blob. For example, I initially drew a link indicating 'Mum's health' influences 'our perception of Mum's needs'. I then realised my sense of Mum's health was mostly about her physical capabilities so I interposed 'Mum's physical capabilities'. That alerted me to the influence between 'Mum's physical capabilities' and 'Mum's ability to take care of herself'.

The meaning of *influences* is quite specific but paradoxically vague. It takes a bit of discipline to ensure arrows always mean 'influences' but within that discipline, defining the influence, or even knowing its nature, is unnecessary.

Understanding an influence diagram

As I drew the influence diagram shown in Figure 10.4. I had very little idea of what I was drawing, except that it was an influence diagram and I was exploring the unease I had experienced as I discussed our concerns for Mum with my sister. This lack of a clear topic at the start is common in diagramming and I could only put a title on the diagram once I finished drawing, could look at it, and could decide what I had drawn.

As I drew, I experienced a deepening understanding of the issues. It had felt ethically uncomfortable talking about Mum 'behind her back', especially as we were talking about decisions that would affect Mum's life in profound, unwished-for and probably irreversible ways. In drawing the diagram, I was able to see that our growing responsibility for decisions mirrored Mum's transition from autonomy to dependency. Sensitive awareness of the issues would ensure that I was not *interfering* so much as *taking responsibility* as Mum's ability to decide declined. Some of this was emotional, as well as cognitive, learning.

As I looked at the finished influence diagram, I noticed the number of influences centred on 'Mum's sense of security and wellbeing' and 'Mum's ability to take care of herself'. 'Mum's health' influenced, directly and indirectly, both of these. I could imagine how, if Mum's health continued to decline, 'our perception of Mum's needs' would become a more powerful influence than 'our perception of Mum's wishes' on 'our willingness to take decisions on Mum's behalf'. 'Mum's health' was one of the key influences that would determine how and when we took decisions on Mum's behalf. 'Our respect for Mum's autonomy' and 'our concern for Mum's welfare' (influenced by information from the helpers) would ensure that our decisions would be centred on Mum's welfare rather than expedience. I had been concerned that my own needs would be an undue influence on any decisions, even though they would be a legitimate concern.

I was reassured to notice the mutual influences between 'Mum's sense of security and wellbeing' and 'Mum's ability to take care of herself'. Initially I had drawn an arrow to note my sense that Mum's ability to take care of herself would depend on her feeling well enough, and motivated enough, to make the effort. Later I realised that as her ability to take care of herself declined, she would feel less secure and happy.

If I ask, 'What did I learn from drawing this diagram?', my answers are disappointingly imprecise. On the other hand, it made sense where none had existed before. Influence diagrams can make sense of poorly understood messes, even when they start from something as simple as stating 'Mum's mental capabilities influence her ability to make decisions'. In this case, I understood, and was thus able to manage, my unease about making decisions on Mum's behalf.

Rules and guidelines for influence diagrams

Influence diagrams have rules. The rules provide a structure against which to test ideas. As with all 'rules' for systems thinking they can be broken with impunity but, in my experience, a temptation to break the rules usually disguises a unwillingness to challenge my woolly thinking. Here are the rules:

1   Blobs represent components that influence other components, or are influenced by them.

2   Words label each component.

3   An arrow joining Blob A to Blob B indicates 'A influences B' (see
     Figure 10.1.). Arrows do not signify any other connection between A
     and B.

4   Double headed arrows are used only if A's influence on B is *identical*
     to B's influence on A; otherwise two arrows are used.

5   Arrows may be drawn as heavy lines to show a strong influence or as
     dotted lines to show a weak, but nonetheless significant, influence.

6   An influence diagram, like a systems map[3], is a snapshot of the
     situation at one point in time.

7   A title is essential to identify the diagram as an influence diagram
     and to identify the situation I am trying to make sense of.

8   System boundaries identify a cluster of mutually influential
     components as a system. They are optional.

Few of these rules need any further discussion. Of Rule 4, I would say
that I have never found a use for a double-headed arrow. Almost always,
if A influences B and B influences A, then two arrows are used. System
boundaries, mentioned in Rule 8, are optional. There was a clearly identifiable
cluster of mutually influencing components in Figure 10.4, for example.
The components: Mum's health; Mum's sense of security and wellbeing;
Mum's mental capabilities; Mum's ability to take care of herself; and Mum's
physical capabilities might have been identified as a subsystem called 'Mum's
capabilities'. It seemed unnecessary to include it, however. Figure 10.5 (below)
shows an influence diagram with a system boundary. The four components
seem to belong together as a system with a purpose.

There are neither rules covering the placement of components nor a direction
for reading the diagram. It helps if components you take to be important are
easy to identify. Arranging components left-to-right or top-to-bottom will help
if there is a sequence of influence you wish to make prominent. In practice,
when you are trying to make sense of a messy situation, there are so many
interconnections it may be impossible to discern a dominant direction.

A good influence diagram makes sense of a messy situation (or part of it, at
least). This means you have to be selective about what to include. Influence
diagrams that have more than, say, twenty blobs are very difficult to read. They
very quickly become 'horrendograms' that do no more than illuminate the
potential impossibility of making sense. It is better to group several components
into a single blob and draw other influence diagrams exploring details. Be
selective about which influences to include. Limit yourself to the strong ones.

You will need to do some disentangling as your diagram develops. Crossed arrows make the diagram harder to read so redrafting to reduce crossings-over are a necessary and valuable part of the sense-making process. On the other hand, arrows that take long detours around the outside are also hard to make sense of. Sometimes you cannot eliminate every cross-over. I am sometimes tempted to omit the last redrawing because 'it's just for me' but it is often the last draft that delivers the Aha! moment when ideas fall into place and I begin to discern some underlying structure in the mess. Using curved arrows makes the diagram much easier to read. Straight lines arrest the eye, keeping it on a single influence couplet and making it hard to see sequences of influence. There is a final informal rule. Rule 9: draft, redraft and redraft again without embarrassment. Drawing diagrams is a way of learning your way to understanding. False starts, blind alleys and red herrings are all part of the landscape through which you find your way to better understanding of the mess.

I usually defer adding a title to my diagram until near the end. As in the example above, I may not know what I am drawing until near the end – I am simply tracking some influences in order to make some sense of a messy situation.

I had been drawing diagrams for years before a helpful client suggested that I write the words first and only then draw the blob around them. Like the best suggestions, it was obvious once pointed out so I felt rather foolish. I pass this suggestion on so you can save yourself a lot of unnecessary tidying up.

Drawing an influence diagram

I now challenge you to draw an influence diagram of your own. You may want to explore a messy situation you are already contending with, or you may want to explore something else[4]. I have tried to tell you everything you might need to know about influence diagrams but I cannot tell you much about how useful they are – you simply have to experience that for yourself.

As you draw, do not worry about 'getting it right'. There is no answer in the back of this or any other book. Influence diagrams are about making sense of messy situations. They usually succeed but only you will be able to tell when it is right. Getting it right is about achieving some understanding that was not there before.

You may want to start with a theme you identified from a rich picture, if you are stuck for somewhere to start. Then ask a question such as *What are the influences acting on …?* As you work, you may find you are answering some other, potentially more profound or more important question. Just keep going. Sense-making is often about finding better questions. Alternatively, you may start with a sense of unease or puzzlement with no clear aim or question in mind. In either case, simply start with a single influence statement from the mess and work outwards asking:

- What else does this influence?

and

- What else influences this?

The only stopping rule is 'stop when it makes sense of part of the messy situation'.

Using influence diagrams with others

Like most diagrams, influence diagrams are powerful communication tools in meetings. Big, informally drawn, influence diagrams will enable participants to understand how you see the situation and will invite contributions that develop the group's understanding. Chapters 9 and 12 give suggestions about how to do this.

More influence diagrams

It was time to evaluate the impact of a high-profile training initiative designed to develop leadership skills in the next generation of managers in the organisation. Participants had enjoyed the workshops and continued to express their appreciation of the insights they had experienced. Participants' managers, however, reported no discernible improvement in participants' performance. The Human Resources Director faced a conundrum. Should she invest more in the popular programme, in the hope that extending it would deliver results? Or should she wind-up the programme? The evidence was contradictory. When she asked me to help, I drew the influence diagram shown in Figure 10.5.

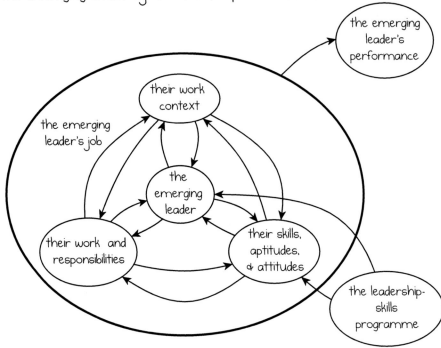

An influence diagram of the leadership-development programme, the emerging leader's job and their performance

Figure 10.5 In this influence diagram, the four central elements are mutually influential: each influences all the others. Taken together, they can be seen as a 'system of practice', indicated by the system boundary. This system, as a whole, influences the element on the top right. The element on the bottom right can only influence the system by influencing two of its sub-systems.

The diagram drew on a generic model of 'practice' I had developed for another purpose (Figure 9.1 also derives from this common source.) The emerging leader's job is a system in which the person, their skills, aptitudes and attitudes, their work and responsibilities and their work context all influence one another. Their 'work and responsibilities' is a catch-all term indicating their tasks, job descriptions and day-to-day and strategic responsibilities. The 'work context' indicates their teams, colleagues, their boss, the resources to which they have access and the organisational culture. The programme could only influence the emerging leader and their skills, aptitudes and attitudes. It could have no plausible direct influence on performance because performance emerges from the job *as a whole*. Of course, there was no way of knowing if my diagram was 'true' in any way but, in discussion, we agreed to investigate whether work tasks, responsibilities and context had any bearing on the performance of the emerging leaders. It transpired that the emerging leaders were frustrated by a lack of opportunities to use their new skills. Inadequate resources and unsupportive bosses often undermined them. A few months later, the organisation ran a programme for senior managers (i.e. the participants' bosses) on 'Supporting Emerging Leaders'. Senior managers and emerging leaders all improved their performance and reported more job satisfaction. The organisation itself reported improved performance.

We drew an influence diagram when we were trying to understand Mum's finances. Money had emerged as a theme in our rich picture about the caring-for-Mum mess[5]. Although the elements representing money were quite diverse, it only took a simple diagram to show how they influenced each other. You can see the influence diagram in Figure 10.6. It helped tie together all the disparate elements representing this theme. It became a means of explaining our decisions to each other.

Influence diagram about financing Mum's future care

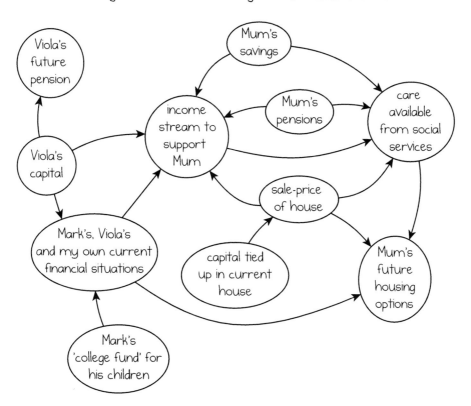

Figure 10.6 *An influence diagram showing the interactions affecting Mum's financial situation.*

MAKING SENSE OF INFLUENCES IN MESSY SITUATIONS

Sense-making plays an important role in systems thinking because messy situations have multiple interconnections. Without making sense of these, intervening to improve the situation risks creating unintended consequences. Diagramming is a powerful tool for making sense because it is able to represent networks of interconnection. The dialogue between the diagrammer and the diagram is a process of articulating the interconnections so that they make sense. The usefulness of the diagram is two-fold: drawing it creates sense and the diagram captures the understanding for future reference. Diagrams such as influence diagrams have a precise grammar, without having to specify in detail what the influence is.

There is no recommended order for drawing diagrams and certainly no necessity for drawing all of them to make sense of a messy situation. It is usually helpful, however, to draw at least one sense-making diagram in the process of understanding a messy situation. This usually means one or more systems maps or influence diagrams. The next chapter builds on sense-making to diagnose what is happening in a messy situation.

NOTES, RESOURCES AND EXPLORATIONS FOR CHAPTER 10

1 *Clay Aiken*

An American pop singer who shot to fame in the 2003 season of *American Idol*, Clay Aiken is a prolific performer on records, musicals and on stage and television. He starred on Broadway as Sir Robin in *Spamalot,* the Monty Python version of the Arthurian legend. He has used his celebrity influence to promote inclusion of children with disabilities in mainstream childhood activities.

2 *Systems that influence*

If something such as an artefact, a technology, a person, a concept, a phenomenon or an organisation can influence something then, by attributing this as its purpose, I declare the 'thing' to be a system.

3 *Influence diagrams and systems maps*

It is sometimes helpful to develop an influence diagram from a systems map. Simply add the influence arrows to a systems map. I prefer to draw them separately, not least because it may take several drafts to create a good influence diagram and I do not want to lose my systems map.

Like systems maps, influence diagrams show blobs because the items identified can be seen, without too much stretch of the imagination, as systems with boundaries.

4 *Practising drawing influence diagrams*

Influence diagrams are brilliant tools for understanding the background to news and current affairs. Here are some universal and timeless issues you can practise with:

- the economy (start with the current issue-of-concern: unemployment, inflation, interest rates, the national debt, etc.)
- 'the drugs problem'
- the effects of, or adapting to, climate change
- the health-care system
- providing emergency aid (overseas or domestic)
- alleviating poverty

Other issues might include office politics, being happy or saving energy.

5 *Caring for Mum*

This rich picture and the mess it relates to are discussed in Chapter 3.

CHAPTER 11

Diagnosing messy situations

Felix qui potuit rerum cognoscere causas.
Happy is he who is able to understand the causes of things.
                                    Virgil[1] (70 B.C.E. – 19 B.C.E.)

To confess ignorance is often wiser than to beat about the bush
with a hypothetical diagnosis.
                                    William Osler[2] (1849 – 1919)

Messy situations often appear in the form of 'something going wrong' followed by attempts to fix it that don't work, or appear to work at first but then cease to work. To understand what is going on when this happens needs *diagnosis*[3]. This chapter explores interactions within messes through the understandascope of *cause and effect*.

We are used to the idea of *chains* of cause and effect but causes and effects rarely assemble themselves in chains and especially not in messy situations[4]. *Multiple-cause diagrams* map the webs of intersecting causes and effects and allow diagnosis of persistent unwanted phenomena and discernment of intervention points for improving the situation. They can also help predict the possible consequences of an intervention, allowing the systems thinker to manage or forestall unwanted consequences.

MULTIPLE-CAUSE DIAGRAMS

Multiple-cause diagrams recognise that events and phenomena rarely have a single cause. They map effects, phenomena and events that cause other effects, phenomena and events in networks of intersecting causation. Unlike systems maps and influence diagrams, which are snapshots, they represent a history and future, as well as a present.

Multiple-cause diagrams have words, arrows and a title. Figure 11.1 shows the form of each diagram 'statement'. The words in the diagram represent effects, phenomena, events or observations rather than entities or variables, so they do not have system boundaries. The arrows indicate causation and read as 'causes' or 'contributes to'. It is tempting to interpret the arrows as meaning 'is followed by' or 'leads to'. Even though we are used to reading arrows as a time sequence, neither of these meanings meets the rules of multiple-cause diagrams. Since arrows have many different meanings in systems and other diagrams, the title of a systems diagram should make clear what type of diagram it is. (I am sometimes irritated when reading books and other documents by the use of un-defined arrows in diagrams. It is sometimes impossible to discern what the arrow means.)

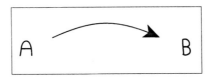

Figure 11.1 In a multiple-cause diagram, the cause and effect pair above reads as 'A causes or contributes to B'. A common mistake is to read it as 'A is followed by B' or 'A leads to B'.

Choosing a multiple-cause diagram

Multiple-cause diagrams are useful for:

- understanding why an effect, observation, phenomenon or event happens or has happened, or why it continues to recur

- understanding why attempts to prevent or stop an unwanted effect, observation, phenomenon or event sometimes fail

- discerning ways of intervening that will improve the situation while minimising unintended and unwanted consequences

- discerning possible unintended consequences of intervening.

Multiple-cause diagrams cannot predict the consequences of an action but they can structure ideas about them.

Making sense with a multiple-cause diagram

When my sister and I were trying to work out how best to 'take care of Mum', a multiple-cause diagram provided us with the breakthrough we needed. As we talked about the rich picture we had drawn[5] about 'taking care of Mum', we noticed we were both talking about our sense of impotence, guilt even, that we were not able to make arrangements we felt were good enough. We wrote down 'guilt' as a theme[6], even though it is not obvious in our rich picture. We started the multiple-cause diagram with 'Viola feels guilty' and 'Rose feels guilty' and worked from there. Figure 11.2 shows where we got to.

A multiple-cause diagram of Viola and Rose feeling guilty

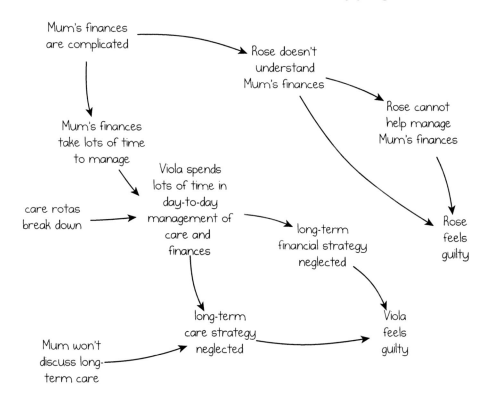

Figure 11.2 *The multiple-cause diagram I drew with my sister as we discussed our vague feelings of guilt. This diagram provided the breakthrough we needed to manage Mum's care well.*

At first sight this diagram seems to suggest only that our guilty feelings traced back to Mum's finances being complicated, Mum not discussing long-term care, and the care rotas breaking down. None of this was our fault and we chose to take our guilt as symptomatic of a desire to do things differently. We noticed that while Viola's guilt came from an inability to address long-term finance and care issues, mine came from an inability to support her. Suddenly a strategy became obvious. I would take on long-term planning and strategy and Viola would continue day-to-day managing. This would, we thought, work well. That is what we did and it was a huge improvement. The impact went way beyond alleviating our sense of impotence. I took a week off and visited several care-homes, putting Mum on the waiting list at some of the most suitable ones, in case she should ever need residential care. I researched annuity options and investments for Mum's changing financial needs. Viola was able to continue managing Mum's day-to-day care as we waited for developments. As with many messes, it was not a solution but we knew we had covered the immediate and medium-term possibilities.

This diagram exemplifies the idea that messes cannot always be 'solved'. We were still not able to discuss the options with Mum and the issues remained unresolved but, if Mum's health improved we knew what the options were, and if Mum's health continued to decline, we had created better options for her care.

We had 'broken the arrow' in the diagram that meant that Mum's unwillingness to discuss long-term care contributed to neglect of the long-term-care strategy. Viola still spent lots of time managing the day-to-day issues but we were no longer neglecting the long-term issues. We felt energised, had more options and more control.

Drawing the diagram was straightforward. At each stage we asked ourselves *What else does this cause or contribute to?* and *What else causes or contributes to this?* In this case, the causes and effects were mostly linear. We needed only one draft. (Figure 11.2 has been tidied up for clarity.) Having started in the right-hand side of the page, the narrative direction emerged naturally from left to right. Curved lines support easy reading.

Diagnosing with a multiple-cause diagram

A multiple-cause diagram supports diagnosis by identifying points for disrupting a sequence of phenomena, events or observations to mitigate an unwanted phenomenon. Figure 11.3 shows a multiple-cause diagram of the spread of flu at work.

The annual flu epidemic hits the UK and people get flu. People will often continue working if their symptoms are mild or there is pressure to continue working. This causes other people to acquire the infection. Setting out this sequence of events in a multiple-cause diagram allows diagnosis and identification of appropriate interventions. Intervening, in terms of multiple-cause diagrams, means either removing an event, phenomenon or observation (represented by words) or removing a causal link between events (represented by an arrow). Either has the effect of breaking the sequence.

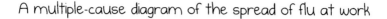

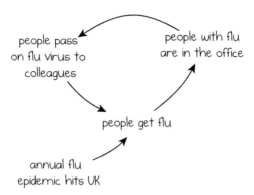

Figure 11.3 *A multiple-cause diagram of the spread of flu at work. Once people get flu, the cycle starts and more people become infected. From the perspective of a manager, the best option seems to be ensuring that people with flu do not come into the office. This would break the loop.*

In the case of Figure 11.3, some effects are more accessible to intervention than others. A manager may decide there is very little he can do about the arrival of the annual flu epidemic. The diagram might then prompt him to ask whether the link between the arrival of the flu epidemic and people getting flu could be broken. Would it be possible to vaccinate staff, for example? It seems inevitable that some people will get flu: is there a way to break the link that causes people with flu to be in the office? Can people be discouraged from coming to work if they have flu? Could they work from home without penalty if they suspect they might have flu? People with flu may be in the office. Can person-to-person contact be minimised? Can face-to-face meetings be minimised? Can we improve hygiene standards? Can we protect non-infected staff in any way?

The diagram suggests many lines of inquiry for dealing with the issue. At the heart of the diagram is a *reinforcing loop*. Once the loop initiates, it has the potential to run until almost everyone in the office has flu. This makes vaccination a good option – in terms of preventing the loop forming – although it may be expensive.

Once the loop starts running, the main option for intervening is getting people to stay at home if they suspect they may have flu, perhaps offering home-working arrangements and, in the office, minimising face-to-face contact and improving hygiene. None of these options excludes any other and many are low-cost compared with high levels of unplanned sick-leave and long recovery times. I have simplified the loop somewhat and I have ignored, for example, the time delay between infection and getting the symptoms and between infection and becoming infectious. There is evidence, nonetheless, that organisations adopting these measures in the face of a flu epidemic lose less time than those with a more aggressive 'come-to-work-until-you-drop' approach to flu[7].

Breaking a causal sequence involves looking at events or phenomena that may restart the sequence of events. For example, there were two sequences of events contributing to 'Viola feels guilty' in Figure 11.2. Two interventions were required to eliminate this unwanted effect: one to engage with a long-term care strategy, the other to engage with a long-term financial strategy.

Another approach would be to tackle 'Viola spends lots of time in day-to-day management of care and finances', attempting to eliminate the effect, perhaps by delegating the task to someone else or by somehow removing the causes of that effect ('care rotas break down' and 'Mum's finances take lots of time to manage').

Persistence, resistance to change, and failed attempts to improve, bedevil messy situations. The following example shows how this resistance arises:

Many small towns in Europe have a farmers' market, a range of specialist food shops and a congenial atmosphere of commercial bustle and personal service. Out-of-town supermarkets threaten the viability of such towns as commercial and shopping centres. Although, at first sight, the arrival of a supermarket appears to offer another shopping option, the effect of out-of-town supermarkets and shopping centres is often to reduce choice and to degrade the life of the town centre and its commercial activity. The out-of-town supermarket is often the beginning of a decline that is hard to arrest and even harder to reverse.

Figure 11.4 is a multiple-cause diagram that summarises some of the effects.

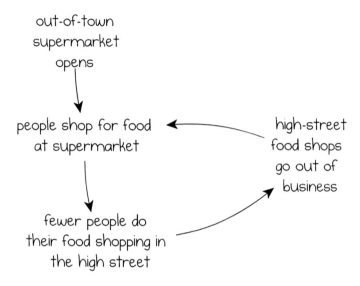

Figure 11.4 *A limited multiple-cause diagram showing the self-reinforcing effects of an out-of-town supermarket on high-street food shops.*

The driver of Figure 11.4 is a reinforcing loop. Once such a loop is present, simple measures such as 'breaking the chain' are unlikely to work. The out-of-town supermarket would re-initiate the loop, even if it were possible to disrupt the loop in some way. Extending the boundary of this diagram reveals potential effects for other, non-food, shops in the high street. It is clear that people will do other 'discretionary' shopping while they visit the high street. If they no longer shop for food on the high street, they trigger another reinforcing loop that results in a decline of non-food shops and a consequent loss of choice.

Both loops in Figure 11.5 are 'resilient'. Loops like this must be treated as a whole and, in this case, demand concerted action by local government and local business. Where local planning laws permit, siting a supermarket within the town works much better. The cost of providing car parking and a large enough site is an investment in the vitality of the town and its community. Competition may mean that some shops close but overall, more shoppers come into town creating opportunities for new shops.

A multiple-cause diagram of deteriorating high street shopping

out-of-town
supermarket
opens

people shop for food
at supermarket

high-street
food shops
go out of
business

fewer people do
their food shopping in
the high street

high-street
shopping becomes
less attractive

less choice
for shoppers

people make
fewer discretionary
purchases on the
high street

high-street
non-food shops go
out of business

Figure 11.5 *A multiple-cause diagram of the effect of an out-of-town supermarket on the high street. The arrival of the out-of-town supermarket initiates a cycle of deterioration for high-street food shops that, in turn, initiates a cycle of decline for other shops. Attempts to halt the decline of the high street are doomed because of the decline in high-street food shopping. Decline in all types of high-street shopping may be inevitable unless the supermarket comes into the town.*

Rules and guidelines for multiple-cause diagrams

Multiple-cause diagrams are, perhaps, the simplest systems diagrams to draw. The 'rules' are simple but nonetheless important because they challenge you to clarify your thinking.

1   Words represent events, phenomena, effects and observations. They may be ongoing effects or specific events in time.

2 An arrow joining AAA to BBB means 'AAA causes, or contributes to, BBB'. Arrows do not signify any other connection between AAA and BBB.

3 No distinction is made between sufficient, necessary or contributing causes[8].

4 Double-headed arrows are not used.

5 Arrows are easier to follow if curved and, in particular, loops are easier to see by drawing arrows to curve around the centre of the loop.

6 The link between each cause-and-effect should be sufficiently obvious that it is clear how AAA causes or contributes to BBB.

7 Sequential events should not be combined in one node.

8 For clarity, a single diagram should have no more than 25 nodes.

9 A title identifying the diagram as a multiple-cause diagram is essential.

10 An optional boundary may identify a cluster of mutual causations as a system.

Rule 2 is clear but easy to break inadvertently. Check each arrow reads as 'causes' or 'contributes to' rather than 'is followed by' or 'and then'. If you discern a loop, then you can make it more obvious by the curvature of the arrows, as for example in Figure 11.6. Rules 6 and 7 ensure important effects are not obscured by bigger conceptual leaps than necessary. Ask whether the statement would be accessible and plausible to an imaginary reader unfamiliar with the situation. Including all the intermediate effects and events offers more possible intervention points. Violation of Rule 8 to the extent of two or three nodes is, of course, not serious but too many nodes make the diagram as messy as the situation you are trying to diagnose. It is helpful, if in obedience to Rule 9, you postpone adding a title until you have finished drawing the diagram.

It is common to find that the topic of the diagram evolves as you draw it. If a multiple-cause diagram shows a cluster of interconnected effects, a system boundary may be helpful (Rule 10), especially if the implied system appears to have a purpose. If the system identified by a system boundary 'does something' then it is purposive and qualifies as a system[9]. The multiple-cause diagram in Figure 11.5 does not include a system boundary although it can be 'a system to degrade the high street' or 'a system to reduce shoppers' choices'.

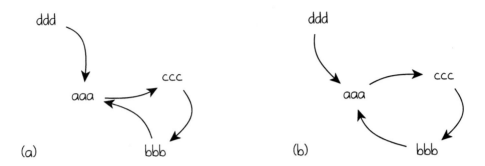

Figure 11.6 *Loops and significant sequences can be emphasised by appropriate curvature of the arrows. The loop in (b) is much easier to read than the loop in (a). Similarly, the eye follows the sequence ddd, aaa, ccc more easily in (b) because the arrow from ddd to aaa flows more naturally on to ccc.*

Drawing a multiple-cause diagram

Diagnosis starts with symptoms. Multiple-cause diagrams start by identifying an effect, phenomenon or event and working outwards. Explore causes by asking 'What causes this?' and 'What else causes this?'. Explore consequences by asking 'What does this cause?' and 'What else does this cause?'. Ask these questions of each node until the next node seems irrelevant. For example, in Figure 11.3, the causes of an influenza epidemic are probably irrelevant to the manager trying to maintain business. Where to stop is a matter of judgement and, as such, remains an open question as the diagram evolves. Other perspectives should be included when asking these questions.

Multiple-cause diagrams are relatively easy to draw but preparing a final draft can be time consuming. They are particularly vulnerable to arrows crossing each other and untangling them may take several drafts. Arrows that fly around the perimeter of the diagram also impair clarity. I notice that when I draw multiple-cause diagrams, it takes many more drafts to 'get it right'. It is worth persevering: the clarity of a simple diagram is always worth the effort.

As a diagram is redrafted, it is worth checking for redundant nodes. It is surprisingly easy to create events that duplicate another you have already included, with slightly different words. In Figure 11.5, I initially had a node for 'shoppers have less choice about what to buy' and one for 'shoppers have less choice about where to shop'. I combined these into 'less choice for shoppers' without losing any meaning.

Any form of systems diagram creates insights as you draw it but multiple-cause diagrams need stand-back-and-review time to understand where and how to intervene in the situation. Look for loops and parallel sequences. Loops need attention as wholes. Intervening in any sequence must address the potential for the sequence to re-initiate itself.

If you are dealing with a mess at present – particularly if stratagems you have tried have not worked, have caused unintended consequences, or have made things worse – now would be a good time to try a multiple-cause diagram. If not, there are suggestions for practising at the end of the chapter[10].

Exploring unintended consequences with a multiple-cause diagram

Taking action in messes is always risky. By definition, messes contain unforeseen interconnections that may generate unintended and unwanted consequences when well-meant interventions trigger them. The risk of unintended consequences can be minimised by thinking through what might happen. This involves calling on the perspectives of other people[11] and extending the boundaries of my own systems-of-interest to see the wider context in which unintended consequences might occur. A multiple-cause diagram is one way of doing this.

A university in South Africa was seeking to increase the diversity of its academic staff who were overwhelmingly white men and disproportionately over 50. They decided to achieve this by setting a compulsory retirement age of 60. This would, they believed, release posts for a more diverse and younger academic body and would better reflect the diversity of the student body. I imagine their thinking ran something like Figure 11.7. The 'system to renew the faculty by ensuring early retirement of existing staff in order to create more diversity' set a boundary to their thinking.

A multiple-cause diagram, if they had used one, should have prompted questions about unintended consequences at each stage. For example, if they had asked 'What else does this cause?' at each point, they might also have noticed other possible consequences of their actions. For example, what skills might be lost, who else might be affected – other than the white males – and whether suitably qualified people could be recruited.

Figure 11.8 shows the impact of the initiative on Auntie Celeste, the elderly 'auntie' of the Mathematics Department who made the tea, did the photocopying, took the post round and generally ensured the smooth running and comfort of the department. Already in her 70s, Auntie Celeste supported nine grandchildren whose parents had died of AIDS. Auntie Celeste was one of many such aunties in the university. They found themselves forced to retire, with no pension, from a vital source of income that supported not only themselves but their grandchildren. The university had unwittingly lost a vital resource for its own smooth running and had deprived some of its least privileged, most needy, and possibly heroic, people of an income. A university official later remarked that no decision taken in South Africa could be isolated from the impact of AIDS.

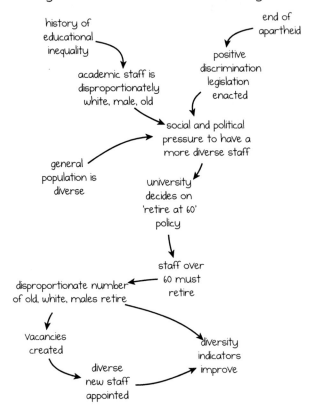

A multiple-cause diagram of an early-retirement diversity initiative at a South African university

Figure 11.7 A multiple-cause diagram of an early-retirement policy that is limited to the immediate intentions of the scheme. No attempt had been made to explore other consequences of any of the items in the diagram and the action thus excluded unintended consequences that might otherwise have been foreseen.

A multiple-cause diagram showing an unintended consequence of an early-retirement diversity initiative at a South African university

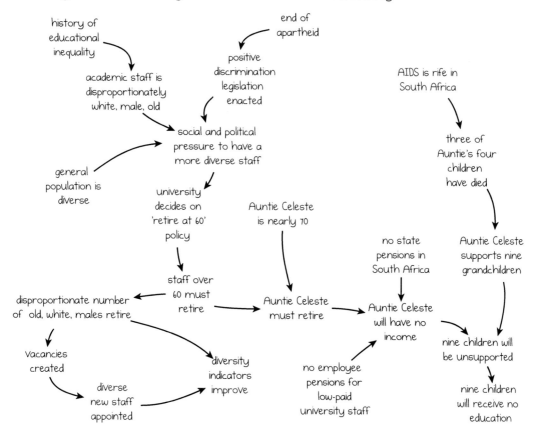

Figure 11.8 A wider view of the early retirement scheme showing the unintended consequences for Auntie Celeste, one of the many elderly aunties supporting grandchildren and thus in great need of employment by the university.

Asking at each stage, *what else does this cause?* alerts the diagrammer to the possible unintended consequences of a proposed action, especially if he or she consciously attempts to extend the question to include other perspectives. Failing to consider other perspectives often gives rise to unintended consequences. Using a multiple-cause diagram is one way to access other relevant perspectives.

Using multiple-cause diagrams with others

Multiple-cause diagrams are excellent for explaining a messy situation in terms of effects, what sustains them and potential interventions. Colleagues or audiences readily understand the simple grammar of AAA causes BBB. Contributions are less easy to manage because even a few crossing arrows, or arrows on circular detours around the margin, can impair readability. Distributing copies of the diagram for annotation may be more effective than inviting additions to the 'public' diagram and preserves the sense of provisionality that invites contributions and discussion.

A fix that failed: another multiple-cause diagram

An interesting diagram emerged from an ill-fated attempt to treat a mess as though it were a difficulty. The Educational Services Trust, employing approximately 100 high-performing and motivated people, became aware that their sickness absence was higher than other divisions in the company – only slightly higher, but enough to motivate the Staff Director to do something. The policy she set in place was not draconian, although staff referred to the 'get tough policy'. Team leaders simply telephoned absent staff to encourage a speedy return to work. The effect was marked: the absence rate increased dramatically. How did that happen?

Counter-intuitive effects characterise interventions that treat messes as if they were difficulties. They signal the presence of a complex set of interactions. I drew a multiple-cause diagram to explore what had happened. Figure 11.9 was the result. It includes the 'flu loop' I discussed above. One of the characteristic behaviours of staff was their reluctance to take sick-leave. Staff were committed, worked long hours, ran to tight deadlines, and were loyal to colleagues. They were reluctant to take sick-leave and returned to work quickly to deal with in-trays that filled rapidly in their absence. The normally energising pressure led to stress when people felt unwell.

Discussing the diagram with the Staff Director illuminated a number of issues. It was clear she had acted with good intentions. She was conscious that prolonged absence imposed even more pressure on the staff that remained and she was seeking to minimise that pressure. It was also clear that she was one of the lucky people with a robust constitution for whom flu was a minor inconvenience if she got it at all.

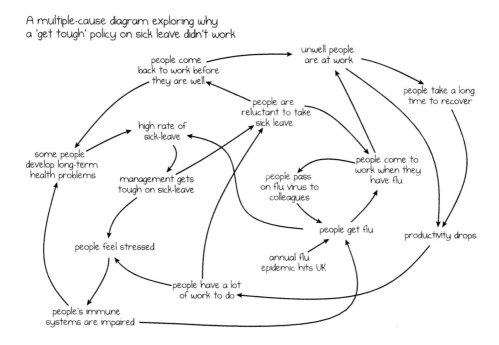

A multiple-cause diagram exploring why
a 'get tough' policy on sick leave didn't work

Figure 11.9 *A multiple-cause diagram showing the looped interactions that raised sick-leave rates when management used a 'get tough' policy to reduce sick leave. The 'get tough' policy brought into being, and then closed, many of these loops.*

The Staff Director had not fully grasped that some staff not only feel unwell when they get flu but are vulnerable to complications and slow recovery because of otherwise-unproblematic medical conditions. The diagram was a revelation. By introducing the get-tough policy, she had unwittingly closed a number of loops in the web of causes and effects. You can trace them in the diagram. For example, now a loop (in the top-left) ran:

> *management gets tough on sick leave → people feel stressed → people's immune systems are impaired → people get flu → high rate of sick leave → management gets tough on sick leave.*

This is a particularly tricky loop since it triggers the 'flu loop' referred to earlier. Another loop closed by 'management gets tough on sick leave' also triggers, and is triggered by, the flu loop. It runs:

> *management gets tough on sick leave → people are reluctant to take sick-leave → people come to work when they have flu →*

> *people pass on flu virus to colleagues* → *people get flu* → *high rate of sick-leave* → *management gets tough on sick leave.*

There are several other loops operating in this multiple-cause diagram. See if you can spot them.

The situation improved only slowly when the get-tough policy was abandoned. More steps were taken, including some of those outlined above. It was not possible to vaccinate staff but those who wished to be vaccinated were granted time off to get it done. Staff discussed and then took absence-proofing measures and re-scheduled some annual tasks to take them out of the typical flu season. Several senior members of staff did a short course on systems thinking.

DIAGNOSIS AND MULTIPLE-CAUSE DIAGRAMS

Multiple-cause diagrams enable the diagrammer to make connections between many observations and build them into coherent wholes that:

- explain why persistent effects or observations occur

- show why these often appear to be persistent and resistant to intervention

- suggest points for effective intervention

- reveal possible unintended consequences of intervention.

Unlike systems maps and influence diagrams, which show a single coherent 'snap shot' from a single perspective, multiple-cause diagrams work best when a multiplicity of viewpoints are brought together to create a diagram that shows change through time.

Multiple-cause diagrams are perhaps the simplest diagrams to understand and construct but they rely on adherence to a strict rule: arrows mean 'causes' or 'contributes to' and never anything else. Practising multiple-cause diagrams develops the intellectual capacity to anticipate unintended consequences, both wanted and unwanted. Through practice, multiple-cause diagrams develop genuinely useful thinking skills.

Notes, resources and explorations for Chapter 11

1   *Publius Vergilius Maro*

This quotation comes from Book 2 (line 490) of Virgil's *Georgics*, the instructive poem on raising crops and trees. The book is a detailed account of tree culture, vine growing and olive trees. Although the poem seems to praise country life and farming, it also contains darker themes, including the struggle between humankind and the earth. Vines, for example, are characterised by Virgil (himself a farmer's son) as overly tender and hard work in contrast to olive trees, which require no attention other than harvesting.

Rerum cognoscere causas (to know the causes of things) is the motto of two UK institutions: Sheffield University and the London School of Economics.

2   *Sir William Osler*

Sir William Osler, M.D., C.M. was the Canadian physician and medical educator who pioneered the patient-focused medical education we know today. He understood that formal lectures and books could not create skilled medical practitioners and started bedside teaching and the residency system of developing diagnostic and care skills at Johns Hopkins Hospital and Medical School in Baltimore, MD.

3   *Diagnosis*

Diagnosis first appeared in modern usage in 1681. It comes from the Greek *dia*, meaning *apart* and *gignoskein*, meaning *to know*. Thus, diagnosis means to discern or to distinguish between. In modern usage it is most strongly connected with the medical sense of 'finding out what is wrong' and it is in that sense that this chapter is offered.

4   *Fishbone diagrams*

Project managers use fishbone diagrams (or Ishikawa diagrams). They group causes into categories to identify the potential or actual sources of defects. The categories are typically:

- People involved in the process
- Methods, including processes, procedures, protocols, rules and regulations
- Machines, including equipment, computers, tools and process-monitoring equipment
- Materials, including raw materials, consumables and energy
- Measurements: any data needed to ensure the quality of the output
- Environment, including location, time, weather and culture within which the product is produced.

The fishbone's structure ensures a comprehensive catalogue of causes but not a systemic one. It cannot allow for the loops of causation that bedevil messy situations because each cause is connected – by a chain of intervening causes and effects – to the effect whose cause is being sought.

5   *Rich pictures*
     See Chapter 3.

6   *Themes*
     See Chapter 4

7   *Managing flu, some reflections on cultural differences*
     I am impressed by the way Japanese people typically respond to flu. At the
     first signs of flu, the average Japanese worker puts a mask over their nose
     and mouth, buys a supply of food and some DVDs, and goes home. Japanese
     culture and etiquette demand that the flu victim does everything possible to
     minimise the risk of infecting anyone else. Japanese workers are far more likely
     than their American or European counterparts to go to their doctor who is
     far more likely to prescribe anti-viral medication. By contrast, European and
     American workplaces support a culture of 'presenteeism' where workers take
     sick leave only in extreme circumstances. They are discouraged from going to
     the doctor unless they experience medical complications.

     In Japan, the 2009 death rate from flu was 2 per 100,000 compared with much
     higher rates in the UK (22 per 100,000) and the USA (32 per 100,000). Other
     factors may have an effect but it is widely accepted that infection rates in Japan
     are lower, as are the number of sick-leave days, compared to countries with
     similar sick-leave entitlements. In the United States, where workers do not
     generally get paid sick leave, it has been estimated that presenteeism costs the
     national economy $180 billion.

     World Health Organization, (2009). Transmission dynamics and impact of
     pandemic influenza A (H1N1) 2009 virus. *Weekly epidemiological record: Relevé
     épidémiologique hebdomodaire*, 84(46).

     Adams, J. (2009). U.S. sick-leave policy promotes infection, swine flu. *San
     Francisco Health News Examiner*.

8   *Causation*
     Causation has been a key discussion in Western philosophy since Aristotle
     (384 B.C.E. – 322 B.C.E.) (*Metaphysics* and *Posterior Analytics*). Logic identifies
     three types of cause, following Francis Bacon (1561 – 1626) and influenced by
     the ideas of scientific knowledge. A *sufficient cause* is one that, on its own, can
     cause the identified effect. Thus, acquiring the flu virus from a colleague is
     sufficient to get flu, even if only mildly. A *necessary cause* is one that is necessary
     to cause the effect. Thus acquiring the flu virus is also a necessary cause of
     flu because without the virus, I do not have flu. Acquiring a flu virus *from a
     colleague* is not a necessary cause, only a sufficient one. It is only necessary to
     acquire the virus from someone or somewhere. A *contributing cause* only makes
     the effect more likely. An impaired immune system makes it more likely that I
     will get flu but cannot give me flu on its own.

     Philosophy also distinguishes between *proximate cause*, the immediate cause of
     an event or effect, and *ultimate cause*, sometimes thought of as the 'real cause'.
     Thus the proximate cause of King Alfred (849 – 899) burning the cakes was

that he left them on the griddle too long. The ultimate cause was the Danes' incursion into Wessex distracting him.

Contiguity is a condition for associating cause and effect. It simply means that there must be a discernible causal connection between events or between events and intervening events. Time-based connections are insufficient. Correlations between stockmarket indices and sunspot activity do not imply causation (in either direction) until some contiguity is established.

9   *Purpose*
     See Chapter 8

10   *Suggestions for practising multiple-cause diagrams*
     Politicians and other commentators often describe episodes of terrorism, violence, civic disorder, teenage misbehaviour, etc. as 'mindless', 'senseless' or 'cowardly'. This is the language of blame (see Chapter 5) and is not improvement-focused. It simply means the speaker has little understanding of what caused the event. Multiple-cause diagrams can be instructive whenever someone talks about an event in these terms. It is also an exercise in accessing someone else's perspective. I suggest you attempt to practise a multiple-cause diagram whenever you hear this language used. The purpose is not to exonerate, nor to blame, simply to find possible intervention points – changes that will improve the situation. This may be a challenging exercise!

11   *Perspectives*
     See Chapter 2.

CHAPTER 12

Thinking about diagramming

Concern for man and his fate must always form the chief interest of all technical endeavors. Never forget this in the midst of your diagrams …

Albert Einstein[1]

SYSTEMS DIAGRAMS

Is there a correct order for doing diagrams when you are dealing with a mess?

There are no rules but thoughtful selection will save time, energy and patience. Thoughtful selection in this case, includes considering:

- the situation, and what has been learned so far

- the diagrammer, their skills and their history of diagrams that worked well in the past

- the purpose of each diagram type.

The purpose of each diagram has already been discussed and the order of the chapters themselves shows how the diagrams might fit into progressively increasing understanding. Figure 12.1 brings all the diagrams together in these terms. I most usually start tackling a mess by drawing a rich picture. With practice, I can draw a useful picture in 15 minutes and, in the process, generate a page or two of notes, ideas and questions. A rich picture allows me the space to come to terms with the mess, to accept some responsibility for improving it where I can, and brings together all the features that make it messy. Alongside any insights and questions that arise as I draw, there is also a process of letting quick-fix solutions go and the dark satisfaction of 'knowing the worst'. A rich picture seems to work because it is unstructured. I draw a spray diagram occasionally, as an alternative to a rich picture, but they only work well when the messiness is limited to discrete bits of a difficulty[2]. I think they impose too much structure too early.

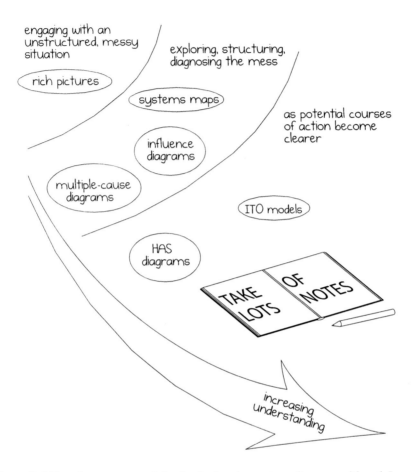

Figure 12.1 *There is no recommended order for drawing systems diagrams, although I usually draw a rich picture first, if I am dealing with a messy situation. After that, systems maps, influence diagrams and multiple-cause diagrams will help explore, structure and diagnose the mess. Where there is a risk of unintended consequences, ITO models and human-activity system diagrams will help with exploring options for action. Throughout the diagramming process, insights, questions and ideas are as valuable as the finished diagram.*

My next diagrams will usually, although not always, be one or more systems maps, multiple-cause diagrams or influence diagrams. Systems maps provide some structure for thinking about the mess simply, without having to simplify my picture of it. Several systems maps can be useful, often taking different themes as starting points. I may also draw a systems map from someone else's perspective, after a conversation with them. If there is a clear sense of something going wrong, or something having gone wrong, a multiple-cause diagram may be the next step after the rich picture, especially if previous attempts to improve the situation have failed or back-fired in some way. Multiple-cause diagrams identify densely interconnected webs of causation that I can think of as *systems of causation* leading to unwanted effects, as well as identifying possible sites for intervention. Where such systems emerge, it can be useful to map them in a systems map. Multiple-cause diagrams also identify possible outcomes of a course of action. They give a messy situation an historical context by tracing the causes of things that went wrong.

The impulse to draw an influence diagram often comes from a perception that everything is interconnected. As well as providing a map of the interconnections, an influence diagram identifies systems of influence that I can then map in a systems map. It may suggest discrete clusters of issues to address without destabilising other parts of the mess.

In all of these diagrams, themes (see Chapter 4) taken from the rich picture provide a useful starting point that should not be held too tightly. Drafting and redrafting will generate new themes for helpful diagrams. Putting dates on diagrams (including false-start drafts) charts progress and helps diagrams to trigger later diagrams. As with all diagrams, drawing systems maps, influence diagrams and multiple-cause diagrams provides food for thought. The notes you take about ideas for action, insights about the mess, questions to ask and so on are also a valuable resource.

Two more diagram types, together with other ideas discussed in the following chapters, enable significant progress even when the mess still offers few ideas about what to do. The *ITO model*, discussed in Chapter 8, is the starting point for a *human-activity system (HAS) diagram* – a diagram of a system that, were it to exist, would be relevant to improving the situation. The following chapters bring these ideas and tools together to build this HAS diagram. The human-activity system diagram is a diagram of a system that creates a transformation through the ordered operation of a number of human activities.

Choosing what diagram to draw also involves the human element – the diagrammer. There are choices. Figure 12.1 is neither a prescription nor a preferred order. In diagramming, the diagrammer develops skills and preferences and brings their own history and ideas to selecting which diagram type to use (or invent). I encourage you to develop your own practice: I offer my own approach as an invitation to devise your own systemic rationale and your own preferred way of diagramming.

Diagramming yields powerful insights into how to manage any particular mess. It is part of the systems-thinking collection of tools and techniques. But above all, diagramming is a means to acquire the ability to see the world systemically. It is an access point to systems thinking itself. As you practise systems maps, for example, you will begin to see the world in terms of systems with their boundaries, environments and subsystems. You will begin to discern webs of interacting influence as you practise influence diagrams. You will learn to look for, and discover, webs and self-reinforcing loops of causation. You will develop systems-thinking skills that enable you to think more effectively, and to improve messy situations without making them worse.

USING DIAGRAMS: STORIES FROM THE FRONT LINE

I, and my colleagues from the Systems Group at the Open University, have been teaching diagramming for many years. Thousands of students have learned to draw the diagrams you see here. If education is what remains when you have forgotten everything you studied[3], then systems diagrams have been part of these students' education. For many of them, diagramming remains part of their practice long after they have passed their exams.

More recently, I was asked by the university to support a wider group of colleagues in becoming systems thinkers. The participants' enthusiasm showed the endeavour was a success, as did their recommendations to other colleagues and their willingness to take on the messy challenges of the university's rapidly changing environment. The appearance of systems diagrams on walls, in meetings, and in presentations shows that diagramming has become part of participants' practice. Rich pictures, systems maps and influence diagrams seem to be particular favourites. As teachers teaching students, my colleagues and I awarded marks for technical accuracy in students' diagrams. In teaching managers and strategists, I learned to be much less precious about adherence to the rules and more interested in *usefulness*. I observed with fascination that the pursuit of useful diagrams led to many more unfinished diagrams and many sheets of notes as participants discovered ways to improve situations that had been unaddressed, often for years. Diagrams appeared in discussion papers and reports but the most valued diagrams were the scrappy ones taken to meetings that were then over-written by new contributions. Managers absorbed diagrams into their practice and displayed them like trophies, evidence of breakthrough moments in mess-management.

This story of diagramming success contrasts with another that highlights the difference between diagramming for communication and diagramming for understanding. In April 2010, stories appeared in the press about a military briefing in Afghanistan. A hapless junior officer had clearly spent many hours creating a systems-dynamics diagram for a PowerPoint presentation to General McChrystal, the leader of US and NATO forces in Afghanistan[4]. It showed the complexities of the Afghan situation that were stalling progress against Taliban resistance. The diagram had more than 100 nodes and would certainly have persuaded anyone of the complexities of the Allies' situation – a real *horrendogram*. The assembled generals dismissed the diagram as incomprehensible.

This is, I think, a story about a diagram rather than about diagramming. The ridicule was a response to the junior officer's failure to tailor the diagram for the audience and its needs. No doubt, the diagram was immensely meaningful to the person who drew it but, unless you participate in drawing it, such a complex diagram conveys little, especially in a presentation. It was as if the map were as complicated as the territory. McChrystal later quipped that, 'When we understand that slide, we'll have won the war.'

The diagram depicted a complex situation, the Counterinsurgency (COIN) Strategy in Afghanistan. In that sense, the diagram does a great job of mapping the complexity in detail. It failed, as a communication diagram, because a briefing cannot deal with the level of complexity it depicts. McChrystal's observation is spot on but perhaps not in the way he meant. If the situation were understood at the same level of complexity as the diagram, and the COIN Strategy were able to respond to that complexity, the outcome of the war might be different. I suspect the military mind would have preferred a simpler diagram. However, simple diagrams do not make the situation simpler. A good diagram makes it *simpler to think about*. My suggestions for improvement would be to cluster the many 'blobs' into no more than 20 clusters with a suite of diagrams, available on request, addressing the details. Such a diagram would show the complexity of the situation but would also be discussable in a briefing. It would literally 'make sense' of the situation.

DIAGRAMS FOR PRESENTATION, DIAGRAMS FOR DISCUSSION

While I would give a prize to the junior officer[5] for the thoroughness of his analysis, clearly his diagram provoked hostility and ridicule in the context of a presentation. Almost everyone who practises diagramming thoughtfully struggles with a conundrum. Drawing a diagram greatly increases the drawer's understanding. Studying someone else's diagram does not increase understanding to the same extent – unless it is accompanied by an invitation to improve it. Diagrams for presentations, reports and military briefings need to convey their message simply.

Computer-drawn diagrams are ideal for final presentation of a simple message but engaging with diagramming software has pitfalls. I wonder, for example, whether the Afghanistan diagram was the result of getting carried away by the software.

My own experience suggests that while computer-drawn diagrams serve the needs of communicating thinking, diagrams for understanding should be hand-drawn, especially when you wish to draw other people into the process. Software can set traps for the diagrammer that inhibit understanding. The software tends to focus attention on getting the diagram to look good. There are, in any case, remarkably few affordable software packages that can draw a decent systems diagram. Indeed, most diagramming packages, including high-end ones, *cannot* draw good systems diagrams. The arrows are often constrained to straight lines, making it hard to discern relationships. Nested blobs are disallowed. The best (by a long way) programme I have found is *yEd*. At the time of writing, yEd is available as a free download[6]. But I remain convinced that hand drawing is a better way of drawing diagrams, in the early stages at least, when you are trying to make sense of a messy situation. It uses both sides of my brain and prevents my thinking getting trapped in my logical-verbal left brain[7].

I use *MindManager*[8] software for spray/spider diagrams and there are similar free downloadable programs such as *FreeMind*.

DIAGRAMS AS TOOLS FOR THINKING ABOUT MY THINKING

Thinking about my thinking, and seeing it reflected in my diagrams, is the key motivation for diagramming. Diagrams become a record of my growing understanding of the messy situation. They also generate a set of notes as I question my own understandings. Have I missed insights or observations? Does my thinking make sense? Am I making progress? It is immensely valuable to have a record of ideas and understandings to return to.

OTHER SYSTEMS DIAGRAMS

If you are interested in systems diagrams, there are more to explore. The book's website[9] has additional systems-diagramming resources.

Notes, explorations and resources for Chapter 12

1   *Albert Einstein*

This quote is attributed to Einstein in one of his talks.

2   *Messes and difficulties*

For a discussion of the differences between difficulties and messes, see Chapter 1.

3   *Education*

John Coulson (1910 – 1990, first Professor of Chemical Engineering at the University of Newcastle upon Tyne) drew this idea to our attention in one of his undergraduate classes. He then gave us an excellent education. The remark is attributed to Albert Einstein.

4   *The infamous Afghanistan diagram*

First reports appeared on the front page of *The New York Times* on 26th April 2010, appearing later in the *Mail Online, The Guardian* and *The Huffington Post*.

Mail Online
http://www.dailymail.co.uk/news/worldnews/article-1269463/Afghanistan-PowerPoint-slide-Generals-left-baffled-PowerPoint-slide.html#ixzz0mlAbTafL

The Guardian
http://www.guardian.co.uk/news/datablog/2010/apr/29/mcchrystal-afghanistan-powerpoint-slide

The Huffington Post
http://www.huffingtonpost.com/meghan-ohara/diagram-of-a-war-strategy_b_555389.html

The diagram rapidly spread all over the Web. Find it using search terms: Afghanistan, diagram, McChrystal, PowerPoint. Some web versions leave off the key, the title and the encouraging label 'Working draft v3'.

5   *PowerPoint Rangers*

Apparently the demand for PowerPoint slides for US military briefings in Afghanistan is such that a cadre of junior officers has emerged to create them. They are known informally as the PowerPoint Rangers.

6   *yEd diagramming software*

yEd diagramming software is available from
http://www.yworks.com/en/products_yed_about.html

It runs on all the usual platforms.

It takes about an hour or so to work out how to use the software effectively but it works efficiently and seems utterly reliable. Its great advantage is that you can rearrange the blobs and words ('nodes') and the arrows ('edges') follow as if they were elastic.

7   *Left brain, right brain*
       For a discussion of left and right brain activity, see Chapter 3.

8   *MindManager*
       MindManager is by MindJet and I depend on it utterly for Things-To-Do lists.

9   *Website*

       www.triarchypress.com/GrowingWings

Part 3: Exploring purposeful action in messy situations

Taking action in messy situations is risky. Changes in one part of the mess propagate through the multiple interconnections between the intersecting elements to trigger changes all over the mess. If the action is well considered, and its possible consequences thoroughly explored, the interconnections have a multiplying effect. The improvements may then be greater than the immediate improvement at the site of the intervention. Ill-considered actions, on the other hand, will create unintended and unwanted effects that make the mess worse. In systems thinking, action is typically postponed until its possible consequences are well understood and there is reasonable confidence that most stakeholders will experience improvement or, at a minimum, no worsening of the situation.

Conceptualising an improvement, in the form of a system of logically-necessary human activities, and specifying its purposes and its fit with the situation, creates a framework for testing ideas for action. The three chapters of Part 3 show how this system can be defined and diagrammed and how the definition and diagram operate as an understandascope for revealing opportunities for action in the messy situation.

The structure of Part 3

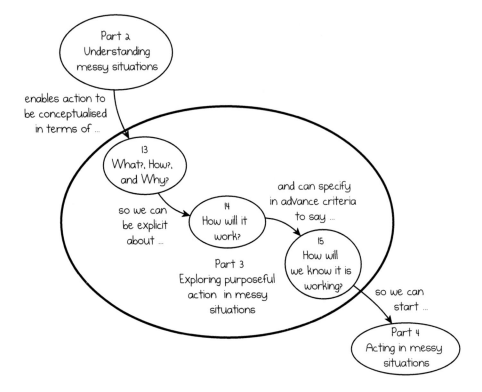

Part 3 addresses the task of conceptualising change. Starting (in Chapter 13) from a systemic understanding of purpose, it specifies 'a system relevant to thinking about the situation' in terms of what it does (What) and locates it in a hierarchy of systems that provide purpose and purposeful activity (Why and How). The next stage specifies the logically-necessary activities the system needs to accomplish its transformative effect (Chapter 14). Finally, performance criteria for the system reduce remaining ambiguities (Chapter 15). This human-activity system becomes an understandascope for discerning opportunities for change that will improve the messy situation.

CHAPTER 13

What?, How? and Why?

Everything should be made a simple as possible, but not more so.
Albert Einstein, *Physikalische Zeitschrift* (1916)

Why do action plans often get nowhere? Why do discussions about 'what to do' go round in circles? This chapter uses the idea of a system to present a simple but elegant way of formulating actions that cuts through the misunderstandings and confusions bedevilling action plans.

Rich pictures, looking at situations holistically and from a number of different perspectives, and diagramming, will all trigger ideas for improving a messy situation. Uncontroversial improvements can be implemented quickly when, for example, a diagram indicates that there is little risk of unintended consequences. Major improvements in a messy situation, however, require careful consideration to avoid unintended consequences and to make the most effective use of resources and opportunities. This chapter, and the two that follow it, focus on developing heuristic devices[1] for finding out what to do and how to do it. The first of these, the system definition[2], clarifies what to do and why, and begins to develop some ideas about how it might be done.

The system definition is an understandascope for looking at the messy situation. It can reveal whether the idea expressed in the definition is feasible or desirable and whether better opportunities are discernible in the messy situation. The system definition starts from the *idea* of doing something relevant to improving the messy situation and conceptualising that action as a system whose subsystems are interconnected human activities that effect an overall transformation. Such a system, being an *idea*, is unlimited by feasibility considerations. It exists only in a conceptual world where feasibility does not matter. It is simply an idea, relevant to the situation, conceptualised as a *human-activity system*. The relevant system may be conceptualised as operating *in* an improved situation or as effecting the transition *to* an improved situation. It is usually sensible to conceptualise several systems with a mix of both types.

Ideas for systems relevant to thinking about improvement can come from notes and jottings created while diagramming or perhaps from *Themes*[3] or *Snappy Systems*[4]. For example, a company supplying knitting kits found itself with insufficient stock when the kits featured in the lifestyle section of a Sunday

213

newspaper. They did a Snappy-Systems exercise for some systems relevant to thinking about improving the situation:

- a system to apologise to customers

- a system to predict demand

- a system to acquire new stock quickly

- a system to assemble kits

- a system to indicate stock levels to website customers.

Some of these systems are relevant to thinking about immediate improvement; others are relevant to a possible future situation that is more robust than the current one.

Once I have an idea for a system relevant to thinking about improving the situation, my purpose in creating a system definition is threefold:

- to articulate it with increasing clarity so that I can think about – and communicate – my ideas more clearly

- to eliminate woolly and wishful thinking

- to understand the messy situation more clearly in terms of what might actually make an improving difference.

A system definition defines the system in ways that challenge my thinking and force me (if I accept the challenge) to think coherently about action that is relevant to the situation.

REARRANGING THE DECKCHAIRS

One of the most lively metaphors to emerge in 'Management Speak' over the last few decades is the idea of *rearranging the deckchairs on the Titanic*[5]. It refers to pointless activity that fails to address the seriousness of the situation; in this metaphor, the imminent peril to the passengers of the sinking ocean liner.

It is a wonderfully evocative metaphor. In my imagination, the orders go out to rearrange the deckchairs and there is a frenzy of activity as sailors run hither and thither with deckchairs. Nothing is achieved. The sailors have been told *what* to do but not *why* they are to do it. Some sailors rearrange the deckchairs so passengers have a better view of the iceberg, some rearrange the deckchairs so as to correct the starboard list, some rearrange the deckchairs so they can be used as flotation aids, and some rearrange the deckchairs to seat the orchestra, still playing as the ship goes down.

Knowing the purpose of an activity creates opportunities to do it well. I need to know *Why*, as well as *What*, in order to decide on an appropriate *How*.

SYSTEM DEFINITIONS

An idea for improving a messy situation, named in terms of a human-activity system, can now be defined as if it were a system.

A simple but unambiguous template for defining a human-activity system – a system in which humans do something – uses the idea of a purpose and subsystems of activity, as in the following template:

> *A system to do <What> by means of <How> in order to contribute to achieving <Why>.*[6]

This format is the beginning of a *system definition*: defining a system with precision and without clutter. Examples might be:

- a system to raise capital by means of obtaining a bank loan in order to contribute to expanding the business

- a system to contain 'rapid oak death' by means of felling affected trees in order to contribute to conserving commercial larch plantations

- a system to pay off the national debt by means of radical cuts in government spending in order to contribute to restoring prosperity in the economy.

Each of these definitions follows the template by specifying What the system does, How it does it and Why it does it, bearing in mind that the system only exists in the conceptual world. It does not describe what exists in the messy situation. It simply defines a system which, if it existed, would be relevant to thinking about the situation.

In order to define an activity, systems thinking asks:

- What is done?

- How is it done?

- Why is it done?

Answering these questions enables the systems thinker to clarify the activity, in terms of its action as a system and its place in a hierarchy of systems. Constructing a system definition is deceptively simple but rigorous and challenging to get right. The challenge is 'to say precisely what you mean and mean precisely what you say' by expressing the essential transformation in its clearest form[7].

The trustees of a national institution asked for my help in re-thinking their role as overseers of the institution's functioning. They sent me a sheaf of paperwork in advance of our meeting. It included the minutes of their most recent meeting. I scanned it for verbs indicating what they did. I was struck by statements such as:

> *Noted: report from the International Outreach Working Group*
> *Noted: publication of five-year development plan*
> *Noted: plans for reconstructing interior of London Office.*

In fact 'noting' was about all the trustees seemed to do. I wondered whether this was a good use of the time and considerable talents of a group of VIPs from the highest levels of public life. Together we worked through some possible system definitions for what they might do. Like many people, the group at first resisted, believing it was obvious what they did and why. As I pushed them gently, they began to realise the deceptively simple template demanded more clarity than they could summon up. 'This is really challenging', someone remarked to me at coffee. It was clear that 'noting' was one of the *Hows* but there were a number of potentially conflicting conceptions of what their task was and why it was important. Nothing was resolved within the hour they had allotted for the discussion but they invited me to their next meeting, nonetheless. In the interim, they must have done some serious thinking and had some good telephone discussions. They presented a system definition for my comment. It was clear, concise and everyone had agreed on it. They had found a more active role for themselves as a source of advice, contacts and 'insider information' for the institution's executive.

The most useful system definitions are those that get close to the heart of the issue. An example arises from the aftermath of the multiple bombings of the Underground rail system and buses in London on 7th July 2005[8]. Fire, police and ambulance crews were operating in a highly uncertain, potentially dangerous situation without adequate communications technology. It later became clear that there was confusion between the services as to each other's roles. For example, the fire-service officer assumed that the first ambulance would transport victims at the station entrance away from the scene as fast as possible. The ambulance officer believed he was there to assess the situation in order to make best use of other ambulance crews as they arrived. As I thought about how to improve the situation (and about improving the situation when the next major incident occurs), my initial ideas were about *clarifying roles* or *directing emergency services* at a major incident. These seemed insufficiently radical to make a big difference. I realised that *clarifying roles* would not ensure that people had the right roles. *Directing emergency services* would not ensure they were directed in the right way. I discovered that I preferred *making the best use of the skills and equipment of emergency services*. It was much closer to the heart of the issue. I had an interesting conversation with myself when I noticed how difficult it was to discern a shared and coherent *Why* for a system that had this as its *What*. Was there a potential conflict between ' … in order to contribute to saving lives' and ' … in order to contribute to treating the injured'? Perhaps the purposes of the emergency services conflicted.

A number of system definitions emerged as coherent understandascopes. It does not matter which, if any, could, should or ought to have been in place. I was looking for system definitions capable of stimulating productive conversations between stakeholders. Working with this possible *What*, any number of possible *Hows* and possible *Whys* came to mind. Combinations of these, assembled into system definitions, can be modelled, and used as 'mediating objects[9]' to explore desirability, feasibility and acceptability.

What	A system to make the best use of the skills and equipment of the emergency services …
Some possible Hows	by means of … … having a skilled director of operations at major incidents, … clarifying the expectations and contributions of each service, … creating a protocol for managing major incidents, … briefing passengers about self-help procedures,
Some possible Whys	in order to contribute to … … minimising fatalities … removing casualties from the scene … minimising risk to emergency crews … getting the seriously injured to hospital quickly … preventing mass panic

Combining these ideas gives rise to 20 distinct system definitions, underlining the importance of saying what you mean and meaning what you say. In casual conversation (and indeed, in many strategic conversations), ideas like this are often conflated and generate misunderstandings.

A system can only be defined in the context of *one* wider system. It may be that the subsystems can, by slight adjustments, enable the system to serve a second *Why*, but for the purposes of clarifying thinking, another *Why* requires another system, albeit similar. One interpretation of the many failings of the UK prison system is a lack of clarity as to its *Why*. Most of the following descriptions of a prison would attract subscribers:

- a system to lock up offenders in order to contribute to punishing them

- a system to lock up offenders in order to contribute to rehabilitating them

- a system to lock up offenders in order to contribute to protecting society

- a system to lock up offenders in order to contribute to isolating them from their criminal milieux

- a system to lock up offenders in order to contribute to removing them from society

- a system to lock up offenders in order to contribute to preventing them engaging in crime.

Each of the definitions above contains the same *What* element of a system definition and a *Why* element. The *Hows* associated with each of these definition differ from the probable *Hows* of the other systems. Indeed, one can speculate that the *Hows* of one system will act against realising the wider purpose of one or more of the other systems. Clearly, a system to lock people up in order to rehabilitate them will have subsystems that conflict with the subsystems of a system to lock people up in order to punish them. Indeed, looked at in this way, it becomes clear that locking up offenders is unlikely to meet any of the intended wider purposes, any one of which, at a minimum, invites consideration of other possible means of delivery.

A system definition that includes *Why* and *How*, as well as *What*, raises questions. For example, assigning a purpose in the form of a *Why* invites consideration of whether the particular *What* is the best way of contributing to the *Why*. So, for example, if my purpose is rehabilitating offenders, is locking them up the best way to do it? Often several purposes are invested in a single activity. Many countries' prison arrangements are messy because they seem to have multiple purposes, meaning none are met well. Working out all the possible purposes invested in a single action will often reveal conflicting *Hows*. By creating a different definition for each *Why*, with associated *Hows*, coherent with the *Why*, any mismatches between *Hows* can then be explored.

Building a system definition

System definitions expressed in this form communicate ideas powerfully and efficiently. We recently recruited four new members of staff. We desperately needed them. We were a team of twenty but had over-committed ourselves. The new recruits were talented people but they would be doing work they had never done before. I needed to make sure they would learn quickly and start contributing. I knew from experience that most people have little capacity for absorbing information when it is not relevant to them and especially when they are meeting new people, in a new organisation and in a new city. I decided instead to make sure the information they needed would be there when they needed it and that they would know where to get it. I decided to embed each of them in several different networks, corresponding to different parts of their jobs. This is the system definition for what I decided to do:

What?   create on-the-job learning opportunities for new staff
How?   embedding them in several knowledgeable and skilled networks
Why?   to contribute to enhancing their ability to contribute independently

The formal statement of the system definition was now:

> *A system to create on-the-job learning opportunities for new staff by means of embedding them in several knowledgeable and skilled networks in order to contribute to enhancing their ability to contribute independently.*

I now knew what I was doing and my simple-but-precise system definition made it easy to communicate to colleagues whose cooperation I needed. They immediately recognised what I was trying to do. We quickly assembled sets of intersecting networks with volunteers who would induct the new recruits into the networks. Project leaders would induct staff into the project networks to learn how we did our projects; PAs would induct each new recruit into networks where they could learn what they needed to know about organisational procedures; and others would induct the new recruits into the social networks of the organisation. When the new recruits arrived, the results were amazing. The new recruits were skilled and knowledgeable contributors within a very short time and had networks whose reach exceeded those of their colleagues. The system definition had been a powerful tool through which I had learned what I needed to do and had been able to communicate with colleagues without ambiguity.

Understanding system definitions

When I first engaged with inducting the new staff, I scoured the internet to find out how other organisations did it. Almost all the processes seemed to build around the idea of *briefing*. Not one of the websites identified any reason for induction or briefing. I deduced the reason as 'conveying essential information'. I guessed the system definition (a 'definition in action', if you like) was something like:

> *A system to brief new staff by means of presenting slide shows in order to convey essential information.*

As I examined the task of induction in terms of this hypothetical system, I began to understand why 'briefing' didn't seem to offer what I needed. A system definition needs to be coherent: the *What?*, *How?* and *Why?* need to make sense in terms of each other. The system does not work as an understandascope when the *How?* and the *Why?* don't work together. For induction, presenting slide shows is not a good way of conveying essential information. Slide shows are good for conveying *ideas* or *small amounts of information* but not the large amount needed to induct a new member of staff to a large organisation.

I can use a ludicrous example to illustrate this need for coherence. Definitions 1 and 2 below work well. Definitions 3 and 4 do not.

> A system to dig a hole in the garden by means of using a trowel in order to contribute to planting daffodil bulbs.

> A system to dig a hole in the garden by means of using a mechanical digger in order to contribute to installing a swimming pool.

> A system to dig a hole in the garden by means of using a trowel in order to contribute to installing a swimming pool.

> A system to dig a hole in the garden by means of using a mechanical digger in order to contribute to planting daffodil bulbs.

The folly of systems defined by Definitions 3 and 4 is not about feasibility. It is simply that the *Hows* do not make sense in terms of the *Whys*. What? How? and Why? form three levels in a hierarchy of systems. One of the characteristics of a system is its place in a hierarchy of systems with sub-subsystems 'below' it and, above it, a system of which it is itself a subsystem. Each of these systems has a purpose, understood in this case as simply what it does[10]. If I define a system in terms of its doing something (*What?*) then its subsystems do things that are the *How?* of the system. The system itself is a subsystem of a higher-level system that meets some higher level purpose, the *Why?* Here are three levels of the system hierarchy for my personnel-induction system:

Why?	to enhance their ability to contribute independently	The system that my system is a subsystem of. Its purpose is the *Why?* for my system
What?	create on-the-job learning opportunities for new staff	The purpose of my system – what it does
How?	embedding them in several knowledgeable and skilled networks	The purposes of my system's subsystems – how my system does what it does

Figure 13.1 shows this idea for a generic system. Every system can be thought of as part of a larger system and as having subsystems of its own. To qualify as systems, the subsystems must also have subsystems; and the higher system must be a part of a still-higher system. The implication of this is that any (or each) system definition can have only one *What* and one *Why*.

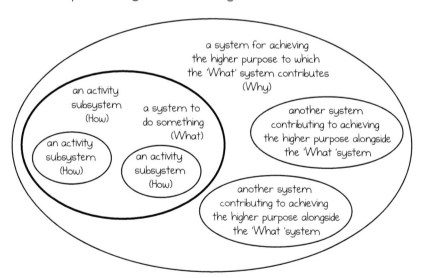

Figure 13.1 A system (shown with a heavy-line boundary) to do something (What) has subsystems that each contribute to achieving the purpose of the What system with their several Hows. The What system is part of a larger system and contributes to achieving what that system does (Why). Other systems contribute alongside the What system to achieving the purpose of the higher system.

When I frame a way of improving a messy situation as a system, I can move my attention up and down the hierarchy of systems. This is a good strategy if system definitions seem somehow not to work. Changing level is often sufficient to clarify my thinking. Taking my own system definition for a system to improve the personnel-induction situation, I can move up and down the system hierarchy to prompt ideas for new system definitions, as shown below and in Figure 13.2.

My original system definition	A system to create on-the-job learning opportunities for new staff by means of embedding them in several knowledgeable and skilled networks in order to contribute to enhancing their ability to contribute independently.
Moving *up* the hierarchy from the original definition	A system to enhance their ability to contribute independently by means of giving new staff on-the-job learning opportunities in order to contribute to improving the quality of our delivery.
Moving *down* the hierarchy from the original definition	A system to embed them in several knowledgeable and skilled networks by means of assigning tasks that engage with multiple networks in order to create on-the-job learning opportunities for new staff.

When I thought about the briefing activities I found from my internet scouring in terms of systems of activity, I began to suspect the systems would quickly run out of Whys as I moved up the system hierarchy. I had already noted that no-one had given a reason for briefing staff and I had a sense that if I had asked why 'conveying essential information' was important, I might be told 'well, it just is'. Rather unsatisfactory. In theory, a system hierarchy goes upwards through an infinite number of systems and downwards through an infinite number of systems. In practice, a few levels up and down suffice. Unlike 'conveying essential information,' some implied purposes are self-justifying. For example, some UK hospitals take 'improving patient care' as self-justifying. Staff are encouraged to challenge the need for bureaucratic procedures by asking *Why?* five times[11]. If the respondent cannot get to 'It improves patient care' within five steps, then the procedure is deemed unnecessary. Asking *Why?* reveals whether the activity really does contribute to the common weal or whether it is merely 'doing something on the off chance it makes a difference'.

Rules and guidelines

The template for a basic system definition is disarmingly simple but stripping away distractions to arrive at a system definition takes patience and commitment. There are a few simple rules.

1   Define an action in terms of a system of human activities. Use the template definition:
    A system to do <What> by means of <How> in order to contribute to achieving <Why>.

2   Use verb forms for *What*, *How* and *Why*.

3   Each system has only one *What*, the primary activity that defines its purpose.

4   Each system has only one *Why*.

System definitions start from ideas about what the system does, specifically to by-pass unconscious constraints arising from existing structures, tools, procedures and roles. This puts verb forms – action words – at the heart of the conceptual system. The verb captures a transformation and meets the same criteria as the transformation used in the ITO[12] model. This rule about verbs is absolute for specifying *What* and *Why* but need not be so strictly adhered to for *How*, provided the *How* is specific enough to indicate what subsystems *do*.

Some verb choices undermine the clarifying power of the system definition. It can be tempting to resort to *Vague Verbs*. Examples of Vague Verbs include:

manage ~ increase ~ communicate ~ support ~ participate ~ coordinate ~ organise ~ review.

While these words do not break the rules, they are not specific enough for a good system definition in most cases. For example, I claim to support a football team. It is not clear, however, what *supporting* is when I do it. It may simply mean I look out for their match results, experiencing pleasure or dismay according to the score. It may mean I invest millions of Euros in the team and broker deals for buying star players through my international business networks. I can detect Vague Verbs that undermine a system definition's effectiveness by asking questions such as 'What changes as a result of this system?' In framing my system definition for induction, I initially had 'support on-the-job learning' but rejected it because its potential meanings ranged all the way from 'take a benign but inactive interest in ...' to 'contrive learning experiences for every moment of the day'.

Creating a system definition

Now is a good point to attempt a system definition of your own. You may want to define a system you know about, or to express an action plan for your own messy situation as a conceptual system for improving the mess. You may also want to define a system in a way that opens up new possibilities. (For example, *a system to show what time it is …; a system to educate children …*).

If you are working with a messy situation of your own, *Themes* or *Snappy Systems* are good places to start. Start with *What* the system will do and then fill in the template definition:

> *A system to do <What> by means of <How> in order to contribute to <Why>.*

Make sure the *What* contributes *directly* to the *Why* in ways that would be readily understandable. For example,

> *A system to clean every hospital ward daily by means of … in order to reduce the risk of hospital-acquired infections*

is better than

> *A system to clean every hospital ward daily by means of … in order to save lives.*

System definitions work best when they define systems with an extended lifespan. For example:

> *A system to join a swimming club by means of …in order to get regular exercise*

will not work as well as

> *A system to swim with the swimming club by means of … in order to get regular exercise.*

The joining is a one-off event, a matter of filling in some forms and paying a fee. The substance of the activity is *swimming*. Aim to get right to the heart of the situation by looking at the main verb. Ask yourself whether the difference it makes contributes directly to the wider purpose.

How will you know when you have 'got it'? As with so many systems ideas, there will be a moment when what you have will seem obvious. This obviousness is a signal, not that it was easy or trivial but that you have arrived at a coherent system definition for a relevant system.

Using What, How *and* Why *with others*

Why do discussions about what to do go round in circles? Group discussions often muddle *What, How* and *Why*. When this happens, disagreements cannot be addressed because proposals about *Why* are countered by objections to *What* or *How*. Because most people do not carry any awareness of systemic hierarchy, it is also hard to spot common ground or even agreement. Systems thinking is sometimes criticised for its lack of attention to conflict. There is some substance to this criticism but *What, How* and *Why* goes a long way towards creating a structure for converging on agreement and isolating sites of disagreement.

Different personal styles also hamper discussions about 'What to do'. Some people prefer to work from the specific and local towards the more general. Others prefer to work from broad aims towards specific actions. *What, How* and *Why* is a useful device for sorting out different systemic layers by enabling people to match their different proposals by ordering each one in a hierarchy. This may involve listening carefully to the many suggestions and ordering them before feeding them back to the meeting, bearing in mind that one person's *Why* may be another person's *How*. Sensitively done this can be a powerful way of creating a dynamic of agreement and accommodation. It subtly shifts the focus from identifying immediately feasible but not necessarily helpful actions to a suite of actions that each contribute to overall agreed aims.

Another valuable insight relates to managing people. Managers who come to workshops report to me that it is frustrating when their managers tell them *What* needs to happen without also saying *Why* it needs to happen. Without that information, it is almost impossible to know how to do it well – except when a senior manager then compounds the frustration by micromanaging the *Hows*. Together, workshop participants and I have concluded that, to do a task well, you need to be told *What* is required and *Why* it is required. Given these two pieces of information, I can safely be left to work out *How* to do it and how to do it well. One manager had a career-long history of poor relationships with his staff. As we talked, he became aware that he had assumed his task concerned strategy (i.e. the *Whys*) and that, to get the job done, he would tell people what to do. He was frustrated by the poor performance of his staff and he often intervened to tell them *how* to do something, because no progress was evident. He agreed to experiment with telling his staff *What* to do and *Why* it was important and to avoid, if possible, micromanaging them as they did it. When I next saw him six months later, he looked ten years younger. His staff were working well and outperforming themselves. Not only was everyone performing better, they were happier too and feeling more confident in themselves, their abilities and their colleagues.

Assuming people don't need to know *Why* seems to be common. Organisational restructuring seems particularly susceptible. As I write this chapter, the UK Government has just announced a radical restructuring of the Police Forces in the UK and the formation of 'Britain's FBI'. There are many reasons why some rearrangement might be useful but, so far, no *Why* for this restructuring is evident, leading me to ask 'To what problem is this a solution?'

DEVELOPING THE SYSTEM DEFINITION: *TWO CAGES*

Eight more elements develop the system definition. The list of elements is set alongside the system definition as a supplement to it. In this section, I describe each of these elements and how to specify them. TWO CAGES[13] is a helpful mnemonic for remembering each item.

Transformation

The first element is the Transformation – the T in TWO CAGES – the system would achieve, were it to exist. It is the essence of what the system would be. Chapter 8 discusses the ITO model as a way of understanding the Transformation. The Transformation (often referred to as simply the *T*) is a verb closely allied to *What* the system does in the *What?, How? and Why?* formulation of the system definition. I imagine the action as a system of human activities. I then imagine what the system does as a transformation of something in one state into the same thing in another state. In my system definition from the section above, *A system to create on-the-job learning opportunities for new staff by means of embedding them in several knowledgeable and skilled networks in order to contribute to enhancing their ability to contribute independently*, the transformation is:

> *on-the-job learning opportunities uncreated* → *on-the-job learning opportunities created*

indicating the Transformation verb is *create*.

To work out the Transformation the system would achieve, ask *What would be changed by this system?* The transformation you specify is the system-definition transformation.

W

The W in the TWO CAGES mnemonic stands for *Weltanschauung* – the belief-set that would make this transformation a meaningful thing to do in this situation. It relates to the *Why* in the system definition and perhaps to several *Whys* above that in the system hierarchy. It is a German word meaning 'world outlook' but carries a deeper meaning than the literal English translation. *Weltanschauung* implies not just beliefs but values, emotions and ethics. It is closely related, therefore, to the ideas that were explored in Chapters 2 and 6. In the context of a system definition it has to explain why the transformation is relevant in terms that do not need to be justified to the person holding that particular *Weltanschauung*[14]. Because its use in a systems definition is a more limited use of the concept of *Weltanschauung*, this element of the system definition is simply referred to as W.

In my system definition, the *W* for my induction system is something like:

> *The belief that contributing independently is a hallmark of the competent professional practice needed from staff.*

Sometimes the *W* is simply a version of the mission or the high-level goals of those involved. For example, 'for the good of the patients' might be sufficient for a hospital-based activity. As before, getting the 'right' *W* is less important than identifying one that is coherent with the rest of the TWO CAGES criteria and with the *What*, *How* and *Why* system definition.

Specifying W thus involves asking *What idea would make this system's Transformation relevant and useful?*

It is helpful to specify the *T* and *W* criteria first. The next few criteria add more detail to the system definition.

W can be a powerful way of exploring different perspectives. Other perspectives take form as other *Weltanschauungen*. This in turn will lead to different Ws for system definitions. It is helpful to ask oneself whether, and how, different Ws will make sense to other stakeholders. Indeed, system definitions imagined from other people's perspectives can be very revealing.

Owners

A human-activity system has decision-making processes. The *Owners* of the system would make the most fundamental decision; whether or not the system should exist. Formally, they are those who would have sufficient power to stop it functioning, although those who can cause its demise by passive veto or by failing to carry out the required activities, don't count. In *Star Trek: The Next*

Generation[15], officers on the bridge of the Starship Enterprise frequently appear discussing options. As they converge on a decision, Captain Jean-Luc Picard will say 'Make it so', knowing his officers will implement the decision without needing his involvement. I think of the Owners of the systems as the person, or persons, with the right to say 'Make it so.'

To specify the owner of the system, ask *Who would give (or withdraw) permission for this system to exist?* Check that the Owner you specify makes sense in terms of the system definition and its *Why*.

Customers

Specifying *Customers* takes a broad interpretation of the word. In this context, *Customers* are the *direct* beneficiaries (or victims) of the system. They are the people on the receiving end of the system's action. Thus, in 'a system to immunise children …' children are the Customers. In a system to 'issue nurses with painless-immunisation kits for use with children …', nurses are the Customers even though the children will, I imagine, benefit from the new technology. In grammatical terms, Customers are the object, direct or indirect, of the verb that describes the Transformation. Look for the object of the transformation verb. If the object of the verb is not a sentient being, look for the words *for* or *to* for clues. It is not necessary that Customers consent to, or benefit from, the Transformation. In *a system to lock up convicted felons*, the felons are the unwilling Customers. The *Why* of the system definition may also be distracting. In 'A system to kill badgers by gassing them in their setts, in order to eliminate the tuberculosis risk to cattle', the unfortunate badgers are the Customers, not the cattle. Customers are connected to the *What* level of the system definition, not the *Why* level.

The Director of Personnel Development of a large organisation was concerned that the management-development programme was having insufficient impact. All the indicators suggested it was an excellent programme and participants were very positive but the political context was messy. The organisation was in a rapidly-changing market and the already skilled staff would need to be focused and adaptable if the organisation was to continue to flourish. Together we developed a system definition for a renewed management-development programme. Everything seemed coherent and the existing programme seemed to match any sensible definition of the system very well. With one exception. We could not work out who the Customers were. Getting stuck is often a clue that a breakthrough moment is imminent. We discussed for almost half an hour until we realised that our confusion matched the organisation's own confusion about whom the programme was for. Once the senior executive decided that the programme was for the direct benefit of the organisation, rather than for participants, a new set of guidelines could be installed for participants and their managers that made participation a priority task rather than a 'perk' for young managers.

Ask: *Who would be directly at the receiving end of the Transformation specified in the system definition?*

Actors

Actors – the A in TWO CAGES – are the people who would enact the various activities that enable the system to effect the Transformation. Actors may include more than one individual or group as different actors perform different activities. The system definition must identify the Actors quite specifically. For example, in the badger-killing system, images of the system in action depend on whether the cattle-owning farmer, or a government agent with powers of compulsion, is the Actor. It may be appropriate to name people, specify an organisation, or to state a profession or degree of skill. Be as specific as possible about the skills and attributes necessary and use real-world names sparingly. Again, getting it 'right' is less important than getting it coherent with the definition and other TWO CAGES criteria. It may be necessary to add Actors to your first attempt as you consider the Subsystems of activity (S in TWO CAGES) later.

To specify the Actors, ask, *Who would carry out the activities which, taken together, will achieve the Transformation?* Do not include people carrying out related activities: include only the people whose actions contribute directly to achieving the Transformation.

Guardians

Guardians are the people who would raise the alarm if the system were to create unintended consequences that adversely affected the system environment. Guardians may not be directly involved with the system, they might not even be aware of it, if it existed. They nonetheless represent the environment surrounding the system. For example, in the badger-killing system, possible Guardians include: farmers in neighbouring areas; farmers on the farms where setts are gassed; walkers enjoying the countryside; conservationists and veterinarians. These people will notice unintended consequences such as: the migration of badgers to neighbouring areas; injured badgers that have survived in distress; changes, if any, in tuberculosis infection in cattle; other injured animals; population changes in animals that badgers eat. Government bureaucrats may also be Guardians: manipulating the population of badgers violates the Bern Convention that prevails in much of Europe[16].

Britain would be in violation of this convention if badgers were gassed, triggering unpredictable consequences for negotiating future conventions, so diplomats too might be guardians. Bureaucrats would be likely to intervene if a government-funded gassing programme became too costly, took too long or simply did not work.

Ask: *Who would notice if this system has unintended consequences?* It may be easier to answer this question after some thought about what those unintended consequences might be.

Environmental constraints

The E of TWO CAGES is Environmental constraints. Environmental constraints set limits for the system's operations. They often deal with things like deadlines and budgets but they must also describe the context the system must fit into. Environmental constraints specify what must be taken as given. Simply list the features of the environment that cannot be changed and will bound the system. For example, in providing sandwiches for archaeologists at a dig with minimal washing facilities, givens may include:

- the archaeologists will use no plates or cutlery

- the archaeologists will have dirty hands

The environmental-constraints element of the system definition strongly determines how the system can, and cannot, work. For example, in a system to take the family on holiday, a budget of $1,000 per person suggests a very different system to one with a budget of $100 each, even if all other elements of the system definition remain the same. To identify environmental constraints, I find it helpful to imagine a fantastical system-gone-mad, taking over the world with its single transformation. It is then easy to list what would keep such a system within bounds. These are the Environmental constraints. Each constraint must be looked at to test whether it is immutable. It is easy to assume that something is given when it is not.

Ask: *What features of the system's environment would be taken as given?, What features in its environment would limit the operation of this system?* and *What context would this system have to fit into?*.

Subsystems of activity

Finally, S is for *Subsystems* of activity. This is simply a list of necessary activities to achieve the system's Transformation. In a system definition, some of the activities are evident in the *How* part of the system definition. Adding additional activities at this point clarifies the workings of the system still further and helps to distinguish it from similar systems. They do not need, at this stage, to be listed in any particular order. Consider the following example:

A system to arrange a face-to-face meeting with the suppliers by means of coordinating people, time, date and venue, in order to contribute to discussing escalating prices.

The subsystems of activity are the logically-necessary activities needed to complete the transformation 'arrange':

- appreciate the purpose of the meeting

- identify participants

- notify/invite participants of date, time and venue

- identify possible dates for essential participants and venue

- assess size of meeting

- choose date and time for meeting

- book venue

- identify an appropriate venue

- collate data sheets on prices

- circulate data sheets

Be wary of listing too many activities. This over-specifies the system, making the idea too rigid. Instead, aim for The 'Magical Number Seven'[17], and certainly no more than 10.

It is tempting to list a number of activities that represent *preparation* for arranging the meeting, with 'arrange meeting' as the final activity. The *activities* should, taken together, constitute the Transformation and the list should include only activities that contribute directly to the Transformation as specified by the transformation verb in the system definition. As with all the other techniques and ideas in this book, keep notes about any thoughts, ideas or puzzles that crop up as you develop your system definition.

Finally, the list should represent logically necessary activities, not necessarily those already happening. The difference between the specified, logically necessary activities and those observable in the situation will trigger useful questions.

AN EXAMPLE

Here is a simple example of a system definition, using the *What, Why and How* template and listing the TWO CAGES elements associated with it. The system defined is just one possible way of providing a lunch for archaeologists.

> *A system to provide sandwiches by assembling bread, butter and fillings in order to feed a team of hungry archaeologists at the dig.*

Although this is only one of many possible system definitions, exploring it can reveal much about the nature of the task, even if the lunches are eventually bought from a supermarket. Here is one possible way of extending the definition by listing some TWO CAGES criteria:

Transformation:	sandwiches unprovided → sandwiches provided
W:	the belief that sandwiches are a good lunch for people who do not have access to cooking facilities or shops
Owners:	the dig's Project Leader
Customers:	hungry archaeologists
Actors:	the volunteer dig-support team
Guardians:	the archaeologists
	the dig Project Leader
	the support team
	the kitchen owner
Environmental constraints	they must be nourishing enough to get the archaeologists through the afternoon
	they must be tasty
	they must generate a minimum of wrapping waste
	the archaeologists will use no plates or cutlery
	the archaeologists will have dirty hands
	a budget of €2.00 per person
	volunteers have the use of the village hall.
Subsystems of activity	find out how many archaeologists to feed
	acquire bread, fillings, butter, wrappings
	prepare fillings
	butter bread
	fill sandwiches
	cut sandwiches
	wrap sandwiches
	deliver sandwiches to site

This would be a good point at which to attempt to identify TWO CAGES elements for your own system definition. Check that the system definition and the TWO CAGES elements make sense, taken as a whole. Make a note of any questions, insights or new lines of inquiry.

System definitions as heuristic devices

Assembling a system definition and listing the TWO CAGES criteria provides many lines of inquiry. The system definition becomes an understandascope for understanding and improving the messy situation.

Here are some of the questions that suggest themselves to me.

Working from the system definition:

- sandwiches? what about soup, casserole, etc.?

- how many sandwiches?

- assembling sandwiches? what about buying ready-made sandwiches fetched from the city, or bespoke sandwiches from a caterer? or booking a mobile hot-dog stand?

- sliced bread or rolls? brown or white?

- what fillings will work well? what fillings will not work well? do we offer choices? do we offer a menu earlier in the day for selecting sandwiches?

- how many archaeologists? will we know in advance of making sandwiches? how hungry are they (measured in sandwiches)?

- do we need to feed them at the dig? can we feed them at the village hall? What options open up if we can? what facilities are there on site? is there a marquee? is there a campfire?

And, working from the associated TWO CAGES criteria and

thinking about the Transformation:

- what else might be provided to supplement sandwiches?

thinking about the W:

- are sandwiches going to be adequate day after day? can we provide enough different fillings?

thinking about the Owner:

- does the project leader have any preferences or alternative expectations? does he or she have access to any alternative facilities or resources?

thinking about the Customers:

- do the archaeologists have any preferences or alternative expectations? do they have any experience from previous digs that will help us meet their needs?

- how will they express their views?

thinking about the Actors:

- does the dig-support team already exist?

- does the dig-support team have any expertise in making sandwiches? how do we set standards? will they need hygiene training? what skills do we need to recruit?

- how many volunteers are there? can they work in teams? is one of them able to transport sandwiches to the site?

thinking about the Guardians:

- how will we know whether the archaeologists are enjoying the sandwiches?

- how does the project leader want the sandwiches delivered?

- when does the project leader want the sandwiches delivered?

- what resources are available at the village hall? what are the expectations about clearing up, other users, food storage, access, etc.?

thinking about the Environmental constraints

- how will we know if the sandwiches are tasty?

- how will we manage wrapping waste?

- can we wrap the sandwiches for eating with dirty hands?

- can we provide wrappings that allow the archaeologists to eat from them?

- what size sandwiches are appropriate if they must be pre-cut?

- can we access any free resources for fillings, bread, etc.?

- what are the costings for bread, butter, fillings, etc.

Of course, many other questions are prompted by examining the situation through the understandascope of the system definition and its associated TWO CAGES criteria. This is just a first pass from the perspective of someone who might be organising the sandwiches. But all of the questions open avenues to potentially better ways of providing lunches for the archaeologists. The understandascope opens up not only a range of possible actions but reveals them as actionable options.

NOTES, EXPLORATIONS AND RESOURCES FOR CHAPTER 13

1   *Heuristic devices*

An heuristic device is a mental tool for finding a way forward. Heuristic comes from the ancient Greek word *heuriskein* meaning discover. It carries the sense of homing in on hidden quarry that may not be glimpsed until the final moment.

2   *System Definitions*

See Note 3 in Chapter 17 for details on the source for system definitions.

3   *Themes*

See Chapter 4.

4   *Snappy Systems*

See Chapter 8.

5   *Rearranging the deckchairs*

This vivid metaphor seems to have passed into popular usage in 1976. Rogers Morton (1914 – 1979), President Ford's campaign manager, was quoted in the *The Washington Post* (16th May 1976) as saying 'I am not going to rearrange the furniture on the deck of the Titanic'. He was explaining why Ford had lost five of the last six primaries.

The metaphor occurred earlier in the *The New York Times* (p.34, 15th May 1972) when Joseph Eger reported that administrators at the Lincoln Center 'are running around straightening out deck chairs while the Titanic goes down'. However, even this seems not to have been its earliest use.

6   *What?, How? and Why?*

I am indebted to my colleague Janet Churchill for this simplified template for a system definition. See also Note 3 in Chapter 17.

7   *Sue Holwell*

I am indebted to my friend and colleague Sue Holwell for the insight of the last sentence.

8   *The 7/7 attack on London's transport system*

On 7th July 2005, four young suicide bombers exploded bombs on three tube trains and a bus as Londoners made their way to work. The blasts killed 52 people and injured approximately 700. Detailed accounts, given by people at the scene and others, emerged at the inquests held in London in 2010.

9   *Mediating objects*

See Note 8 of Chapter 3.

10   *Purpose*

See Note 8 in Chapter 8.

11   *Five Whys*

The Five Whys approach described here relates activities back to some fundamental mission. It should not be confused with another version of Five Whys that is concerned with finding the 'root cause' of some problem. This latter, rather simplistic, approach works well for difficulties but much less well for messes where a single chain between something going wrong and a root cause is unlikely. In a mess, a multiplicity of interacting causes is much more likely. The Five Whys described in this chapter has the advantage of being systemic and thus better matched to messy situations.

12   *The ITO model*

See Chapter 8.

13   *TWO CAGES*

I am indebted to my colleagues in the Systems Development Institute in Australia for the TWO CAGES mnemonic.

14   *Weltanschauung*

As someone who is struggling to speak (and understand) German better, I find this word intriguing. It has emergent properties, as many German words do, that are more than the sum of its parts. (See Chapter 8 for a discussion of emergent properties.) Like all German nouns, it has a capital letter. The stress falls on the *an* sound in the middle. Velt AN show (rhyming with cow) ung. Its plural is *Weltanschauungen*. Or you can simply call it *W*. Other systems thinkers will know what you mean.

15   *Star Trek: The Next Generation*

The American TV series ran for seven seasons from 1987, and maintained huge audiences. Created by Gene Roddenberry, who had created an earlier version of Star Trek, it is set in the twenty-fourth century. As its crew 'boldly go where no-one has gone before' they meet complex situations, make decisions and deal with the consequences. The English Shakespearian actor, Patrick Stewart, plays the uber-cool Captain Jean-Luc Picard.

Star Trek: The Next Generation (1987 – 1994) Created by Gene Roddenberry and produced by Gene Roddenberry, Rick Berma and Michael Filler (Paramount TV)

16   *Convention on the Conservation of European Wildlife and Natural Habitats (1979)*

The convention, which has been in force since 1982, forbids manipulating the populations of named species.

17   *The Magical Number Seven*

See Note 2 in Chapter 6.

CHAPTER 14

How will it work?

You have your way. I have my way. As for the right way, the correct way, and the only way, it does not exist.

Friedrich Nietzsche[1] (1844 – 1900)

Aut inveniam viam aut faciam
Either I shall find a way or I shall make one.

(Latin saying)

This chapter is about conceptualising how a system might work using diagrams of a *human-activity system*. There are two ways to use a human-activity system (HAS) diagram. The first is to use the diagram, alongside a system definition[2] for a relevant system, as an understandascope for looking at a messy situation to discern options for action. The second is to conceptualise how possible action to improve a messy situation might work. In both cases, constructing an HAS diagram follows from creating a system definition. In the first case, neither the system definition nor the HAS diagram refers to a proposed system. They simply define, and conceptualise the activities of, a system that is relevant to improving the situation in some way. In the second case, the system definition may refer to an action plan and the HAS diagram then expresses more detail for the plan. The HAS and the system definition (with its TWO CAGES criteria) form a conceptual rehearsal for taking action that ensures unintended consequences are minimised.

An HAS diagram models the activities, carried out by humans, that logically follow from the system definition. It is simply a diagram providing one possible answer to the question, 'How might we do this?'. It conceptualises the system in terms of the human activities that are *logically necessary* to effect the Transformation specified in the system definition. It identifies both the necessary activities and the relationships between them. Although simple in structure, HAS diagrams are challenging to construct because they force one to think about logical necessity; they transcend preferences, notions of feasibility, how it is at present, and detailed 'how to's'. The HAS diagram has blobs, words, arrows, a system boundary, a monitoring-and-control function to check it is working, and a title. Figure 14.1 shows an HAS diagram. Providing sandwiches is not an activity that normally requires modelling but, as a well understood process, it serves to explain the ideas.

A human-activity system to provide
sandwiches for archaeologists

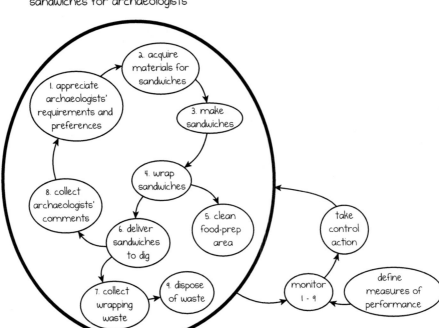

Figure 14.1 *A human-activity system to deliver wrapped sandwiches to a team of hungry archaeologists at a dig. It shows a sequence of activities in a logically necessary order with arrows representing contingency. A system boundary encloses the system and a monitoring and control system regulates individual activities and the system as a whole. The numbering of the activities simplifies labelling and does not refer to an order. Each activity is monitored and controlled, together with the whole system.*

Activities that contribute to accomplishing the system's overall transformation appear in the diagram as subsystems labelled using verbs in the imperative mode: *acquire, make, wrap, deliver,* etc. Taken together, and completed in logically necessary order, the activities make up the transformation process: the *What* that the system does[3]. Activity subsystems are numbered for convenience but the numbering does not imply any order.

Arrows show the logical dependency between the activities. Thus, in Figure 14.1, the arrow indicates that 'make sandwiches' is logically dependent on – and cannot happen without – 'acquire materials for sandwiches'. Although this logical ordering usually means the activity at the arrow's head happens after the activity at the arrow's tail, the arrow does not mean 'is followed by …'

In Figure 14.1, for example, the next activity in a time sequence after collecting the wrapping waste, may be to clean the food-preparation area. The arrows in an HAS diagram have the strict meaning shown in Figure 14.2.

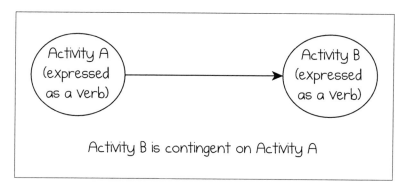

Figure 14.2 *The meaning of arrows in an HAS diagram. The activity at the head of the arrow is contingent on the activity at the tail of the arrow.*

Each system has an associated monitoring and control function, ensuring that each activity plays its role well enough to complete the transformation that is the function of the whole system. Criteria or measures of performance can be set for each activity, plus another for the functioning of the whole system. Chapter 16 discusses this function in more detail and shows how the ideas behind it provide ways to ask 'How will we know the system is succeeding?'

An HAS diagram is a way of thinking about an action, or a proposed action. It allows me to understand the action in terms of key elements of the transformation, without being constrained by 'the normal way of doing things', organisational structures or unfounded assumptions. By staying at the conceptual level of the strictly necessary, the diagram transcends feasibility and detail so that any proposed way of enacting the system can be tested for necessity and logic. Diagramming a transformation in this way cuts through the complexity of real processes to what is strictly necessary.

BUILDING HUMAN-ACTIVITY SYSTEM DIAGRAMS

A key system definition emerging from the review of a cardiology clinic concerned the management of routine check-ups for low-risk patients:

> '*A system to appraise low-risk patients by regular tests and consultations in order to spot changes in their condition.*'

Many registered patients were in reasonable health, some maintained by medication. Of this group, most were on a quarterly, six-monthly or annual cycle of tests and appointments with the consultant cardiologist. Before the review, patients would receive notification of a series of appointments for various tests, followed by an appointment to see the cardiologist. Each group of technicians or radiologists would manage their own appointments. The system often went wrong. If a test had not been completed, perhaps because the patient was unable to attend at the appointed date, it would be discovered only at the consultant's clinic. The appointment would be wasted and a second consultant-appointment would be needed to complete the patient's check-up cycle. Patients hated the many appointments, often as many as five or six, to complete all the tests and the complicated bus journeys or expensive taxi rides to get there.

During an 'away day' meeting between the cardiology technicians (who did many of the tests), the receptionists, the consultant and the clinic nurses, it was easy to say what was wrong but harder to focus on ideas for improving the situation. Then someone remarked that 'perhaps we should think of an appointment with the clinic rather than an appointment with the consultant'. Interestingly, this remark had not been intended as a suggestion but it was a breakthrough moment.

The cardiology team quickly established that almost all this group of patients needed the same group of tests at each routine check-up. The team began to experiment with the idea of carrying out all the tests at one clinic appointment.

The system definition was now:

> '*a system to appraise low-risk patients by means of tests and consultations carried out in one morning, in order to spot changes in the patient's condition*'.

The list of activities ('S' in the TWO CAGES list[4]) for each cycle was:

- decide on further tests for this cycle
- review results of tests
- decide on necessary tests for next cycle
- create treatment plans
- meet patient (take history, examine patient, explain results of tests, discuss emerging issues, review medication, etc.)
- decide interval before next appointment

- decide on any necessary intervention
- do echo cardiogram
- do ECG tests
- measure blood pressure
- weigh patient

This list was indicative of the kinds of activity the team imagined happening in the clinic. It formed the basis of an HAS diagram. Not all the activities eventually appeared in the HAS diagram and the TWO CAGES list was later amended. The group clustered the tests under one heading and identified a list of logically necessary activities for a single-appointment system. They drew the list as a circular arrangement, much like that shown in Figure 14.3. The group then drew in arrows to show logical dependency for the activities.

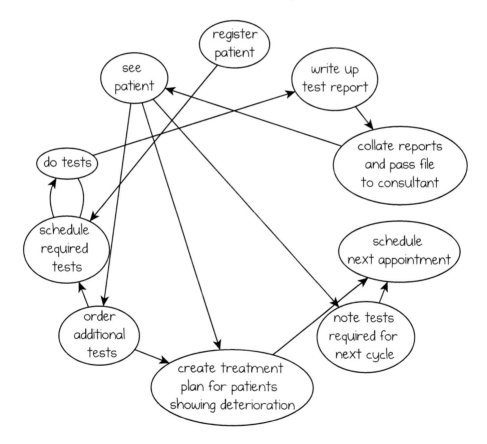

Figure 14.3 *The preliminary stage of building the HAS diagram for a Cardiology Department 'routine check-up' clinic. In this optional stage, arranging the constituent activities in a circle makes it easier to decide on a logical arrangement for the activities.*

All that then remained was to disentangle the diagram to turn it into a HAS diagram. A system boundary and a monitoring function were added and the HAS diagram then looked like Figure 14.4.

A human-activity system model of a single-morning clinic for patients having routine check-ups

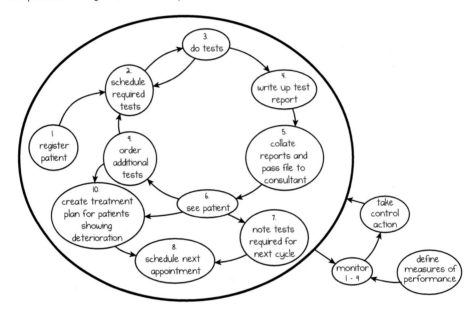

Figure 14.4 *The Cardiology Department's HAS diagram to monitor low-risk patients by means of regular tests and consultations, carried out in one morning, in order to spot changes in their condition.*

Using this diagram, the group imagined scheduling a regular clinic *for routine check-ups only*. The patient would be registered on arrival and the receptionist would consult their screen to determine what tests had been requested at the previous appointment. She would then schedule tests so that, within 90 minutes of the patient's arrival, the patient would have completed the tests. Technicians and equipment for completing the most commonly requested tests (electrocardiograms, ultrasonic 'echo' imaging, weight checks and blood-pressure measurement, for example) would be available in the department. Other tests (mostly X-ray examinations) would be fast-tracked by the Radiology Department for that morning. Cardiology technicians would write up the results immediately, noting any changes in the patient's condition, and returning their report immediately to the receptionist for filing with other patient notes. Once the tests were completed, the receptionist would pass the notes to the consultant cardiologist, who would see patients as they completed the scheduled tests. The cardiologist would thus have a complete set of test results when he saw the patient. In most cases, the cardiologist would request the same set of tests for the next routine appointment. If the patient needed further tests, the receptionist would try to schedule them for that morning. Only if this were impossible would the patient come back for another appointment to complete the check-up cycle. The consultant would outline a treatment plan during the consultation for any patient whose condition had deteriorated and, if necessary, would refer the patient to another cardiology clinic.

The team then looked at the current situation in the light of the diagram they had created. The diagram highlighted the delays at every stage between scheduling the required tests, doing the tests, writing up the test report and passing it to Patient Records, who would file it in the patient's file. This attenuated process required a separate stream of activities for each test. It suddenly seemed like pure luck that it worked as often as it did. Comparing the diagram with the situation revealed current activities as potentially changeable. It is very easy to assume that current ways of doing things are 'just the way things are'. In all previous discussions, staff had taken for granted that doing, and writing up, tests took several days and that getting test reports into the file took at least a week because the file first had to be extracted from the rack, checked, the test results inserted and then the file re-racked. The idea that patients, consultants, test equipment, technicians, test results and patient records would be 'held in close proximity' for a whole morning appealed to everyone.

The department adopted the single-morning clinic. The receptionists managed Activities 1, 2 and 5 by slotting patients into the various tests as technicians, equipment and patients became available. Technicians did the tests and wrote up their reports immediately (Activities 3 and 4). The receptionist ensured all the test results were available before passing the patient's clinical notes to the consultant. The consultant cardiologist examined the patient and decided when the next check-up should be and what tests would be needed (Activities 6 and 7). If necessary, he scheduled additional tests (Activity 9) or created a treatment plan (Activity 10).

The improvement was immediate. Patients attended only once in each check-up cycle (except when additional tests could not be completed on the day). They knew they might be there for several hours but surveys later showed they spent only slightly more time than they did before (when they just saw the consultant). Consultations were more efficient and less frustrating for both consultant and patient because everything the consultant needed to make clinical decisions was in front of him. Patients missed fewer expensive appointments because each cycle of check-ups needed fewer appointments. There was a sense of gaiety at the clinic. Patients chatted more with each other and were less grumpy. They experienced an efficient process of testing and consultation rather than waiting about.

As time went by, the Cardiology Department adjusted the frequency of its 'check-up only' clinics because they were able to see nearly 20 per cent more patients, leaving more time for other clinics and for patient care in the hospital's Cardiology Ward. The consultant did not need to see the patient's notes until immediately before the patient's next appointment. The receptionists, excited by their enhanced role, designed a form for the consultant to fill in. The consultant had proved unreliable about making clear the interval to the next check-up and the tests needed. If he did not fill in the form, the receptionists picked it up immediately. Receptionists became efficient at expediting patients through the test schedule. The whole department valued the new arrangement, so they allowed receptionists to keep everyone up to speed on clinic day. The department has already saved several hundreds of pounds annually per patient in the 'routine check-up' category. It is taking steps to improve the efficiency of its other clinics. Staff report greater job satisfaction and there is even evidence of better clinical outcomes, although it is not yet clear whether, or how, this relates to improved clinic management.

RULES AND GUIDELINES FOR HUMAN-ACTIVITY SYSTEM DIAGRAMS

The rules of HAS diagrams are strict in the sense that only determined adherence will deliver an understandascope that reveals options for change.

1   Verbs, in the imperative form[5], describe the activity so words represent an activity carried out by an actor or actors.

2   Activities are specified in general, abstract terms, focusing on *what* happens rather than *how* it happens.

3   Arrows represent the logically necessary relationship between activities needed to accomplish the overall transformation. They do not indicate relationships such as 'is followed by…', leads to …' or 'contributes to …'.

4   The diagram includes a title.

5   The diagram includes a system boundary and a monitoring and control function.

6   If the diagram models a system definition, it must be coherent with the system definition.

7   The activities, taken together, represent the overall transformation of the system.

8   The diagram may contain iterative loops.

9   The diagram should contain between five and nine activities.

The reasons for, and implications of, most of these rules has already been discussed but several need further discussion.

Rule 5 refers to a monitoring and control function. The diagram represents a system of activity and, because the system must be self-regulating, through human activity, activities to monitor and control the system lie outside the system boundary as in Figure 14.4. This form is standard in HAS diagrams.

Rule 6 requires that the activities in the HAS diagram, taken together, will achieve the Transformation specified in the system definition in the manner indicated by the list of subsystems in the TWO CAGES list. For coherence, the list of subsystems may need amendment. The diagram should also be capable of interpretation as meeting the needs of Customers, with the Actors specified, with the same Owners and Guardians. The diagram should also fit into the W specified in the system definition.

Beginners often make the mistake of diagramming preparatory activities, including the transformation they are diagramming as the final activity. For example, slice bread, butter bread, make fillings, and finally 'make sandwiches' may appear, incorrectly, as the activities for a sandwich-making system. *All* the activities should be part of the process of making sandwiches. No activities should be included that are not part of the transformation. To comply with Rule 7, ask of each activity whether it is part of the overall transformation.

As allowed by Rule 8, some human-activity systems, particularly those concerning ongoing processes, contain loops. Figure 14.4 shows two examples. In Figure 14.4, the consultant sees the patient with three possible outcomes. Whether the consultant creates a treatment plan or requires tests for the next cycle, the system terminates, for the patient, when the receptionist schedules the next appointment. Sometimes, however, the consultant may order additional tests and, if the tests are available that morning, the patient rejoins the cycle of activities as the receptionist schedules the test. In principle, the loop can act on the patient as many times as it takes until the consultant is able either to create a treatment plan or note the tests required for the next appointment. The second loop shows that as soon as a nurse or technician has completed a test, the receptionist can schedule another for that patient until completion of all their prescribed tests.

Rule 9 has two functions. It refers to the Magical Number 7: Miller's observation that the human mind can only deal with around seven concepts at once[6]. It keeps the diagram manageable. The rule also imposes a discipline that keeps the activities in the diagram at a very general level, avoiding spurious detailing. Notice that the Cardiology Department's HAS diagram had 10 activities. Rule 9 is not a strict rule although I have noticed that the usefulness of an HAS diagram declines dramatically if more than 10 activities appear in it.

DRAWING HUMAN-ACTIVITY SYSTEM DIAGRAMS

As with learning many other human skills (riding a bicycle, drawing systems diagrams, etc.), reading about HAS diagrams will only get you some of the way. In this case, I believe their usefulness is proportional to the challenge of drawing any particular diagram. There is no doubt that a good HAS diagram is challenging but you know when you have it. There is surprise and delight in realising a good HAS diagram.

You may already have a system definition you wish to explore, or you may wish to draw an HAS diagram using one of the suggestions at the end of the chapter[7]. The best way to practise is to start with a system definition (with its associated TWO CAGES criteria) and create a diagram to match. You can do either first.

The list of Subsystems of activities, from the TWO CAGES mnemonic, together with the *How* from the system definition, is a good place to start. Alternatively, you can start by listing the activities that make up the Transformation your system will do. Simply ask, 'What minimum set of activities would be needed to accomplish this Transformation (from the TWO CAGES list), in line with the system definition?'. If you have more than nine items, look for different verbs. For example, if in a sandwich-making system I have 'peel cucumbers' and 'slice cucumbers', I can merge these activities into 'prepare cucumbers', because they are activities that relate immediately to each other.

Some people are happy to go straight into the diagram. Others prefer to arrange the activities around a circle first (as in Figure 14.3). Either way, simply start by identifying an activity that does not depend on any other activity. Then look for activities about which you can say 'and then I can <activity>'. Be careful to check backwards as well, asking 'What does this activity depend on'. Be prepared to draft and redraft, adding activities to your list if necessary.

When you are near completing your arrangement of the activities, review your diagram and compare it with the system definition. Modify either or both of these so that they are coherent with each other, even if this means you have a slightly different system from the one you intended. If necessary, don't be afraid to start again or to re-write the system definition. The system does not have to be the 'right' one, nor even one you favour. It simply has to be relevant to the situation, internally consistent and consistent with the system definition.

For your final draft, add a system boundary, a monitoring and control function and a title. Check the title is coherent with the system definition and with the HAS diagram itself.

CHOOSING A HUMAN-ACTIVITY SYSTEM DIAGRAM

The advantages of an HAS diagram arise from its being *conceptual*. It does not represent anything I perceive in the messy situation. It exists only in the conceptual world as a logical device. It does not even represent a system that could, should, or ought to, exist. It is simply one conception of the minimum set of activities needed to accomplish a transformation.

Two possible uses make drawing an HAS diagram a useful option. If ideas about improving action already exist, they can be tested against the HAS diagram and the messy situation. If there are no clear ideas about action, using the HAS diagram as an understandascope will generate options for action.

When you already have some idea of possible action to improve a messy situation, diagramming the idea as a human-activity system shows how the transformation might be achieved using a minimum set of interconnected activities. Diagramming the transformation in this way, logical necessity replaces assumptions, 'the usual way to do it', and the way it is currently done (if it is) in my thinking about improving the situation. It articulates a set of logically necessary and logically linked *Hows* for ideas about *What* to do. It forces me to refine my ideas by exposing weak options such as 'things to do because I can do them'.

The HAS diagram can also be used as an understandascope for looking at the mess. It allows me to ask questions about action in the messy situation. Such questions might include:

- Is such a transformation desirable?

- What alternative transformations might be more desirable?

- Is such a transformation feasible?

- What alternative transformations might be more feasible?

- Is this transformation happening in the messy situation?

- What activities in the situation contribute to the transformation?

- Are they logically necessary?

- Are they logically connected?

- What activities, named in the HAS diagram, already happen in the situation?

- Would it be possible to link them differently to achieve the transformation?

- Does each activity in the situation meet the contingencies of subsequent activities?

Like system definitions, HAS diagrams can become understandascopes in a social process. Where the HAS diagram differs from what is perceived in the situation, stakeholders can debate these differences with a view to creating accommodations around agreed changes to the messy situation. In working with these questions, the HAS diagram has the capacity to be a powerful 'mediating object'[8] for conversations about what to do, especially when used in conjunction with a systems definition. In this sense, the diagram works best, as with most diagrams, when it invites others into the conversation by its informality. Such informality belies the careful work of preparing it[9].

USING HUMAN-ACTIVITY SYSTEM DIAGRAMS WITH OTHERS

The subtleties of an HAS diagram, alongside its associated system definition, make it difficult to create with a team of novices. It is usually more effective to create the system definition with the team and then generate the HAS diagram only with those who have a clear idea of what is required. Many practitioners generate both system definition and HAS diagram outside of team meetings. If possible, I prefer to generate the system definition collectively, listening carefully for clues about how the team imagine the system might work. I then generate an HAS diagram for each system definition, outside the meeting. My experience has been that team members then say the HAS diagram represents exactly what they had in mind. For others, it enables them to articulate where they differ. As long as the system definition and the HAS diagram are coherent, the HAS diagram will serve its purpose. It becomes a means by which team members can articulate what they like and do not like, and where they see problems. Working this way may involve planning meetings so that I, or the team working with me, can generate HAS diagrams for each system definition in an interval between two meetings.

Once the HAS diagram has been constructed, it can be used like any other diagram. Most people will be able to read the HAS diagram accurately, although they may need reminding about the very specific meaning of the arrows. A large flipchart diagram, informally drawn, will invite other ideas and suggestions. I have found photographing the original HAS diagram provides a useful record of the starting point. HAS diagrams may go through a lot of crossing out before the team reach satisfactory accommodations[10].

Discussion of the HAS diagram may be heated. This is not a cause for alarm. HAS diagrams typically surface different Ws (*Weltanschauungen*), even when these do not come out directly in discussion of the system definition. They expose strongly held values and the differing meanings that stakeholders attach to the messy situation. These differences can be acknowledged and discussed and, with patience, accommodations emerge.

Notes, explorations and resources for Chapter 14

1   *Friedrich Nietzsche (philosopher)*

Nietzsche deserves to be far better read than he is. *Thus Spake Zarathustra* is a dense philosophical novel exploring Nietzsche's key ideas through the voice of a fictional prophet. The quotation comes from the end of Chapter 55, *The Spirit of Heaviness*. *Thus Spake Zarathustra* is always in print and the full text can be found online. (Search for 'Nietzsche Forum').

2   *System Definition*

See Chapter 13.

3   *What?, How? and Why?*

A system definition 'template' is ' A system to do <What?> by means of <How?> in order to contribute to <Why?>.' Each element describes an activity. See Chapter 13.

4   *TWO CAGES*

TWO CAGES is a mnemonic for elements that supplement and complete the system definition. See Chapter 13.

5   *Imperative verb forms*

Imperative comes from the same root as *imperator*, the Latin for *emperor*. Imperative verb forms are thus like orders: 'prepare my bath', 'pour more wine'; 'invade Gaul', etc.

6   *The Magical Number Seven*

See Note 2 in Chapter 6.

7   *Suggestions for practising human-activity system diagrams*

organising a retirement party

reducing the number of staff to cut costs

deciding where to go for a family holiday

reducing your domestic energy consumption by half

funding your child's education

closing the detention facility at Guantanamo Bay

sending a manned mission to Mars

You need not attempt to diagram the topic as a whole. Any system that seems to be relevant to the issue can be diagrammed as a human-activity system. It is helpful to work with a suite of relevant systems related to the same topic to generate a suite of corresponding HAS diagrams.

You may find it helpful to develop a system definition for your chosen system. Alternatively, develop a system definition alongside your HAS diagram. HAS diagrams work at the level of logical necessity so you do not need to work out details. This makes it possible to practise diagramming ambitious systems.

8   *Mediating objects*
        See Note 8 of Chapter 3.

9   *Diagramming*
        See Chapter 9 for more on this.

10   *Accommodations*
        See Chapter 2.

CHAPTER 15

How will we know it is working?

Do What You Do Do Well, Boy

Ned Miller[1] (b. 1925)

Any successful purposeful action will succeed at three levels. Firstly, it will do what it is supposed to do. Secondly, it will do what it is supposed to do with a minimum of fuss and using a minimum of resources. Finally, it will contribute to achieving some higher purpose. The successful action will be *Efficacious, Efficient* and *Effective*.

If I think of an action as a system of human activities working together to achieve a Transformation[2], then I can relate success to three systemic levels. First, the system will effect the transformation. It will accomplish *What* it does. *Efficacy* measures whether it does. Secondly, the success of the system depends on the *Efficiency* of the activities that achieve the transformation. The system will need a performance measure to measure its use of resources, including time, energy and enthusiasm as well as money and physical resources. Finally, to be successful the system must contribute to a wider purpose, the purpose of the wider system of which it is part. *Effectiveness* measures how well the system meets this wider purpose. *Efficacy, Efficiency* and *Effectiveness* are the *3Es* that represent the three levels of system performance. A successful system will be efficacious in doing what it does, efficient in its use of resources, and effective in contributing to the realisation of some higher purpose.

3Es, 5Es

The idea of the 3Es is to specify criteria or measures, as part of the human-activity system diagram, to monitor and control the system's efficacy, efficiency and effectiveness[3]. The 3Es appear in the HAS diagram[4] as the monitoring and control function. In the system represented by the HAS diagram, the monitoring and control function is conceptualised as a set of measures and controls related to the logically-necessary activities of the system. The general idea that success occurs at three systemic levels is applicable to any proposed course of action, or any system of activities, intended to improve a messy situation. The 3Es invite me to consider how I will know whether a human-activity system, or a proposed course of action, is efficacious, efficient and effective. This means going beyond simply asking whether the system is efficacious, efficient and effective. It means identifying *measures* of performance, or *criteria* for performance.

In the last chapter, I discussed the experience of a Cardiology Department in improving its clinic for routine check-ups. Their system definition[5] was:

> a system to appraise low-risk patients by means of tests and consultations carried out in one morning, in order to spot changes in the patient's condition

I can identify a measure of performance for efficacy by asking questions like: 'Does the system appraise low-risk patients?'. Probing further, I might wish to ask how many of the patients in the low-risk category were checked, at the required frequency, over the course of a year. Clearly, if the new system monitored fewer patients than before, it would not be succeeding. Patients may remain unmonitored for several reasons. They may move out of the area without informing the clinic, or they may for whatever reason not turn up for appointments. But it seems that measuring the number of patients monitored on schedule, each year, as a proportion of the total number of expected patients would be a sufficient performance indicator for efficacy.

Efficiency is the measure of how well the system works in terms of resource use. I might ask about the resources used by the system. The system would be not be a success if, for example, it cost twice as much per patient to run the clinic in this way or if it dramatically increased the time consultants, technicians, radiographers and receptionists took to see each patient. It makes sense therefore to monitor cost per patient and time per patient. Either or both of these measures could be used to measure efficiency. In fact, both measures improved. Fewer appointments were wasted through patient non-attendance or by consultants not having test results.

Finally, effectiveness measures ensure that I do not 'do the wrong thing righter'. My activity may be happening and it may be efficient but unless it contributes to a higher purpose, then it is not succeeding. For example, in the Cardiology Department, rearranging the clinic would only be successful if patients' emerging problems were spotted before they became serious. The department already had data on the clinic's performance in this respect. They decided that, for the present, they would continue to collect data in this way and set a minimum standard equal to their previous arrangements. In the event, they proved rather better at picking up problems early. Hospital administrators detected this 'improvement' as more patients were referred for treatment in the first year. (More patients were being monitored, so the proportion of early detections increased, leading to more referrals.) To hospital administrators, this looked like a problem but the cardiology consultant persuaded them to give the clinic a few more months. As the surge subsided, referrals returned to their previous levels and, because treatment referral happened earlier, patient outcomes improved. The hospital administration had initially been reluctant to offer fast tracking of laboratory tests for the single-morning clinics but the significantly improved patient outcomes persuaded them to make the arrangement permanent.

Checkland[6] proposes two additional Es – *elegance* and *ethicality*. Engineers use the word *elegance* to describe aesthetically attractive solutions to engineering problems. It suggests beauty, ingenuity and 'I wish *I'd* thought of that'. One workshop participant, an IT specialist, struggled with the idea for a moment and then said, 'Ah! You mean the opposite of clunky.' This captures the idea of elegance very well, I think. Elegance is a fourth criterion for success. It may not be easy to measure, but you usually know when you achieve it. In the Cardiology Department, they felt they had achieved elegance when patients, doctors, nurses and technicians expressed their *enjoyment* of clinic morning. The fifth E, *ethicality*, can be more specifically linked to criteria. It is an invitation to set criteria for keeping the ideal human-activity system, or the proposed action, ethical. Individuals often have a very specific sense of what is ethical and what is not. There is usually, within a group, considerable overlap. Often it is easier for people to express ethical values in terms of what would be unethical. The Cardiology Department had a long discussion about ethicality. Medical practice sets specific requirements for ethical treatment of patients but the Cardiology Department wanted to go beyond these. Members of staff expressed their desire that patients should not be 'messed about'. In a series of conversations, staff explored together their experiences of when and how they observed patients being messed about. Several themes emerged from these conversations. Patients felt messed about, staff thought, when they were told to expect one thing but experienced another; when appointments were changed at short notice; when they saw a different doctor to the one they had expected to see; and when they were given no indication of what to expect next. Some of these were outside the control of the Cardiology Department but they made a conscientious effort to reduce 'messing about'. They ensured patients saw the doctor named on their appointment letter whenever possible and that the letter itself indicated the possibility of a late change in unexpected circumstances. Receptionists undertook to explain to patients why any particular doctor was not available. Patients seemed content to see another doctor if they knew, for example, that the doctor they had been expecting to see was dealing with an emergency elsewhere. Nurses carrying out a patient's initial 'weigh-in' would brief the patient about the tests scheduled for them that morning.

Setting the 5Es criteria – for being efficacious, efficient, effective, elegant and ethical – took the Cardiology Department beyond the implementation of a new clinic system. Asking 'how will we know if this is working?' in terms of the 5Es enabled them to articulate exactly what they were trying to achieve and pointed the way to continuous improvement. By exploring what success would look like, they refined and built on their initial successes and gained political capital by having objective measures of their success.

Guidelines

Sometimes people misunderstand the 3Es and simply ask themselves: *Is it efficacious?, Is it efficient?* and *Is it effective?* The 3Es are a prompt to consider not only whether a system or an action is efficacious, efficient and effective but *How will we know?* and *Are we progressing towards efficacy, efficiency and effectiveness?* In other words, the 3Es invite us to specify how we will measure success against these three (or five) criteria. There are very few rules.

1   Efficacy measures whether or not the transformation at the heart of the action is happening at all. I can record it in terms of a criterion for success or in terms of a measure of progress towards achieving the transformation.

2   Efficiency measures the transformation against the resources used to make it happen. Resources may include physical quantities of materials or energy, or may include time, enthusiasm and human energy, or I can measure it in terms of financial costs. Ideally, I would measure it so I could see improvements or deteriorations in efficiency.

3   Effectiveness measures the contribution of the transformation to some higher purpose, the *Why* in the system definition. I can specify this in terms of a criterion or the value of the contribution. I should specify effectiveness to make clear that the transformation is 'the right thing to do'.

4   Elegance measures the aesthetic qualities of the transformation and the means by which it is achieved. It may be politic to specify elegance to meet the approval of particular stakeholders.

5   Ethicality measures the extent to which it conforms to specified ethical criteria.

Measurable standards for the 5Es can be tricky but, where I can specify them, they help establish that the action or system is working and identify improvements under each of the five measures. But of course, measures can take on a life of their own and usurp the real purposes of what you are trying to do. For example, my local general practitioners' surgery has performance targets based on seeing patients within two days of a request for an appointment. In order to improve their performance, they now offer appointments only on the day of the request, making it almost impossible for patients who work to get appointments without taking sick leave. The performance measures have hijacked the aim of patients getting prompt appointments to see their doctor. Efficacy, efficiency and effectiveness, taken together, address success at three different systemic levels and offer some protection against the measures displacing the transformation. It is, nonetheless, a danger to be aware of. If measures seem not to fit naturally, then it may be that criteria-based assessments of efficacy, efficiency and effectiveness are more appropriate. It can be helpful to keep a question in mind: 'How will we know the action or system is efficacious, efficient and effective?'.

Specifying the 3Es, or the 5Es, is not simply an add-on process to specifying a plan of action. The criteria may themselves prompt reconsideration of the action, its means and its purpose. Specifying a plan of action and specifying criteria for success can be an iterative process to achieve coherence between the two, using the insights generated in specifying each one.

Specifying the 3Es for the system defined by the system definition, and diagrammed in the human-activity system diagram leads to a three-way dynamic between the 3Es, the system definition and the HAS diagram. Here too, the recursive process of creating coherence generates better understanding and possibly refinement of the system definition, the HAS diagram and the 3Es. Specifying the 3Es is an activity in the HAS diagram. They become criteria for the monitoring and control function that is part of a fully articulated human-activity system.

Setting performance criteria for the 3Es

This would be a good point to consider some performance criteria. You might want to devise free standing 3Es (or perhaps even 5Es) for a plan of action you have in mind or, if you have a system definition for a system you consider relevant to a particular mess, then you may wish to devise 3Es criteria for it.

Start with the Transformation. How will you recognise that the transformation has happened or is happening? Can you express it as a criterion or as a measure of Efficacy? For many years, UK television featured a commercial for soft-timber treatments, claiming 'It does exactly what it says on the tin.' A good criterion for efficacy shows whether the system does exactly what it says on the tin. In an HAS diagram, you can also monitor each activity for efficacy. If you have an HAS diagram, you may want to practise by setting efficacy criteria for each of the activities as well as for the system as a whole.

The next question concerns Efficiency. How would you recognise efficiency for your plan of action or for the system depicted in your HAS diagram? There may be clues in the system definition. It may be appropriate to monitor some of the same inputs mentioned as Environmental constraints[7]: financial cost, time, energy, resource use, and so on. It is often sensible to specify Efficiency for the most precious of the inputs but you can specify additional measures. Once you have decided what efficiency means for your action plan or for your system, you will need to decide on a measure for it. Efficiency is usually about minimising inputs but can also measure waste production or CO_2 footprint. It is rarely possible to combine multiple measures to produce a single efficiency measure but several measures will provide a 'dashboard' for monitoring improvement. If you are working with an HAS diagram, you can also set efficiency criteria for the individual activities.

Effectiveness is realised at a higher systemic level than the system itself. It may link to the *Why?* in the system definition, if you are working from there. If you are specifying your 3Es without a system definition, first ask about your action plan *Why is this a sensible thing to do and to what will it contribute?* Whether you are working with an action plan or a system definition of a relevant system, next ask how you will know whether the action plan or relevant system is contributing to the higher purpose. You can then ask how you will measure it. You can also measure the effectiveness of the activities specified in the HAS diagram of the system. In this case, their effectiveness will be a measure of whether or not they contribute to the Transformation of the system.

I find elegance is often difficult to specify in advance and always difficult to measure. It is, nonetheless, worth considering what would constitute elegance and how you would recognise it. It may, for example be worth considering *who* would find it elegant. Whose opinion will you value? The Owners[8], perhaps? Or perhaps the quiet satisfaction of the Actors? Customers are usually too interested in the output of the Transformation to concern themselves with the elegance of its production. When I planned this book, I realised I would need some critical readers to comment on early drafts so that I could redraft before handing the manuscript to the publisher. I took it as an elegance criterion of my 'planning the book' system that I had enough critical readers without needing to ask anyone. As I described my plans to friends and colleagues, some volunteered to be critical readers.

Finally, ethicality. As before, the first question to ask is about ethicality itself in relationship to the system or the planned action. Ask, 'What would I (or a Guardian) need to see in order to say this system or action was ethical?'. This question is fundamentally about personal values – the province of ethics rather than of morals[9]. Ethics is a huge subject and well beyond the scope of this book. In working with systems ideas, however, I have reached the conclusion that while I *aspire to be* ethical in my practice, it is not for me to claim *to be* ethical. Ethicality seems to make more sense as an emergent property of a relationship between me and people experiencing my behaviour. It is for other people, observing me, to say whether I am ethical. All I can say is that I am trying to be ethical. This is, in part, why Guardians appear in the TWO CAGES criteria for a system definition. Guardians observe the system and notice unintended consequences – including the ways in which the system is experienced as unethical.

Once you decide on ethical values for the system, ethical standards are surprisingly easy to measure. Much has been learned from the new field of ethical monitoring: the process by which enterprises claim to be ethical in their operations. You may choose to monitor progress on, for example, eliminating exploitation from the supply chain, sourcing from fair-trade accredited suppliers, affirmative action and staff diversity, reducing the system's CO_2 footprint or being polite to customers. These measures do not guarantee ethicality but they monitor progress towards standards that express your values. Be careful that 'improving ethical standards' is separate from the transformation. The point is for the system to operate ethically, rather than be a system to improve ethicality.

Choosing the 5Es

The 5Es are part of the mediation between the HAS diagram, the system definition with its associated TWO CAGES criteria, and the 5Es themselves, which becomes an understandascope for looking at the messy situation to discern opportunities for improving it. I can use any part of the understandascope to test the others and make adjustments to each until they are coherent each with the others. The 5Es challenge me to refine a plan of action by asking how success will be realised at *three* systemic levels. Identifying success criteria for these three levels checks not only that the plan will do what it is supposed to do, but will do it efficiently and, perhaps even more importantly, is the right thing to do. It is an insurance against the danger identified by Russ Ackoff[10] of 'doing the wrong thing righter'.

Using the 3Es and 5Es with others

Participants in workshops have found the 3Es exceptionally useful. Stories began to emerge of unexpected usefulness when people negotiated tasks with senior executives. The 3Es are relatively easy to carry in one's head and so, in the course of conversations about upcoming projects or tasks, people were able to frame questions about efficacy, efficiency and effectiveness without extensive note-taking or feats of memory. They simply asked about what would be recognised as success.

About efficacy	'You have asked me (or my team) to undertake <task>, what would you need to see in order to say we were doing it successfully?'
About effectiveness	'What does this <task> need to fit in with? and then 'What would you need to see in order to say <our task> had contributed effectively to <higher-level task>?

People rarely found it necessary to ask about efficiency. The advantage, they said, of the 3Es idea was that they could ask questions of clarification without appearing to interrogate the executive. The questions supported the executive in being more explicit about what they needed.

Bosses also found it useful when explaining a task or project to their own staff. Firstly, it enabled them to be clear about what they wanted and secondly it clarified communication with the people who would actually do the job.

Insight and the 3Es

I was working with a large organisation to develop its capability for systems thinking. I felt there was lot at stake for me personally, not least because of my identification with systems thinking. It was not clear what was needed or how it should be done but finding out was part of the project. In many ways, it was a messy situation, although few in the organisation were prepared to acknowledge it. I failed to ask the right questions about what success would look like to the key stakeholders. I was simply told to 'give us the numbers to prove it's working'. As tensions began to surface about what was wanted, I began to think seriously about how I would recognise success and demonstrate it to the project sponsors.

Thinking about success in terms of the 3Es, it seemed the request for numbers arose from a need to demonstrate activity – in other words, it seemed to be about efficacy. I kept a record of the numbers of people who had engaged in different ways with the project, the numbers of requests for help I received, and the number of workshops or similar engagements I was involved with. The numbers seemed acceptable and the project was judged a success. I was far from convinced. I wanted to make a difference to the organisation and its staff so I was interested in *effectiveness*. I also wanted, in the spirit of systems thinking, to extend the sponsors' conception of success beyond simple efficacy. Finding a way to measure how people were using systems thinking seemed tricky. If people find systems thinking useful, they use it without noticing. It becomes a natural way of doing things and they do not attribute their improved performance to systems thinking. None of this would be easy to measure. Then I noticed that people were engaging with systems thinking because of recommendations by previous participants. People were seeking to develop their own skills because they saw the difference it made to other people. Third-party recommendations became my measure of effectiveness.

Efficiency was a little trickier. I had a tight budget and few resources. Efficiency would involve creating the maximum benefit from the few resources I had. I decided I would have to focus my efforts on where it would have maximum impact and influence. I could not measure efficiency directly but I had a strategy for being efficient.

SOME EXAMPLES OF 3ES CRITERIA

In each of the following examples, notice how your understanding of the system, and what it is doing, is enhanced.

A system to cut 20 per cent from public expenditure by means of passing much service provision to the private sector in order to contribute to reducing the national debt.

	Indicator	Questions to answer
Efficacy	measure public expenditure	Is it reduced?
Efficiency	measure the number of services passed to the private sector	Are enough services being transferred?
		Is it happening quickly enough?
Effectiveness	measure the national debt	Is it reduced?

A system to engage in conversation with local Afghani villagers by means of teaching selected soldiers conversational Pashto, in order to contribute to better understanding of local concerns.

	Indicator	**Questions to answer**
Efficacy	measure number of face-to-face conversations between villagers and soldiers	Is it increasing?
Efficiency	record number of soldiers able to reach conversational standard in Pashto	Can enough soldiers reach conversational standard to make a difference?
		Does this improve on using English-speaking Pashtuns?
	measure cost per soldier of reaching conversational standard in Pashto	Is this good value for money?
	measure hours per soldier to reach conversational standard in Pashto	Is this good value for time?
Effectiveness	ask senior officers to rate their understanding of local concerns	Is it improved?
	ask villagers to rate their perception of allied forces' understanding of their concerns	Is it improved?

Notes, explorations and resources for Chapter 15

1   *Ned Miller*

Ned Miller is a country singer and songwriter. His song *Do What You Do Do, Well* was an international hit. Capitol Records released it on the album *The Best of Ned Miller* in 1965.

2   *Transformation*

Chapter 8 discusses the idea of transformation: what the system does. A system's transformation expresses, in verb form, what the system does when it transforms something in one state into the same thing in another state. Thus a system that transforms a rough diamond into a cut diamond is characterised by its transformation – cutting.

3   *The origins of the 3Es*

See Note 3 in Chapter 17.

4   *Human-activity system diagram*

See Chapter 14.

5   *System definitions*

For a discussion of system definitions and their associated TWO CAGES criteria, see Chapter 13.

6   *Checkland on monitoring and control*

See Note 3 in Chapter 17.

7   *Environmental constraints*

Environmental constraints form part of the system definition as one element of the TWO CAGES criteria. See Chapter 13.

8   *Owners, Customers, Actors and Guardians*

Owners, Customers, Actors and Guardians are all people in relation to a relevant system defined by a system definition captured by the TWO CAGES criteria. See Chapter 13.

9   *Ethics and Morals*

See Note 13 of Chapter 5.

10   *Doing the wrong thing righter*

See Note 2 of Chapter 1.

Part 4: Inquiring through action

In the final part of the book, I invite you to review the tools and techniques of previous chapters and to see how linking them can create synergies and additional value.

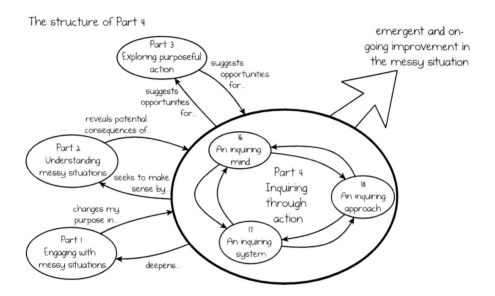

In systems thinking, action is enfolded in inquiry and is not the culmination of the inquiry process but a part of it, so that improvement in the messy situation is an emergent property of the inquiry system. This part of the book sweeps in all the previous parts of the book by exploring the stance of the systems thinker themselves (Chapter 16) and the system of inquiry that provides a model for inquiry in this book (Chapter 17). Finally, it summarises the characteristics of systems thinking itself by asking some questions about it (Chapter 18).

In this part of the book, Chapter 16 explores the systems thinker through the lens of some characteristic stances and habits. Chapter 17 looks at systems methodologies as systems for inquiring into how to improve a messy situation, bringing together many of the ideas introduced earlier in the book. Chapter 18 concludes and summarises the book by bringing together some questions frequently asked about systems thinking.

CHAPTER 16

An inquiring mind

> To the extent that philosophical positions both confuse us and close
> doors to further inquiry, they are likely to be wrong.
> Edward O. Wilson[1], biologist (b. 1929)

Using systems ideas and systems tools, techniques and approaches does not
make someone a systems thinker. On the other hand, it is almost impossible to
define a systems thinker. A systems thinker, I believe, has some characteristic
habits that I can attribute to a genuinely systemic way of thinking about messy
situations. I infer from these habits that the systems thinker sees and thinks
about the world in a particular way. Figure 16.1 indicates some of these habits.

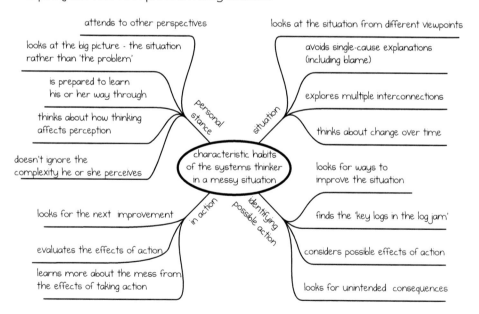

Figure 16.1 *Characteristic habits of systems thinkers indicate their thinking style. A systems
thinker adopts a particular stance in relation to a mess, addresses the situation differently, identifies
possible action in a particular way and, even in taking action, is learning more about the situation.*

I want to examine the characteristics of a systems thinker through four lenses: enthusiasm, humility, curiosity and respect.

ENTHUSIASM

One magic ingredient makes it possible to achieve much. Obstacles can be overcome, the reluctant engaged, despondency banished and energy continually renewed. The magic ingredient is, of course, enthusiasm. The etymology of *enthusiasm* is illuminating. It comes from the Ancient Greek *en theos*, having a god inside, and then *enthousiázien*, to be inspired by a god.

> *Nothing great was ever achieved without enthusiasm.*
> Ralph Waldo Emerson[2] (1803 – 1882)

If Emerson's dictum is true, then an enthusiasm check might be in order before taking action in a messy situation. Here are some questions for checking that you have enough enthusiasm for the challenges of creating change in a messy situation.

- Are you enthusiastic about acting to improve the messy situation? Enthusiasm is likely to come from two directions: enthusiasm for improving the situation and enthusiasm for the action you have decided on. Which of these is strongest for you, in this context?

- If you have more enthusiasm about taking a particular course of action than for improving the situation, are you the right person to initiate the changes you have identified?

- If you have less enthusiasm for the particular course of action you have chosen:

  o is this symptomatic of insufficient planning?

  o have you also given appropriate thought to the process of engaging other people?

  o is the change you wish to make radical enough? If not, then develop more radical system definitions and human-activity system (HAS) diagrams[3].

  o do you need to fill out your understanding of the action you have chosen?

     o   have you assembled the right resources?

     o   are other people willing and able to play their part?

- What are the risks inherent in the changes you propose?
  If you have not already done so, now is a good time to itemise risks.
  The systems-thinking ideas already described should have alerted you
  to some of the potential pitfalls but, in a messy situation, unforeseen
  consequences may still emerge. Unless you identify the things you
  fear, they can undermine your enthusiasm. Expect the unexpected and
  take steps to minimise the impact by providing yourself with support.
  Someone with whom to talk things through, safety nets and long-term
  recovery plans may all help to build your enthusiasm.

- What will life be like when the messy situation is no longer a big
  worry?
  Sometimes 'owning' a big insoluble problem is almost addictive. It
  provides an excuse for putting off other tasks and a blame story[4].

Taking action to improve a messy situation may not be unconfined joy but
enthusiasm can be a powerful indicator. Watching your own and other people's
level of enthusiasm can alert you to things going wrong, emerging worries or
a need to change direction. Changes in enthusiasm provide feedback before
people are able to articulate, even to themselves, a sense that things are not as
they should be: so enthusiasm becomes an early and sensitive form of feedback.

HUMILITY

It seems to me that systems thinkers need a certain humility. Or, perhaps more
precisely, I often observe that those who struggle to grasp systems ideas are
frequently unwilling to acknowledge that they 'don't know' in the encounter
with a mess. They seem to prefer the false certainty of 'knowing what they are
doing' and what the situation is 'really like' to the open-minded receptiveness
that only comes with recognising uncertainty and incomprehensible complexity.
False certainty is one way of ignoring a mess.

If I discipline myself not to pretend to have more certainty that I do, then I can
develop a tolerance for ambiguity that opens me to other perspectives and to
new insights. Often, of course, the frustrations of trying to deal with a mess
strip away any illusions. Indeed, Marcia Salner[5] has concluded that learners

only begin to grasp systems thinking when they encounter a situation that frustrates all their previous problem-solving strategies. When I engage with other people's messy issues in a consultancy context, I always have to pass through a panicky period where I feel I have nothing to offer, am out of my depth and that the situation is too complex to be improved. I have learned that this is an important part of my engagement. It strips away certainty and creates a space for real understanding to develop. ('Trusting the process' of systems thinking usually leads to a satisfactory outcome and mitigates the fear.)

Humility is about recognising need – for other perspectives, for other knowledge and understanding, and for more engagement with understanding the situation. Humility thus turns to respectful curiosity.

CURIOSITY

Purposeful and respectful curiosity is more than accumulating facts. In a messy situation, the purpose of inquiry is always to understand more about how elements of the situation are connected and how they influence each other; building different perspectives and viewpoints into a more holistic picture. Making sense of all of these, using various understandascopes, is at least as important as collecting facts.

> *Learning is the only thing the mind never exhausts, never fears,*
> *and never regrets.*
>   Leonardo da Vinci, all-round renaissance genius, (1452 – 1519)

In this quote, Leonardo seems to connect learning and enthusiasm. In systems-thinking terms, taking action in a messy situation is never an end in itself. In acting *to improve* the situation, I am also *finding out how to improve* the situation. I keep my eyes open for clues about additional routes to improvement, about the unintended consequences of what I am doing and about the mess itself. One of the biggest mistakes is 'making a plan and sticking to it'. This is not to say that there should be no plan, nor any commitment to it. Instead, the plan should be at the level of learning the way forward through vigilance, investigation and testing. The model here is the steersman[6] who steers the ship through rocks, adjusting the direction continuously in response to eddies and currents. System definitions and human-activity system diagrams are not The Plan but devices for structuring discussions about feasible changes, and understandascopes for viewing unfolding events. 'When the facts change, I change my mind[7].'

Changing one's mind means that some uncertainty is inevitable but certainty comes instead from the process of continuous review and deliberation.

RESPECT

Accessing other perspectives will almost certainly involve other people. They will have their own preferred outcomes, their own ideas about what to do, and their unique viewpoint. Gaining access to this wealth of knowledge, insight and wisdom requires more of the systems thinker than a commitment to working with multiple perspectives. Unless people experience my respect, then whatever I access is not their perspective. Why do I believe this? Accessing someone else's perspective involves attempting to appreciate the situation through their eyes. The impossibility of this task does not invalidate the attempt. Part of anyone's perspective is the way they wish to be treated. Treating them with less respect than I would give myself thus prevents my access to their perspective. Respect involves, for example, assuming their wish to be treated as an autonomous individual who holds their opinions and preferences for good reasons. Most other assumptions will reflect stereotypes rather than autonomy as a *legitimate other*[8]. To treat other people simply as sources of other perspectives or understandings is self defeating and a form of social strip-mining that prejudices later cooperation in changing the situation. This precludes such organisational phenomena as *empty consultation* in which a group of people are consulted about change and then find no evidence that their input influenced the outcome. The need for access to other perspectives makes it desirable to work collaboratively to improve messy situations.

However diligently you have worked out the changes you want to make or however robust your system definition and your HAS diagram, it literally makes no sense to claim that you know what to do, if no-one else wants those changes. Ideally, systems thinking is a collaborative venture but must, perforce, often be done alone, especially when mess-avoiding strategies[9] are at work. However, you have no action plan at all unless other people understand it and can accommodate it in their understandings and plans.

People are autonomous and exercise their autonomy in unpredictable ways. Lewis Carroll's *Alice's Adventures in Wonderland*[10] (1864) shows a wonderful example of this. In Figure 16.2, Alice finds herself in a croquet game[11] invited by the imperious Queen of Hearts.

Figure 16.2 *In Tenniel's illustration, Alice prepares to hit the rolled-up hedgehog under her foot while another hedgehog wanders off. The flamingo, whose neck and head are supposed to be the mallet, is more interested in looking at Alice. The croquet lawn is very uneven and balls would roll in all sorts of unintended directions.*

Alice thought she had never seen such a curious croquet-ground in her life: it was all ridges and furrows: the croquet balls were live hedgehogs, and the mallets live flamingos, and the soldiers had to double themselves up and stand on their hands and feet, to make the arches.

The chief difficulty Alice found at first was in managing her flamingo: she succeeded in getting its body tucked away, comfortably enough, under her arm, with its legs hanging down, but generally, just as she had got its neck nicely straightened out, and was going to give the hedgehog a blow with its head, it would twist itself round and look up in her face, with such a puzzled expression that she could not help bursting out laughing; and, when she had got its head down, and was going to begin again, it was very

*provoking to find that the hedgehog had unrolled itself, and was
in the act of crawling away: besides all this, there was generally
a ridge or a furrow in the way wherever she wanted to send the
hedgehog to, and, as the doubled-up soldiers were always getting
up and walking off to other parts of the ground, Alice soon came to
the conclusion that it was a very difficult game indeed.*

*The players all played at once, without waiting for turns,
quarrelling all the while, and fighting for the hedgehogs; and in
a very short time the Queen was in a furious passion, and went
stamping about, and· shouting, "Off with his head!" or "Off with her
head!" about once in a minute.*

People (and flamingos and hedgehogs) cannot be moved around like chess
pieces as Alice's experience clearly demonstrates. Plans that neglect the
complexities of real people, their interests, diverse motivations and divergent
visions of what is needed, rarely work as predicted, especially in messy
situations. Managers have a choice[12]. Some managers assume people are
reluctant workers and must be compelled by a mixture of sanctions and
incentives to do the job. A more effective management style seeks to engage
workers with the task. People, whether employees, colleagues or allies, are
more effective in creating change if they acquire an interest in that change. One
of the most powerful ways of acquiring a stake in change is contributing to the
change process, even if that contribution is very small. In Ellen Langer's[13] classic
experiment, test subjects bought $1 tickets for a fictitious lottery. Experimenters
then offered them the opportunity to trade their ticket. Those who had chosen
their own ticket – decorated with the badges of a football team – wanted, on
average, $8.57 for their ticket. Those who had simply received a random ticket
wanted only $1.96. The exercise of choice had given them a stake in the outcome
that was more valuable than an equal chance in a $50 lottery prize. I tell this
story, not to demonstrate the 'illusion of control' but to show how exercising
choice creates commitment to the outcome of an event.

Respect means it is your responsibility to explain, not other people's to strain
to understand. Engaging others in creating change requires tact and patience,
separating explanation from persuasion. Even so, in a messy situation, people
will often feel stressed and suspicious. They too experience bewilderment
in confronting a mess they would prefer to ignore. However carefully you
explain, there is a risk that people will misunderstand and then disagree with
their own misunderstandings. If this happens, do not argue. Ask people to
explain what they have understood from your proposal and then correct any
misunderstanding, without judgement. You can eliminate many details and
resolve disagreements by creating common understanding.

The most fundamental disagreements usually cluster around *Weltanschauungen*. Each person's *Weltanschauung* reflects closely held values. Arguing with someone's values and principles is unlikely to effect change and, because values are personal and precious, argument risks being perceived as an attack. Persuasion is a tricky path. The key to success is searching for *accommodation* rather than consensus. In this context, accommodation is participants' tacit give-and-take agreement to changes that don't prejudice their own interests. Accommodations create more room for manoeuvre. Participants gain from improvements elsewhere, even if indirectly, and negotiate improvement of their own situation as new opportunities arise.

A key skill for reaching accommodations is the ability to separate What, How and Why[14]. For example, people will often object to a *What* because they cannot see *How* it might be achieved.

| Proposer: | Extended warehouse loading bays would allow us to accept 42-tonne trucks. It would dramatically improve our delivery times to retailers. |
| Warehouse Manager: | We cannot do that because if we extend our bays there will be insufficient room for trucks to turn around. |

This very typical exchange highlights some of the skills needed to create acceptance of change. The proposal (accepting 42-tonne trucks) elicits a very typical response – a reason why we cannot or should not do it. The need to allow for trucks turning is an important consideration but it relates to *how* we would accept 42-tonne trucks, not *whether* we should. The proposer on this occasion, recognised the usefulness of the contribution without accepting it as a reason for not pursuing the proposal.

| Proposer: | Thank you. We will have to look into how we make room for trucks to turn around. |

A quick conversation with the warehouse manager established that accepting 42-tonne trucks would allow for fewer loading bays while still achieving improved delivery times. Knocking out some of the loading bays created turning space for larger trucks *and* created space for extending the small-packages area. Ideally, stakeholders should be involved in conversations throughout the process of identifying change.

Enthusiasm cannot be given to someone. It must be *brought forth*. Coercion is disrespectful and kills enthusiasm. If other people are unable to respond with enthusiasm, your ideas may be less powerful that you imagined. If enthusiasm is not evident, then suggest something else. I suggest, too, that courses of action that diminish rather than increase the options available to others, might be considered unethical. People are most likely to be enthusiastic if they perceive that their interests have been recognised, valued and accommodated. If they have contributed insights from their own learning, they will be energised and committed.

All of this suggests that the very best outcomes occur when people work together. Collective diagramming, sharing knowledge and information, and the collective creation of system definitions can all be shared activities. HAS diagramming is trickier, though possible, but diagrams created by one person from collectively constructed system definitions seem to elicit ready agreement.

NOTES, RESOURCES AND EXPLORATIONS FOR CHAPTER 16

1   *Edward Wilson*

Wilson's influence extends far beyond his groundbreaking studies of ant behaviour that led to the ideas of sociobiology, a term coined by him. He showed that much ant behaviour made sense only if genes were the basic unit of survival rather than the ant itself. Wilson was thus at the centre of the controversy that surrounded the emergence of sociobiology in the 1980s and 1990s. Wilson's work also draws attention to evolution as an *epic*, an 'intrinsically ennobling' grand narrative in which humans are heroes of their own narrative but only in relationship to a much bigger cosmological story. Edward Wilson is also an ecologist and conservationist.

Wilson, E. O. (2006). *Nature Revealed: Selected Writings, 1949-2006*. Baltimore, MD: The Johns Hopkins University Press.

2   *Ralph Waldo Emerson*

The quotation comes from Emerson's 1941 essay on *Circles*. Emerson, the American essayist, is perhaps one of the best loved thinkers of the nineteenth century. You can find the full text of *Circles* online.

3   *System definitions and human-activity system diagrams*
See Chapters 13 and 14.

4   *Blame Stories*
See Chapter 5.

5   *Marcia Salner*

Salner describes an *epistemological crisis* that learners encounter when they cannot resolve a messy situation. This is often the point in their encounter with systems thinking when they begin to 'get it'.

Salner, M. (1986). Adult cognitive and epistemological development in systems education. *Systems Research and Behavioral Science, 3*(4), 225-232.

6   *The steersman*

In Ancient Greek, this is the *kubernetes*, the pilot. This is the derivation of *cybernetics*. Cybernetics is the study of adjusting the state of a something to fluctuations in its environment, also known as *feedback*. For example, humans adjust their metabolisms to external temperature in order to maintain their body temperature within very narrow limits. Turbines for electricity generation automatically regulate their speed to match the frequency of the electricity grid (60 cycles per second in North America and northern South America, 50 cycles per second elsewhere).

The word was first used by André-Marie Ampère (1775 – 1836), after whom the measure of electrical current is named. The French mathematician, scientist and polymath used the term *cybernétique* to refer to a theory of government. *Cybernetics* entered common usage in 1948, coined by Norbert Wiener (1894 –

1964), the American mathematician, who seemed to be ignorant of Ampère's usage. *Cyber-* has since become a generalised prefix denoting 'something to do with computers' although it originally referred to the ways that computers can respond to changing conditions in automated manufacturing. Wiener's work on control and communication laid the foundations for cybernetics and information theory. He was a fascinating man who led an extraordinary life.

Conway, F. & Siegelman, J. (2005). *Dark Hero of the Information Age: In Search of Norbert Wiener – Father of Cybernetics.* New York: Basic Books.

7   *John Maynard Keynes (1883 – 1946)*
See Chapter 7.

8   *The legitimate other*
This term comes from the work of Humberto Maturana. (See Chapter 7 for more on this important thinker's work.)

9   *Mess-avoiding behaviour and strategies*
See Chapter 1.

10   *Lewis Carroll's 'Alice in Wonderland'*
Lewis Carroll was the pseudonym of Charles Dodgson (1832 – 1898), an English clergyman who lived in Oxford. He was a mathematician and photographer but is chiefly remembered for *Alice's Adventures in Wonderland* (usually known as *Alice in Wonderland*) and *Alice Through the Looking Glass*. Both are unsettling stories of Alice's experiences in fantasy dream worlds. They draw on images taken from playing cards and from chess respectively. Although much loved, not least by adults, some children find them too weird to be enjoyable. John Tenniel (1820 – 1914) illustrated the original books. He also drew political cartoons for the satirical *Punch* magazine.

There is far more to the Alice books than meets the eye. I suggest Martin Gardner's *Annotated Alice*, which contains the full text of the Alice books with Tenniel's illustrations, annotated by Gardner to reveal the depth of Lewis Carroll's extraordinary stories.

Gardner, M. (Ed.). (1965). *The Annotated Alice:* Alice's Adventures in Wonderland *and* Through the Looking Glass *by Lewis Carroll.* Harmondsworth: Penguin Books.

11   *Croquet*
Croquet is an English lawn game in which players take it in turns to hit wooden balls through a series of arches using mallets. The rules of croquet were formalised in 1856 but are freely adapted to local conditions. Although played in genteel circumstances, croquet is notorious for the vicious competitiveness it brings out in otherwise well-mannered players.

12   *Theory X and Theory Y*
Douglas McGregor (1906 – 1964) identified two contrasting ways of thinking about employees in relationship to their work. In Theory X, employees are assumed to be reluctant, lazy and unmotivated workers whose work must

be closely controlled by their managers through rewards and punishments. At the opposite end of the spectrum, in Theory Y, workers are assumed to be motivated, to have much to contribute and to be willing to do their best. Theory X and Theory Y had their heyday in the 1960s and are now rarely discussed explicitly. However, the underlying ideas are not lost but inform many current management theories.

McGregor, D. (1967). *The Professional Manager*. New York: McGraw-Hill Inc.

Theory X approaches demonstrably produce worse performance than Theory Y approaches. While most managers espouse Theory Y, many nonetheless behave in ways that suggest their theory-in-use is Theory X. Argyris and Schön have written much about espoused theory and theory-in-use and provide food for thought for systems thinkers interested in thinking about their own thinking.

Argyris, C. & Schön, D. A. (1974). *Theory in practice: Increasing professional effectiveness*. San Francisco: Jossey-Bass.

13   *The Illusion of Control*

Langer has lately become famous for her work on aging but her earlier work on the illusion of control set her on a career path that is recognised as both brilliant and groundbreaking. She is a professor of Psychology at Harvard.

Langer, E. J. (1975). The Illusion of Control. *Journal of Personality and Social Psychology, 32*(2), 311-328.

14   *What, How and Why*

See Chapter 13.

CHAPTER 17

An inquiring system

It's what it isn't that makes it what it is[1]

Advertising slogan, Guernsey Tourist Board, 1997

Most of the chapters in this book describe systems ideas that you can use independently of one another. Using them has a double effect: they help you work out what to do to improve a messy situation and they help you acquire the ability to see the world in terms of connections and interactions, as well as in terms of entities. This, and the ability to move freely between holistic and detailed views, and to work with many different perspectives, are the hallmarks of a skilled systems thinker.

In this chapter, I want to explore putting together the ideas in this book in particular ways. Thoughtful and purposeful assembly of a sequence of systems tools constitutes a *methodology*. The structure of this book reflects a prototype methodology, a system of connected activities for inquiring into how to improve a messy situation. In this inquiring system, you first engage with a mess by considering it as a whole, recognising a variety of perspectives as well as your own. Then you seek a deeper understanding of the mess by looking for elements of systemicity within it and by diagramming it. From these two phases, possible ideas-for-improvement begin to emerge. In the next phase, these ideas can be further articulated either as possible plans-for-improvement or as understandascopes for discovering other possible actions-for-improvement.

Out of this prototypical methodology, I can conceive a more specific inquiring system which might be carried out as follows:

1. Recognise messiness for what it is – something that you can choose to deal with as messiness or that you can choose to ignore.

2. Engage with the situation by finding out everything you can about it, recognising and exploring other perspectives and exploring holistic as well as detailed views.

3. Represent the situation as richly as possible using a rich picture: this helps to escape from traps set by prejudging what the problem 'really is'.

4.   Deepen your understanding of the situation by:

- exploring different ways of thinking about it using systems maps, influence diagrams or both

- exploring your own role in the mess by exploring your own perspective and complexities, noting any possible traps you may have fallen into

- noticing that other people in the situation have similar complexities and have good reasons for saying what they say and doing what they do

- diagnosing it by drawing multiple-cause diagrams

- making notes of ideas-for-action to think about later, as your understanding of the situation deepens.

5.   Developing ideas-for-action using system definitions, with their associated TWO CAGES criteria, and HAS diagrams. These tools can be used to refine the idea-for-action or as understandascopes for looking at the messy situation in order to discern other possible ideas-for-action to discuss and develop. In either case, the ideas-for-action can be further refined, or the understandascope more finely focused, by considering how you will know that the action is working at three different systemic levels.

6.   Working with others to establish a plan-for-action, enacting it and then, recognising the situation is now different, returning to Stage 2 (or perhaps Stage 1) of the methodology to seek further improvements.

This inquiring system is only one way to work out how to improve a situation. You might develop one of your own with practice - I don't believe that what works well for me will always work well for you. Observe what works well for you, your situations and your skills, and then, once you work out why it works for you, you have a methodology.

If a system for inquiring into how to improve a mess is to have learning as an emergent property, then it would be foolish to enact it by slavishly following each stage step-by-step. Any sequential presentation disguises the importance of *iteration*. At each stage, it may be necessary to re-do, amend or refine any of the preceding stages so that, while jumping forwards is rarely sensible, jumping back is not only sensible but essential as developing understanding demands it. As with all systems thinking, a good 'system for inquiring into how to improve a mess' does not tell you what to do but instead helps you find out. It is not a simple step-by-step algorithm[2] that delivers answers for improving the situation. 'Knowing how to find out' rather than 'knowing how ...' becomes the basis of the systems thinker's expertise.

A number of different methodologies have emerged in systems thinking. Perhaps the best articulated and pre-eminent is Soft Systems Methodology[3] (SSM). SSM, itself a system for inquiring into improving a situation, inspired many of this book's ideas – although the approaches used in SSM are used differently here. SSM has been a major source of inspiration for much of my own systems practice.

Notes, resources and explorations for Chapter 17

1   *It's what it isn't that makes it what it is*

This slogan has been around for a while in the advertising industry. It was used by the Guernsey Tourist Board ('Guernsey: it's what it isn't that makes it what it is') in 1997.

2   *Algorithms*

Algorithms are clearly defined, step-by-step procedures for solving problems. They are used in mathematics and computing for such tasks as sorting random words into alphabetical order. Algorithms can be expressed formally, allowing computers to perform the necessary steps, following programming code. They are, in fact, systems of activities for carrying out routine tasks. David Harrell has written a wonderful book that, although not for the novice, explains the principles of computer algorithms.

Algorithms remind me how very sophisticated the human brain is. It is unlikely that the human brain uses the same kind of algorithms as a computer but the extent and complexity of, for example, an algorithm for selecting the best match for paint, using manufacturers' colour sample cards, is cause for wonder when the human brain seems to complete this task so easily.

Algorithms are named after Abu Ja'far Muhammad ibn Musa al-Khwārizmī (c. 780 – c. 850), one the earliest scholars of the Golden Age of Islamic science. Al-Khwārizmī was a Persian from Khwārizm, in what is now Uzbekistan. He was a geographer, astronomer and mathematician. Latin translations of his work brought the decimal point to European mathematics from India. His book *Kitab al-Jebr* gave us algebra, as well as a name for it. In *Kitab al-Jebr*, Al-Khwārizmī gave us an algorithm for solving quadratic and other equations. Jim Al-Khalili's excellent book has more about Al-Khwārizmī and the remarkable flowering of science in Baghdad.

Al-Khalili, J. (2010). *Pathfinders: The Golden Age of Arabic Science*. London: Allen Lane.

Harel, D. (2004). *Algorithmics: the Spirit of Computing* (3rd ed.). Reading, NJ: Addison Wesley.

3   *Soft Systems Methodology*

SSM emerged out of engagement – by Peter Checkland, his colleagues and students – with 'real-life' messes over a period of more than 30 years. Its development is recorded in the 1991 edition of *Systems Thinking, Systems Practice* (see below).

SSM is a system of interconnected activities which have the emergent property of learning through exploration and action-to-improve. It has rigorous theoretical underpinnings.

SSM takes practice and a clear understanding of its theory but once mastered, even when I have no idea what to do in a particular messy situation, I can trust the process to enable me to move forward.

Rich pictures came into systems thinking through SSM. Checkland and Scholes (see below) give a definitive account of their use in SSM and more recently Checkland and Poulter have added more detail.

The ITO model, systems definitions, HAS diagrams and the 5Es in Part 3 are used in this book for testing and articulating ideas. They are similar in construction to root definitions, conceptual models and the 3Es and 5Es measures of performance in SSM but their use here is different from their use in SSM. I use the terminology *system definition* and *human-activity-system diagram* to distinguish between the uses I describe here and their use in SSM.

SSM is a powerful methodology. If you want to find out more about it, there is plenty of information available but SSM has suffered from more than its fair share of misunderstandings and misinformation. I suggest the books of Peter Checkland and his immediate colleagues. Good places to start are:

Checkland, P. & Scholes, J. (1999). *Soft Systems Methodology in Action*. Chichester: John Wiley & Sons.

Checkland, P. and Poulter, J. (2006). *Learning for Action*. Chichester: John Wiley & Sons.

The classic text *Systems Thinking, Systems Practice* was reissued in 1999 with a 30-year retrospective.

Checkland, P. B. (1999). *Systems Thinking, Systems Practice*. Chichester: John Wiley & Sons.

If you are particularly interested in Information Systems, the application of SSM to this frequently messy field is explored in:

Checkland, P. and Holwell, S. (1998). *Information, Systems and Information Systems: Making Sense of the Field*. Chichester: John Wiley & Sons.

CHAPTER 18

An inquiring approach

*I would like to beg of you, dear friend, as well as I can, to be patient
with all that is unresolved in your heart. And try to love the questions
themselves. Do not seek for the answers that cannot be given. [...]
And the point is to live everything, live the questions now [...]*
Rainer Maria Rilke[1], poet (1875 – 1926)

When I run systems-thinking workshops, I set aside time at the end for
participants' questions and for comparing notes and experiences. So here,
towards the end of the book, this chapter addresses some of the questions that
come up about systems thinking and about managing messy situations.

Some questions are asked regularly, others take me by surprise. Participants
work with their own messes throughout the workshop so, by the time we get
to the questions and reflections session, participants themselves have some
experience of systems thinking and often provide new and exciting insights as
we discuss the questions. In many ways, I hope I have already answered some
of the questions but I hope to crystallise the ideas, perhaps in a slightly different
form, in this chapter. In the spirit of developing your own understanding, you
may wish to think about your own answers to the questions.

HOW DO YOU DEFINE SYSTEMS THINKING?

I am never very comfortable with this question. It seems to imply that one
might stick a probe into someone's thoughts, to see whether their thinking
met the definition of systems thinking. Systems thinking is a multifaceted
phenomenon and so I am inclined to say, 'I recognise it when I experience it'.
The question is a reasonable one nonetheless and deserves a more considered
answer. One answer is represented by Figure 16.1 but I cannot claim reliability
in all these habits myself.

Picture one of many social gatherings. I find myself in conversation with a stranger. Often the conversation, after the usual pleasantries, goes something like this:

Stranger: And what do you do?

Me: I teach / write about / practise systems

Stranger: Oh! That's something to do with computers isn't it?

Me: Well, not really. (I become tongue-tied because I am reluctant to bore my new acquaintance by offering a full account of what I think systems thinking is. I start scanning the social horizon for an escape.)

I found myself in this conversation trap more often than was comfortable and could not discover a simple way of explaining systems thinking to meet the need of social small talk (which I'm not very good at anyway).

How could I explain systems thinking simply? I owe my answer to Open University students who attended the week-long Systems Summer Schools. It often fell to me to give the valedictory lecture but I came to believe that, after a week of intense activity and learning, I could add very little to students' understanding of systems thinking at the last moment. Instead, I presented them with the scenario I have just given you and asked them to come up with a suitable answer. Lecture halls are not good places for group discussions but, despite the difficulties, the conversation was always animated. No-one ever came up with a ready-made answer but we often converged, after an hour's intense discussion, on something like this:

> *Systems thinking is a style of thinking that attends as much to the connections between things as to the things themselves, and to the connections between things and their wider context, and looks at things and their connections from more than one perspective.*

There may be more rigorous definitions but this statement seems to capture well the essential qualities of systems thinking. It finished the summer-school week on a high note and met my need for a meaningful account of 'what I do'.

WHAT ARE THE ADVANTAGES OF SYSTEMS THINKING?

In a mess, when you do not know what to do, systems thinking reduces the chances of making things worse. Examples of expensive mistakes are legion. In public life, there are examples of projects that cost many times the original budget because there was no clear and agreed understanding of *What* they were supposed to do and *Why* (see Chapter 13). Often such projects fail to match their contexts or take no heed of the Customers (also in Chapter 13) and their circumstances. It is as if the focus has been exclusively on the *How* with very little attention to *What* and even less to *Why*.

I believe that one of the biggest, though often invisible, advantages of systems thinking is realised through costs avoided by not making expensive mistakes. Even with this huge advantage, it is hard to make a case for systems thinking based on avoiding mistakes: there is no experience of 'what would have happened' against which to measure the advantage.

I make the case for systems thinking by noting the comments of workshop participants who have become systems thinkers.

Most often, people simply say, 'I tried systems-thinking ideas and I was able to …' There is no way of knowing whether or not they could have done whatever it was in some other way. It is not easy to measure the quality of decisions people make in messy situations so we have to rely on the observations of those who know the messy situation the best. There is simply no way of comparing 'outcomes using systems thinking' (which have happened) and 'outcomes without using systems thinking' (which have not). But one of the outcomes of using systems thinking that people consistently report is their belief that they made better decisions and managed their mess 'better'.

Perhaps even more fundamentally, there is evidence that people who have systems-thinking skills will attempt to manage messes rather than ignore them (or make expensive mistakes by treating them as difficulties). One person told me it was a relief not to have to bang her head against the wall of a previously unrecognised mess. 'I now understand why we made so little progress and I'm ready to try something different.' People who were previously trapped, either by the sheer messiness of a messy situation, or by their own thinking (see Chapter 5), report similar relief: 'Suddenly there were all these possibilities I hadn't seen before'.

For many people the issue of perspectives moved from being a peripheral to a fundamental issue. One person said, 'Once I realised that other perspectives can reveal other options, I shadowed the customer process. I should be embarrassed

I didn't do it before. It was so obvious how we could improve things.' Finally, people report that systems thinking makes it easier to run their teams. It provides a framework through which everyone can contribute to the collective understanding of the mess, representing it through diagrams, and formulating possible actions for improving the situations. Diagrams can be a powerful way of sharing understanding and simply establishing *What* the team is doing and *Why*, allows everyone to coordinate their activities. It is elegance[2] in action.

I'm not sure I can count the following observation as an advantage of systems thinking but on numerous occasions, people have remarked that 'systems thinking is fun'. So I simply report it as part of the experience of becoming a systems thinker.

WHAT ARE THE CHARACTERISTICS OF SYSTEMS THINKING AND ITS APPROACH TO A MESS?

The characteristics of systems thinking are what enable me to 'know it when I see it'. This list is what I observe when I believe someone is using systems thinking[3].

- an ability to see parts and whole in relationship to each other and to move between these two views

- a balance between the processes of finding out and conceptualising human-activity systems that create the potential for action

- an ability to abstract from complexity so that organising structures are revealed rather than imposed or assumed

- an ability to balance flexibility and real-world change against the conceptual need for stable system boundaries and parameters

- a command of multiple problem-solving understandascopes as opposed to employing a limited range of uncontextualised algorithms[4]

- an awareness that the map is not the territory; that the systems thinker's understanding is not the same as 'the way it is'

- and an ability to be provisional in the use of models.

In a mess, systems thinking is characterised by five main features, as shown in Figure 18.1.

Characteristics of a systems-thinking approach to managing messy situations

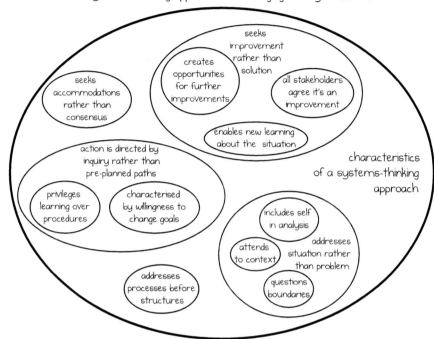

Figure 18.1 *A systems map of some of the characteristics of a systems-thinking approach to a mess.*

Surely improvement is just second best, why can't systems thinking solve a mess?

It is in the nature of a mess to have no single solution. One person's 'solution' may be another's worst-possible outcome. Or, as in the example of caring for my mother, where there was no solution without a major improvement in her health, the solution may lie in an 'if only ...' realm beyond human reach.

Systems thinking does not falter when there is no solution. It is profoundly realistic and searches instead for improvement in the overall situation. My experience has often been that the shifts that occur as the first improvement is implemented often result in self-sustaining improvement. Teams work better as a result of their participation in a learning process, there is clarity about what to do and why, and people understand much more about the situation. This frees up more time, energy and enthusiasm for improving another part of the mess.

IS SYSTEMS THINKING JUST FOR MESSES?

No. I chose to focus on messes in this book because it provides a strong framework for exploring a wide range of issues.

I should perhaps say first that I have mostly assumed, and have perhaps allowed you to assume, that messes are always nasty. Admittedly, most of my experience has been concerned with nasty messes but consider the situation if you were to win € 40 million on the lottery. I imagine most people would experience this eventuality as A Good Thing. But how do you decide what to do with all that money? As soon as you start considering the impact on family, friends, job, lifestyle and where you want to live, then the choices all begin to look messy. Indeed, there is evidence that key personal relationships are frequently, and profoundly, damaged by very large lottery wins. Messy situations can arise when a multiplicity of opportunities presents itself.

Beyond messes, systems thinking is used in, for example, ecology, climate science, strategy, environmental science, social science, medicine, family therapy, systems engineering and policy formation[5]. In such fields, the traditional, reductionist approach only shows part of the picture. Complex fields of inquiry require a holistic approach to parallel the reductionism, and an ability to move between the two.

WHY ISN'T SYSTEMS THINKING MORE WIDELY USED?

This question has troubled me for some time[6]. Figure 18.2 is an attempt to assemble what I have learned through reflecting on my engagements with senior managers.

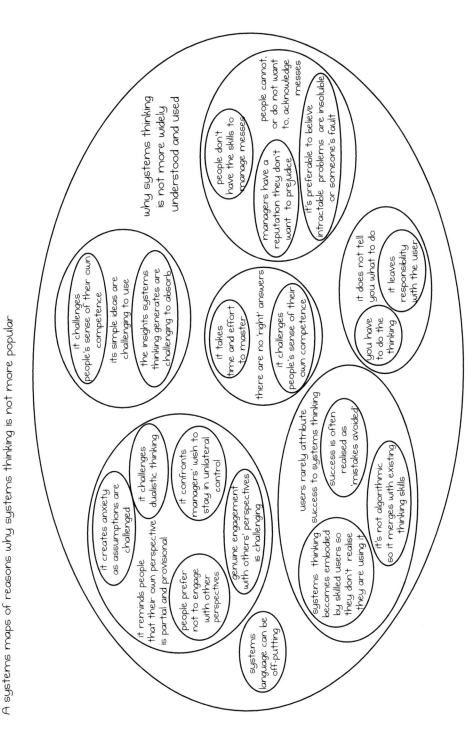

A systems maps of reasons why systems thinking is not more popular

why systems thinking
is not more widely
understood and used

people don't
have the skills to
manage messes

people cannot,
or do not want
to, acknowledge
messes

managers have a
reputation they don't
want to prejudice

it's preferable to believe
intractable problems are insoluble
or someone's fault

it challenges
people's sense of their own
competence

its simple ideas are
challenging to use

the insights systems
thinking generates are
challenging to absorb

it takes
time and effort
to master

there are no 'right' answers

it challenges
people's sense of their
own competence

it does not tell
you what to do

it leaves
responsibility
with the user

you have
to do the
thinking

it creates anxiety
as assumptions are
challenged

it challenges
dualistic thinking

it confronts
managers' wish to
stay in unilateral
control

it reminds people
that their own perspective
is partial and provisional

people prefer
not to engage
with other
perspectives

genuine engagement
with others' perspectives
is challenging

users rarely attribute
success to systems thinking

success is often
realised as 'mistakes avoided'

systems thinking
becomes embodied
by skilled users so
they don't realise
they are using it

it's not algorithmic
so it merges with existing
thinking skills

systems
language can be
off-putting

Figure 18.2 *Some possible reasons why senior managers are reluctant to engage with systems thinking.*

It is tempting to believe that people do not engage with systems thinking because there is something wrong *with them*. This would be falling into a trap. Another way of looking at this problem is to see that the community of systems thinkers, especially those of us who have a professional responsibility to teach and practise it, has failed to explain systems thinking well enough. If this is the case (and I suspect it is), then it is a lamentable failing at a time when strategists, politicians, executives and environmentalists are calling for systemic approaches to managing human affairs in an unjust world facing environmental catastrophe. This book is part of my contribution to putting this right.

IS SYSTEMS THINKING JUST FOR CONSULTANTS?

Absolutely not. There are business and management consultants who use systems thinking as part of their practice but many systems thinkers are simply using systems thinking to do whatever they do in the light of systems thinking. I believe systems thinking is helpful to *anyone* who manages messy situations, whether professionally or not.

IS THERE A FIXED ORDER FOR DOING THINGS?

No, in the sense that there is no procedure that must be followed but *Yes* in the sense that it is sensible to understand as much as possible about the complexity of a situation before taking action that might create unintended and unwanted consequences. The parts of this book suggest a sequence of *Engaging with messy situations* and *Understanding messy situations*, followed by *Exploring purposeful action in messy situations* and *Inquiring through action*. Making appropriate selections of systems-thinking ideas or tools depends on three things: the systems thinker (you), the situation you are dealing with and your role in the situation. There are no 'rules' which say 'in this situation use this tool'. The selection must also depend on the skills and preferences of the practitioner. Of course, that means that having a good range of tools, techniques and ideas that can be used competently and confidently, will increase the chances of getting useful insights. The main criterion for selection is the possibility of helpful insights, so if, after some perseverance, nothing emerges, it may be time to try something else but not, of course, discarding work that might make more sense later.

Notwithstanding the above, systems thinkers may decide to use a methodology such as SSM (see Note 3 in Chapter 17). A systemic methodology is simply a 'learning system' that generates insights by connecting systems-thinking activities in specified ways to create a system that shows emergent learning[7].

HOW WILL I KNOW WHEN I HAVE THE RIGHT ANSWER?

It is a feature of messiness that there are no right answers in a mess.

The question implies a belief that somewhere, undiscovered, there is a right answer waiting to be found. Such an idea makes no sense within the logic of messes. It calls on a philosophy that held sway for generations: that of Plato[8]. For Plato, the muddle of everyday experience hides a world of 'pure forms', uncontaminated by the world of the senses but providing a sort of superstructure for the world we see. In such a world, the pure form of 'the right answer' would correspond to the 'real problem' hidden behind the experience of a mess. For many areas of human inquiry, especially those built on science and mathematics, the notion of the pure form still informs how the inquiry is practised. For example, when I was studying engineering as a student, we were often set questions about, for example, storage tanks and how they should be constructed. To answer such questions, one needed the skill to spot that this was 'really' a question about internal pressures and stresses in the metal. A few equations that connected these 'pure forms' could then be manipulated to find a 'pure-form answer'. There would be a few extra marks for translating that answer back into the context of storage tanks. Platonic problems have answers that can be put at the back of the book so we, or our teacher, can check we have the right answer.

Messes are not like the Platonic problems we are set during most of our education. There are no 'answers at the back of the book' for a mess. It is impossible to discover the 'answers' to a mess. They have to be *invented* from the raw material of our evolving understanding of the mess.

A useful 'answer' is more valuable that a right 'answer'.

WILL SYSTEMS THINKING HELP ME GET MY WAY?

Having 'my way' in mind will stop systems thinking happening at all. A certain amount of modesty is involved in accepting that I do not have everything I need to make a good decision in a mess that involves other people. Systems thinking involves exploring and respecting other perspectives because, pragmatically, it will allow better outcomes for everyone involved. Getting my own way usually results in short-term improvements only or systemic failure.

DOES SYSTEMS THINKING TAKE A LONG TIME TO MASTER?

Yes and No. I have been learning and practising systems thinking for more than 20 years and I often feel I am only skating on the surface of an ocean of possibilities and approaches. So yes, it might take many decades before I mastered it. On the other hand, it does not take long to make a difference.

In the course of teaching systems thinking to beginners, I have seen them making major differences as they became aware of new and better options for managing the situations they found themselves in. For example, one workshop participant was captured by the idea of the 3Es (see Chapter 15). Somehow, the hierarchic structure of 'working well' opened up a world of systems thinking and she was able to arrest the cycle of failure in a software-development enterprise. Not only did the 3Es work well as a tool but somehow they had bounced her into a different way of seeing the world. Even beginners can think differently – better – than before.

Developing your systems-thinking skills and repertoire is nonetheless valuable. When messy problems hit unexpectedly, skilled systems thinkers will respond effectively from a repertoire of well-practised skills. They know what to do, without conscious thought, because their experience has been embodied – literally become part of their body. Practitioners of the martial art of *aikido* repeatedly practise *kihon*, the basics. Even aikido masters return again and again to practising the simplest moves, reconnecting with their breathing, attaining the right attitudes and focus. Such repetition builds 'muscle memory' and the ability to access rapidly the state of mind that leads to a beneficial outcome in *randori*, the circumstances of a real attack. A research colleague[9], drawing on his experience as an aikido practitioner, undertook to improve his systems-thinking skills by practising HAS diagrams daily until he could quickly visualise them well enough to manage disagreements on a software-development team.

How can I learn more about systems thinking?

This is a tricky question to answer because the scene is changing quickly and because searching for 'systems' on the web, for example, will generate all kinds of stuff irrelevant to the question. I suggest searching for 'systems thinking' to avoid all the very generic uses of 'systems'.

Courses

In terms of courses, there are relatively few providers in higher (tertiary) education. The UK Open University and the University of Hull both have long traditions of systems-thinking courses, the former using distance teaching for studying in your own time. Other universities provide systems-thinking courses alongside other subjects, often management or information-systems related. Many courses have a strong systems-dynamics[10] bias. Throughout the English-speaking world, systems-thinking courses usually result from the enthusiasms of a small group of people and cease when they move on.

Shorter courses are also available. There is a lively informal adult education sector in many parts of the world and local and residential adult education colleges may run full-time systems-thinking courses for a week or less, or for a term or more on one evening a week. Look for these in adult education brochures produced by individual colleges, universities and regional education authorities.

Consultants

Consultancies are another source of skills development and quality varies widely but, after reading this book, you will be in a good position to judge whether any particular person or group will be able to help.

The Internet

The Internet provides some very useful resources as well as plenty of low-quality material. The following are useful offerings whose web addresses may change but look likely to have some longevity:

- OpenLearn at the (UK) Open University provides extracts from a range of Open University systems-thinking courses

- *Principia Cybernetica* is somewhat academic but provides a very useful *Web Dictionary of Cybernetics and Systems*

- *The BBC* has a systems-practice website

- *The American Society for Cybernetics* has lots of systems related materials and discussions

- *Mind Tools* have quick tools available for download

Links to all these resources can be found at this book's website: www.triarchypress.com/GrowingWings

Books

There are many, many books on systems thinking although the range runs from the populist-but-useless to the impenetrably academic, with variable quality characterising the whole range. I have cited the books that are important to me in the notes at the end of each chapter but you might also want to explore the work of some of the following:

- Chris Argyris (learning in organisations, learning as a systemic phenomenon)

- Gregory Bateson (cybernetics, psychology and systems theory)

- Mary Catherine Bateson (life-long learning, making sense of lived experience)

- Stafford Beer (the viable system model, another systems core concept)

- Fritjof Capra (emerging systemic paradigms in physics)

- Jay Forrester (systems dynamics)

- Ray Ison (systems practice[11])

- Michael Jackson (methodologies)

- Kambiz Maani and Bob Cavana (systems dynamics)

- Gerald Midgley (methodologies)

- Magnus Ramage and Karen Shipp (the contributions of systems thinking's founding parents)

- Donald Schön (reflective learning from professional experience)

- John Seddon (systems thinking in the public sector)

- Peter Senge (systems dynamics and learning in organisations)

Conferences

Systems-thinking conferences happen regularly. International bodies such as the American Society for Cybernetics, the Australia and New Zealand Systems Society, the International Society for the Systems Sciences and the UK Systems Society run some of the best. Many other international organisations host conferences in languages other than English.

I DON'T HAVE TIME TO DO SYSTEMS THINKING

This is an objection I hear often, especially from people under pressure. The smart answer is 'Have you got time *not* to use systems thinking?' I avoided saying this for a long time but once, caught in a moment of irritation, I asked the question. The effect was interesting. It was clearly a moment at which the objector realised that making progress in a messy situation was contingent on doing things differently. Even a beginning systems thinker recognises that stopping and thinking, however briefly, before acting will reveal potential pitfalls that will cause delays or create further problems. For example, it will always save time if you are clear about what you are doing and why. It will save even more time if that clarity is shared by all those involved.

Doing systems thinking can be very quick; becoming skilled enough to do it quickly takes longer. Like learning to ride a bike, it takes time and practice but, once learned, saves time compared with walking. I urge you to consider that a little practice will give you skills that will repay the time you put into learning them many times over.

When you are a beginner, it takes longer to do what an experienced systems thinker can do quickly but there are very simple tools that take no time to learn. My own observations suggest that rich pictures, used to clarify one's own thinking and then as a means of sharing learning, save time by eliminating misunderstandings and ignorance. Multiple-cause diagrams, and *What? How? and Why?* are powerful emergency tools for newcomers.

Systems thinking is too difficult. Isn't there a simpler way to deal with messes?

I'm astonished when people object that systems thinking is too difficult or too challenging. Why would anyone expect dealing with a mess to be easy? Even if they are unfamiliar with the distinction between difficulties and messes, the evidence of their own struggles with a mess should surely alert people to the intractability of their problem. The human desire for quick and easy answers is universal and I am as vulnerable to that trap as anyone else. I cannot claim that systems thinking is easy but, as human beings, we have tremendous resources of intelligence and diligence and the fate of ourselves and our planet seem to be in our own hands. My hopes are that we can learn to relish that challenge and that systems thinking can contribute to improving the situation.

What happened to Mum?

People sometimes ask what happened to my Mum, after my sister and I had our 'what to do' discussion. Messes change and evolve through time. A few months later, Mum broke her hip; a common occurrence in older people for whom a simple fall can fracture weakened bones. As she recovered, she was assessed as needing full-time care because she was incapable of independent living. The hospital refused to discharge her until a place for her could be found in a care home. After my conversation with Viola, I had spent a week looking at around 20 care homes, looking for clues about the quality of care provided, and had placed Mum's name on the waiting list of four of the best ones. We were very thankful that the offer of a place came up after only a few weeks waiting in hospital. Mum was, by now, very confused and, although initially she was unhappy, she quickly began to believe she was in her own home. Viola continued to manage Mum's day-to-day finances and care-home fees while I looked after the longer term strategic issues. Mum died in 2007.

NOTES, EXPLORATIONS AND RESOURCES FOR CHAPTER 18

1   *Rainer Maria Rilke*

Rilke is one of the best-loved poets writing in German. His work in translation has spread his haunting images around the world. This quotation comes from Letter 4 of his *Letters to a Young Poet*, written to Franz Kappus, the eponymous young poet, between 1903 and 1908.

Rilke, R. M. (1993). *Letters to a Young Poet*. New York: W. W. Norton & Co.

2   *Elegance in action*

For a discussion of elegance, see Chapter 16. In systems thinking, elegance usually refers to the elegance of a human-activity system but when people work harmoniously together and choreograph their activities around each other and a shared sense of what they are doing, individually and collectively, elegance can be perceived in the actions.

3   *Marcia Salner*

I owe this list, at least in part, to the work of Marcia Salner who has been an important influence on my systems-thinking teaching.

Salner, M. (1986). Adult cognitive and epistemological development in systems education. *Systems Research and Behavioral Science, 3*(4), 225-232.

4   *Algorithms*

See Note 2 in Chapter 17.

5   *The Munro Review of Child Protection*

Child protection is a contentious issue in many countries as social workers seek a balance between early, and possibly intrusive, intervention to prevent child abuse and waiting until stronger evidence emerges, by which time the child may be injured. Getting the balance wrong results in disciplinary action, inquiries and vilification by the press and the social-work profession has suffered as a result. The Munro Review's first report on child protection in England has taken a systemic approach to the situation as a whole.

Munro, E. (2010). *The Munro Review of Child Protection, Part 1: A Systems Analysis*. London: Department for Education.

The document is also available online.

6   *Found difficult and left untried*

For a fuller account of this issue, see:

Armson, R. (2008). Found Difficult and Left Untried: why senior managers seem reluctant to engage with Systems Thinking, *The 14th ANZSYS Australia New Zealand Systems Society Conference*. Edith Cowan University, Perth, Western Australia.

7   *Emergence*

For a discussion of emergence see Chapter 8.

8   *Plato*

Plato's Theory of Forms emerges form several of his Socratic Dialogues in which his teacher, Socrates, is involved in dialogues with various interlocutors and discussants. The theory appears in: *Meno* (on defining virtue); *Phaedo* (recording Socrates last day before he is compelled to drink hemlock in punishment for corrupting the youth of Athens and his discussion of the afterlife); *The Republic* (concerning government of the ideal state); *Phaedrus* (in which Socrates discusses love, rhetoric and reincarnation with Phaedrus); and *Parmenides* (in which a youthful Socrates questions the elders Zeno and Parmenides on forms).

See also Note 15 in Chapter 5.

9   *Aikido*

I am indebted to David Leonard for his insights into the parallels between aikido and systems thinking. He explores these ideas and how they might be incorporated into professional information-systems practice in his forthcoming doctoral thesis (Open University).

10   *Systems Dynamics*

For more about Systems Dynamics see this book's website: www.triarchypress. com/GrowingWings

11   *Systems Practice*

Systems practice can be any kind of 'doing' informed by systems thinking. In systems practice, systems thinking ideas are informed by learning from practice and practice is informed by systems ideas in an on-going dialogue that develops practice skills in the systems thinker and others.

The roots of systems thinking

Many ideas have shaped systems thinking, from antiquity to the great syntheses of ideas after World War II and the present. In this appendix, I have assembled some of the key influences, as I understand them, on systems thinking.

Inevitably, this assembly is a personal choice[1] and many people would want to argue that I have left out key people and that I have included some who should not be included. This is simply a reflection of the different perspectives from which systems thinkers understand systems thinking[2].

Some of my exclusions arise from breaks in the intellectual lineages of the systems tradition. Thus, for example, Bogdanov[3] is not included because his influence on later systems ideas was limited. Most of the people identified here are from English-speaking systems traditions. This does not exclude, however, the many contributions from Europe. Systems ideas began to emerge in Europe at the same time as Nazism began to select ideas and people to extinguish. Many European intellectuals thus joined the ferment of intellectual life in the United States in the 1930s and 1940s.

Historical influences in contemporary systems approaches

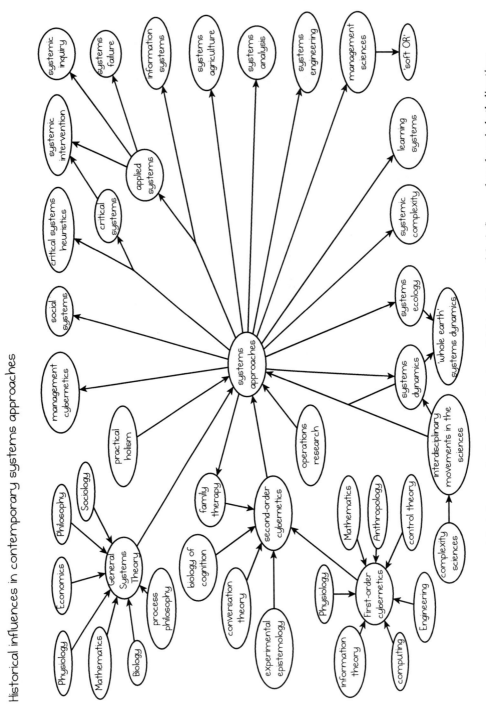

Figure A.1 *Some of the influences that have shaped systems thinking. Many of the influences have been in both directions.*

It is clear from Figure A.1 that cybernetics and General Systems Theory (GST) had a profound influence. The wartime experience of scientists, mathematicians and others of working on multi-disciplinary projects in US universities and government-funded enterprises such as the Manhattan Project, met with the emerging technologies of computing, control systems and management to create fertile ground for new ways of thinking about human concerns. From this ground sprang the Macy conferences[4] and the Society for General Systems Research[5], founding cybernetics and GST respectively. Operations research and systems dynamics developed independently from cybernetics and GST but both soon influenced, and were influenced by, systems ideas. Tables A1 and A2 list some of the people who 'carried' the influences. Their work is described, in most cases, by Wikipedia.

Table A1. Intellectual fields that influenced contemporary systems ideas.

Intellectual field influencing contemporary systems approaches	Contributor[#] making the link to systems approaches
Anthropology	Margaret Mead, 1901-1978, USA
Biology	Ludwig von Bertalanffy, 1901-1972, Austria, USA
	James Miller, 1916-2002, USA
Biology of cognition	Humberto Maturana, b.1928, Chile
Complexity sciences	Ross Ashby, 1903-1972, UK
	Ilya Prigogine, 1917-2003, Belgium
Computing	Warren McCulloch, 1898-1969, USA
Control theory	Julian Bigelow, 1913-2003
	Arturo Rosenblueth, 1900-1970, Mexico
	Nobert Wiener, 1894-1964, USA
Conversation Theory	Gordon Pask, 1928-1996, UK
Economics	Kenneth Boulding, 1910-1993, USA
Engineering*	
Experimental epistemology	Gordon Pask, 1928-1996, UK
Family therapy	Murray Bowen, 1913-1990, USA
	Paul Watzlawick, 1921-2007, USA
First-order cybernetics	Gregory Bateson, 1904-1980, UK, USA
	Paul Watzlawick, 1921-2007, USA
General Systems Theory	Ludwig von Bertalanffy, 1901-1972, Austria, USA
	Kenneth Boulding, 1910-1993, USA
	Howard Odum, 1924-2002, USA
	Geoffrey Vickers, 1894-1982, UK

Information theory	Claude Shannon, 1916-2001, USA
	Warren Weaver, 1894-1978, USA
Mathematics	Ross Ashby±, 1903-1972, UK
	Anatol Rapoport*, 1911-2009, USA
	Norbert Wiener±, 1894-1964, USA
Operations research	Russell Ackoff, 1919-2009, USA
	Stafford Beer, 1926-2002, UK
	C. West Churchman, 1913-2004, USA
Philosophy	Georg Wilhelm Friedrich Hegel, 1770-1831, Germany
Physiology	Walter Cannon+*, 1871-1945, USA
Practical holism	Jan Smuts, 1870-1950, South Africa
Process philosophy	John R. Cobb, b.1925, USA
	Heraclitus of Ephesus, 535-475 B.C.E., Greece
	Alfred North Whitehead, 1861-1947, UK
Second-order cybernetics	Heinz von Foerster, 1911-2002, Austria, USA
	Humberto Maturana, b.1928, Chile
Sociology	Walter Buckley, 1922-2006, USA
	Niklas Luhmann, 1927-1998, Germany
	Talcott Parsons, 1902-1979, USA

#	Countries show where most of the contributor's work was done, not nationality or birth. Where no date of death is given, the person is still working and contributing to the development of systems ideas.
*	influencing General Systems Theory
+	influencing second-order cybernetics
±	influencing first-order cybernetics
*	Engineers were using negative feedback to stabilise engineering devices before feedback theory was developed. James Watt (1736-1819), for example, used steam governors to regulate the speed of steam engines. Servomechanisms have been used to regulate position, velocity, temperature using feedback from pressure, hydraulics, magnetism or springs.

Table A2. *Intellectual fields that have been influenced by contemporary systems ideas.*

Fields influenced by systems approaches	Contributor making the link# from systems approaches
Applied systems	Peter Checkland, UK
	The Open University, UK
Critical systems	Robert Flood, UK
	Michael Jackson, UK
Critical Systems heuristics	Werner Ulrich, Switzerland
Family therapy	Paul Watzlawick, USA
Information systems	Frank Stowell, UK
	Trevor Wood-Harper, UK
Learning Systems	Chris Argyris, USA
	Mary Catherine Bateson, USA
	Kurt Lewin, USA
	Donald Schön, USA
	Eric Trist, UK, USA
Management cybernetics	Stafford Beer, UK
Management sciences	Russell Ackoff, USA
	Ian Mitroff, USA
	Ralph Stacey, UK
Social systems	Eric Trist, UK, USA
	Geoffrey Vickers, UK
Soft operations research	John Mingers, UK
Systemic complexity	Fritjof Capra, USA
	Santa Fé Institute, USA
Systemic inquiry	Ray Ison, Australia, UK
Systemic intervention	Gerald Midgley UK, New Zealand
Systems agriculture	Richard Bawden, Australia
	Colin Spedding, UK
Systems analysis	RAND Corporation, USA
Systems dynamics	Jay Forrester, USA
	Peter Senge, USA
Systems ecology	James Lovelock, UK
	Howard Odum, USA
Systems engineering	Bell Telephone Laboratories, USA
	NASA, USA
Systems failure	The Open University, UK
'Whole earth' systems dynamics	Jay Forrester, USA
	Joanna Macy, USA
	Donella Meadows, USA

#	Countries show where most of the contributor's work was done, not nationality or birth. Where no date of death is given, the person is still working and contributing to the development of systems ideas.

WHERE IN FIGURE A.1 IS THIS BOOK LOCATED?

To my surprise I found this difficult to answer but then realised that the book's location depends on the interaction between it and the reader, as well as between the author and the book she is writing. Instead, I have attempted to give an account of the influences I am aware of as I write. Both general systems theory and cybernetics (especially second-order cybernetics) have influenced my thinking and the book reflects this. In writing the book, my key concerns have been to make available practical tools for dealing with messes so the cluster, at the top right of Figure A.1, that includes applied systems, systemic inquiry and systemic intervention, is probably where the book fits best. I have also drawn less explicitly on ideas about management learning.

Notes, resources and explorations for the Appendix

1 *Acknowledgement*

I am indebted to Ray Ison for much of the material in this appendix. I nonetheless take responsibility for the choices I have made and for any errors.

Ison, R. L. (2008). Systems thinking and practice for action research. In Reason, P. W. & Bradbury, H. (Eds.), *The Sage Handbook of Action Research Participative Inquiry and Practice* (2nd ed., pp. 139-158). London: Sage Publications.

Ison, R.L. (2010). *Systems Practice: How to Act in a Climate-Change World*. London: Springer.

2 *Mapping influences on systems approaches*

In addition to Ison's work (see above), other attempts to assemble the influences upon contemporary systems approaches include the following:

Emery, F. E. (Ed.) (1969). *Systems thinking: Selected readings*. Harmondsworth: Penguin.

Beishon, R. J. and Peters, G. (1972). *Systems behaviour*. London: Harper and Row.

Midgley, G. (Ed.). (2003). *Systems Thinking*. London: Sage.

Ramage, M. & Shipp, K. (2009). *Systems Thinkers*. New York: Springer.

Of the many books competing for space on my desk, Ramage and Shipp has been a constant companion. It includes outlines of the work of 30 systems thinkers and a reading that gives a flavour of their thinking.

3 *Alexander Alexandrovich Bogdanov (1873-1928)*

Bogdanov was an early revolutionary and Lenin's rival for control of the Bolshevik faction of the Social Democratic Labour Party. After Lenin expelled him from the party, he continued as a Marxist theoretician, alongside his work as a doctor in Moscow. He took no part in the 1917 revolution but continued writing on philosophy, economics and art and, at the University of Moscow, researched blood transfusion as a means of rejuvenation. He wrote science fiction in the utopian tradition, exploring his political ideas. From 1913, he worked on a system of ideas he called *tektology*, a prototype for General Systems Theory, but his work remained untranslated until the 1970s. There is speculation about whether Norbert Wiener and Ludwig von Bertalanffy read his work. It is unclear how he died but he remained outside Leninist (and, later, Stalinist) orthodoxy as that orthodoxy became increasingly intolerant of alternatives.

4 *The Macy conferences, 1946 – 1953*

The Macy conferences were a series of interdisciplinary conferences initiated by Warren McCulloch that aimed to generate an understanding of the human mind. From this broad brief, the invited attendees laid the foundations of what became cybernetics. The list of attendees reads like a who's who of twentieth century 'greats' in the history of ideas.

5   *The Society for General Systems Research*

The society was founded in 1956 to explore systems ideas applicable to more than one domain of knowledge. In 1988, it became the International Society for the Systems Sciences. The list of early past presidents overlaps with the Macy conferences.

Glossary

actor	A person who carries out activities necessary to achieve the Transformation in a human-activity system, as specified in a system definition. A in the TWO CAGES mnemonic.
autopoiesis	The process by which a system produces itself or self-organises.
balancing loop	A cycle of events, phenomena or effects that tend to stabilise each other.
boundary	The conceptual line that separates a system from its environment.
conceptual system	A system that exists only in the conceptual world as an idea of a potential activity. It does not purport to represent anything observed.
connection	Connections in a system may include direct physical connection or more conceptual influences such as causation, 'belonging to', contingency, dependency, etc.
constructivism	The idea that we construct reality in our minds by making sense of what we perceive.
customer	The direct beneficiaries (or victims) of a conceptual human-activity system, as specified in a system definition. C in the TWO CAGES mnemonic.
cybernetics	The study of the mechanisms of adaptation and change, especially of a system or organism in response to its environment. The word derives from the Greek *kubernetes*, the steersman of a ship who sets and maintains a course through changing winds and currents.
diagnosis	The process of finding reasons why problems have occurred, or continue to occur and, by extension, discerning how to improve the situation.

diagramming	The practice of drawing diagrams. The benefits of diagramming arise as much from the practice ('a conversation with the diagram') as from the finished diagram, hence the emphasis on diagramming *as a practice.*
diagram	See *systems diagram.*
3Es	Three ways in which a conceptual system must meet its purpose and for which criteria must be set. Efficacy, Efficiency and Effectiveness.
5Es	Five ways in which the success of a conceptual system can meet its purpose and for which criteria must be set. Efficacy, Efficiency, Effectiveness, Elegance and Ethicality.
effectiveness	One of three ways in which a conceptual system must meet its purpose and for which a criterion must be set. The third E of the 3Es.
efficacy	One of three ways in which a conceptual system must meet its purpose and for which a criterion must be set. The first E of the 3Es.
efficiency	One of three ways in which a conceptual system must meet its purpose and for which a criterion must be set. The second E of the 3Es.
elegance	An additional characteristic by which a successful system is recognised. The opposite of 'clunkiness', The fourth E of the 5Es.
emergent property	A systemic quality or property arising from the way system components are assembled which does not exist if one of the parts is changed or connected differently.
environment, system environment	Anything outside the system boundary. The system environment influences the system.
environmental constraint	A feature of the environment that is taken as a given in conceptual human-activity systems, as specified in a system definition. The E in the TWO CAGES mnemonic.

epistemology	The branch of philosophy that deals with how we know what we know about. The idea of epistemology is extended in this book to include knowing about our knowing, thinking about our thinking and understanding our understanding.
epistemological awareness	Awareness that epistemology is an issue and that, therefore, choices can be made about how to think about the issues that arise in any situation.
ethicality	An additional characteristic by which a successful system is recognised. The fifth E of the 5Es.
ethics	The philosophy of discerning what constitutes 'good' behaviour and the principles that guide it.
feedback	Information, cause or influence that results from an effect, phenomenon or system that influences its action.
guardian	A person who will become aware of unwanted effects of a conceptual human-activity system, as specified alongside a system definition. The G in the TWO CAGES mnemonic.
hierarchy, systems hierarchy	The arrangement of systems within larger systems, and of the subsystems that are component parts of each system.
HAS	See human-activity system.
HAS diagram	See human-activity system diagram.
holon	See *whole*.
human-activity system	A system of purposeful, interconnected, human-enacted activities that achieves a Transformation relevant to improving a situation.
human-activity system (HAS) diagram	A diagram of a human-activity system and its associated monitoring and control system showing between five and nine logically necessary activities that will achieve the system's intended Transformation. The diagram has blobs, arrows, a system boundary, a monitoring activity and a title. Arrows indicate contingency.

influence diagram	A diagram showing the influences acting between entities and using blobs, arrows and a title. A system boundary is optional and indentifies an observed 'system of influence'. Arrows read as 'influences' and nothing else.
ITO model	A model of a system in terms of its Transformation of an Input into an Output.
legitimate other	A person whose experience and understanding is taken to be as legitimate, meaningful and rich as one's own.
magical number seven	The idea that the brain can consciously deal with seven, plus or minus two, concepts at once.
models	Representations (physical, graphic, mental, computer, etc.) that represent some but not all of the features of the entity being modelled.
multiple cause diagram	A diagram showing the effect of one event, phenomenon or observation on another using words, arrows and a title. Arrows read as 'causes' or 'contributes to' and nothing else.
negative feedback	Information about the effect of the behaviour of a system that tends to stabilise that behaviour.
owner	A person who can withdraw permission for the operation of a system in a conceptual human-activity system, as specified in a system definition. The O in the TWO CAGES mnemonic.
perspective	A viewpoint that includes position, role, concerns, information available, expertise, previous experience, values and preferences.
positive feedback	Information about the effect of the behaviour of a system that tends to promote that behaviour.
POSIWID	Beer's notion that the 'purpose of a system is what it does'.
purposeful, purposive	Systems have a purpose, attributed to them by an observer. They are thus purposive, rather than purposeful in the narrower sense. See also *higher purpose*.
reinforcing loops	A cycle of events, phenomena or effects that tend to reinforce each other.

rich picture	A rich representation of a situation using pictures and symbols with a title.
second-order cybernetics	The branch of cybernetics that explicitly addresses the role of the observing observer.
self-production	The process by which a system creates its own ability to adapt to its environment by producing or organising its own internal processes.
sinister systems	A variant of the snappy systems technique for generating names for systems, based on what the system does, as if its unwanted effects were intentional.
snappy systems	A technique for generating names for systems based on what the system does.
soft systems methodology (SSM)	A methodology, devised by Peter Checkland, for tackling problem situations where the desirability of any particular goals or outcomes cannot be taken as given.
spray diagram	A diagram showing relationships between ideas. Also known as a spider diagram.
SSM	See soft systems methodology.
stake, stakeholding, stakeholder	A stakeholder is simply someone who has an interest (a stake or a stakeholding) in a situation and is not indifferent to its fate.
subsystem	A component part of a system, within the system boundary, that is itself a system.
system	A set of elements connected together to form a purposive whole with properties that differ from those of its component parts.
systematic	Orderly, methodical and according to some system.
systemic	Attending to relationships within an entity and between an entity and its context.
systems diagram	A diagram, not necessarily of a system as such, that systemically represents features of a situation of interest.
system definition	A definition of a system of activities carried out by humans, usually accompanied by a list of criteria for the system (see TWO CAGES) that complies with the template: A system to <What?> by means of <How?> in order to contribute to <Why?>.

systems map	A map of aspects of a situation conceptualised as a system and its associated subsystems.
systems thinking	A style of thinking that attends as much to the connections between things as to the things themselves, and to the connections between things and their wider context, and looks at things and their connections from more than one perspective.
subsystem	A system component that is itself a system.
subsystems of activity	Subsystems of activity that indicate the human activities necessary to achieve a transformation.
	The S in the TWO CAGES mnemonic.
theme	One- or two-word phrase that names a significant part of a messy situation without judgement.
transformation	The action of a system that takes something (entity, artefact, idea, plan, etc.) in one state and transforms it to another state, as specified in a system definition.
	The T in the TWO CAGES mnemonic.
trap	In systems thinking, an assumption, habit or feature of the situation or of the thinker, which limits their thinking about a situation.
trigger	Change that initiates another change but does not cause it.
truth claim	A statement about the 'real world' that claims to be true.
TWO CAGES	A mnemonic for the criteria listed alongside a system definition. (Transformation, *Weltanschauung*, Owners, Customers, Actors, Guardians, Environmental constraints and Subsystems of activity).
understandascope[1]	A conceptual tool created using system ideas, through which I can look at a messy situation in order to understand it better.
variable	In systems dynamics, a quantity that can vary. Something that can be expressed as a number (at least in principle) and can thus increase or decrease (e.g. temperature, profit, toxicity, happiness, etc.).
vague verb	Verbs that undermine the power of a system definition because they have too many meanings.

W	*Weltanschauung.* The set of beliefs that makes any particular conceptual system a meaningful one to consider.
	The W in the TWO CAGES mnemonic.
What?, How? and Why?	Another name for *system definition.*
whole, holon	A collection of interconnected entities that can be treated as one entity because it has an emergent property that defines it as an entity with properties of its own.

NOTES, EXPLORATIONS AND RESOURCES FOR THE GLOSSARY

1   *Understandascopes*

This delightful invented word deserves to be part of systems language. It comes from the Michael Leunig cartoon shown in the introduction to Part 2. The word is not in widespread use but my experience indicates that most people know what it means.

Index

About the author

Rosalind Armson is a systems practitioner, scholar and teacher, having worked for many years as Senior Lecturer in Systems at the Open University in Milton Keynes (UK). She has extensive experience of using systems ideas to support individuals and organisations facing complex and uncertain situations. She also supports students and others in learning Systems Thinking.

Rosalind started her career as an engineer working in the power-plant construction industry. Her increasing concerns about nuclear-power policy led her to research energy policy at the Open University. She completed a PhD modelling the outcomes for various energy supply scenarios. She taught Engineering before moving to the Open University Systems Group.

Rosalind and her colleagues have designed and delivered Systems Thinking courses to thousands of Open University students. Her big motivation in teaching is students' excitement when they 'get it' and are able to see the world in a richer way.

Rosalind has a long-standing interest in how our thinking both enables and limits the opportunities we can see and take. She has worked with individuals, organisations and institutions seeking to survive and thrive in a world that presents enormous challenges. She is an independent consultant using her systems-thinking skills to enable others to work out what to do and how to do it. This has brought her into contact with development agencies, banks, governments, businesses, health-care practitioners, the voluntary sector, ethical monitoring agencies, energy providers and many others facing radical change. She aims to 'leave the skills behind' at the end of each consultancy engagement by building managers' systems-thinking capability.

Rosalind has delivered systems-thinking workshops in the USA, Canada, Australia, New Zealand, UAE, and South Africa and in Europe. In her workshops, she draws on ideas, stories, images and her own extensive experience as a systems practitioner to provide lively and challenging learning experiences. Many of the ideas draw on the world-leading work of the UK Open University Systems Group.

About Triarchy Press

Triarchy Press is an independent publishing house that looks at how organisations work and how to make them work better. We present challenging perspectives on organisations in short and pithy, but rigorously argued, books.

Through our books, pamphlets and website we aim to stimulate ideas by encouraging real debate about organisations in partnership with people who work in them, research them or just like to think about them.

Please tell us what you think about the ideas in this book at:

www.triarchypress.com/telluswhatyouthink

If you feel inspired to write – or have already written – an article, a pamphlet or a book on any aspect of organisational theory or practice, we'd like to hear from you. Submit a proposal at:

www.triarchypress.com/writeforus

For more information about Triarchy Press, or to order any of our publications, please visit our website or drop us a line:

www.triarchypress.com

We're on Twitter:

@TriarchyPress

and Facebook:

www.facebook.com/triarchypress

Other Systems Thinking titles from Triarchy Press

Russ Ackoff

One of the founding fathers of Systems Thinking was Russ Ackoff, who died in 2009. An acknowledged genius, who often found himself in those lists of the most influential business thinkers and 'gurus', he was a pre-eminent consultant, practitioner, researcher and academic in this field.

Triarchy Press had the good fortune to publish four of his books:

~Management f-Laws
How organisations really work

Russell Ackoff ~ with Herbert Addison. Responses by Sally Bibb

We've all heard of Sod's (or Murphy's) Law - if anything can go wrong, it will. Most of us know Parkinson's Law – work expands to fill the time available for its completion. Now *Management f-LAWS* brings together a collection of 81 of Professor Russell Ackoff's wittiest and most subversive insights into the world of business.

> *"If you ever need a reality check after stumbling out of some appalling management meeting, or just need cheering up on a long business trip, this is the book for you. Just about every myth or pompous delusion about management gets punctured..."* **Stefan Stern, *The Daily Telegraph***

> *"This book is fun - not something one can often say about a management book. It's also a compact piece of distilled wisdom... Many of the 81 f-Laws are obvious when you think about them, but are too often ignored or neglected. Yet they matter. Take No. 4: 'There is no point in asking customers, who do not know what they want, to say what they want.'"* **Charles Handy, *Management Today***

> *"This book offers profound thoughts in digestible bites. It is easy to read and entertaining, yet full of wisdom. How much better our organizations would be if managers could really learn these lessons!"* **Michael C Jackson, Professor of Management Systems, Hull University Business School**

2007, 180pp., paperback, 978-0-9550081-2-2, £18.00

~Systems Thinking for Curious Managers
With 40 new Management f-LAWS

Russell Ackoff ~ with Herbert Addison and Andrew Carey

This more recent title added 40 new f-LAWS to those previously published as *Management f-Laws*. The book also includes plus an insightful, extended introduction to Systems Thinking as developed by Russ Ackoff.

2010, 96pp., paperback, 978-0-9562631-5-5, £18.00

> For managers, leaders and their victims as well as MBA students, these two books of *f*-Laws offer the essence of Ackoff at his sparkling and most digestible best.

~Memories

Russell Ackoff ~ Foreword by Peter Senge

You might think *Memories* would be the fond autobiography of a grumpy old guru. Not a bit of it! There <u>are</u> stories of his chats with the Queen of Iran, his introduction of theme parks to the US, appearing naked in front of his commanding officer in World War II… but they're all there to do a serious job. Ackoff knew his students remembered stories better than teachings, so he uses them to deliver a succession of principles and aphorisms relating to management, organisations and work that he had developed during his life.

> *"Russ was an incisive, lifelong critic of the modern organizational form. He saw its limitations and argued for radical redesign. He was an advocate for major re-visioning and processes of change that started with helping people see what they truly valued and where they truly wanted to get - and then working backwards to see what it would take to get there."* **Peter Senge,** from his Foreword to *Memories*

2010, 120pp., paperback, 978-0-9565379-7-3, £16.00; hardback, 978-0-9565379-9-7, £25.00

~Differences that make a Difference
An annotated glossary of distinctions important in management

Russell Ackoff ~ Foreword by Charles Handy

Towards the end of his life, Russ Ackoff determined to explain how some of the apparently insignificant misinterpretations of language and meaning he observed during his long years of research can, in practice, have far-reaching consequences. His aim was to **dissolve** (not **solve** or **resolve**) some of the many disputes in professional and private life that revolve around such misunderstandings. In this last manuscript that he was to complete before his death he does exactly that.

2010, 144pp., paperback, 978-1-908009-01-2, £14.00

John Seddon and Systems Thinking for public services

~Systems Thinking in the Public Sector

John Seddon

The best-selling analysis of why public services in the UK and around the world so often don't work – and how to fix the mess. This is the book that made a laughing stock of the UK Audit Commission (now abolished), famously ridiculed the culture of targets and 'deliverology' that for years has characterised public services in England and set in train the conversion of the public sector to systems thinking. The reviews say it all:

> *"One of the strengths of Seddon's diagnosis is that, as a consultant, he has seen almost every public service from the inside. From trading standards to planning and housing repairs, all exhibit the same dysfunction, being forced to conform to a work design that starts from the wrong end – the requirements of government rather than those of the citizen."* **Simon Caulkin, *The Observer***

> *"This book provides the public sector with the means to deliver higher levels of public value and the opportunity to be seen to be doing so in a robust way with measurable results, high customer satisfaction and high morale."* **Jim Mather, Scottish Govt. Minister for Enterprise, Energy & Tourism**

2008, 224pp., paperback, 978-0-9550081-8-4, £20.00

~Delivering Public Services That Work

Systems Thinking in the Public Sector: Case Studies

Peter Middleton ~ Foreword by John Seddon

Six detailed and specific Case Studies which convincingly demonstrate that John Seddon's recipe (above) actually works and delivers the results he promised.

2010, 132pp., paperback, 978-0-9562631-6-2, £15.00

William Tate and applying Systems Thinking to organisations

~The Search for Leadership

An Organisational Perspective

William Tate

This Systems Thinking approach to leadership asks us to look beyond individuals, managers, leaders and management training programmes. Using the analogy of an aquarium (where water quality determines the health of the fish), Bill Tate reviews a range of issues like:

Distributing authority ~ management vs. organisation development ~ the structural gaps that account for waste, rework, poor communication and failure ~ transferring learning ~ organisational competence ~ accountability ~ the organisation's culture and shadow-side.

> *"Full of practical tips and insights... a 'must read' book for any leadership or organisational development practitioner who wants to make a difference to business success."* **Linda Holbeche,** *CIPD*

> *"...offers a practical road map for understanding and improving organisations and the way they are led."* **Prof. John Storey,** *The Open University Business School*

> Used in conjunction with the *Toolkit* (below), this is a practical book for HR and other senior executives who want to run an open, effective, responsible and empowering organisation – but aren't quite sure where to start. It's also a powerful stimulus to fresh thinking for business students.

2009, 324pp., paperback, 978-0-9557681-7-0, £28.00
Hardback, 978-0-9557681-8-7, £40.00; e-book, £40.00

~Systemic Leadership Toolkit

William Tate

Designed for use in conjunction with *The Search for Leadership* (above) this toolkit presents nine self-assessment questionnaires in nine separate modules – designed to give any organisation a complete picture of itself: Management Development ~ Organisation Development ~ Learning ~ Competence ~ Culture ~ Decline ~ Systems ~ The Shadow ~ Accountability

2009, 152pp., paperback, 978-0-9562631-2-4, £55.00; e-toolkit, £95.00

CPSIA information can be obtained at www.ICGtesting.com
Printed in the USA
LVOW051222171012

303217LV00006B/1/P